GROUP PROCESS TODAY

Adelphi University
Postdoctoral Program in Psychotherapy
Conference Series

GROUP PROCESS TODAY

Evaluation and Perspective

Compiled and Edited by

Donald S. Milman, Ph.D.

*Professor of Psychology and Co-Director, Postdoctoral Program
in Psychotherapy, Institute of Advanced Psychological Studies
Adelphi University
Private Practice
East Norwich, New York*

and

George D. Goldman, Ph.D.

*Clinical Professor of Psychology, Supervisor of Psychotherapy
and Director, Postdoctoral Psychotherapy Center
Institute of Advanced Psychological Studies
Adelphi University
Private Practice
New York, New York*

CHARLES C THOMAS • PUBLISHER
Springfield • Illinois • U.S.A.

Published and Distributed Throughout the World by
CHARLES C THOMAS • PUBLISHER
Bannerstone House
301-327 East Lawrence Avenue, Springfield, Illinois, U.S.A.

© *1974, by* CHARLES C THOMAS • PUBLISHER
ISBN 0-398-03046-4
Library of Congress Catalog Card Number: 73 19627

Printed in the United States of America
C-1

Library of Congress Cataloging in Publication Data
Main entry under title:

Group process today.

(Adelphi University. Postdoctoral Program in
Psychotherapy. Conference series)
1. Group psychotherapy—Congresses. I. Milman,
Donald S., 1924-   ed. II. Goldman, George David,
1923-   ed. III. Series: Adelphi University,
Garden City, N. Y. Postdoctoral Program in Psycho-
therapy. Conference series. [DNLM: 1. Group pro-
cesses—Congresses. 2. Psychotherapy, Group—Congresses.
WM430 G8823 1974]
RC488.G69   616.8'915   73-19627
ISBN 0-398-03046-4

CONTRIBUTORS

ROBERT U. AKERET, Ed.D.: In private practice. Graduate, William Alanson White Institute.

MILTON M. BERGER, M.D.: Assistant Clinical Professor, College of Physicians and Surgeons, Columbia University; Director of Training and Coordinator of Professional Services, Center for Adults Plus; Educational Director, The Association for Group Psychoanalysis and Process.

THOMAS L. BRAYBOY, M.D.: Director, Youth Development Center, Newark, N.J.; Associate Professor in Psychiatry, North Jersey Medical College.

BARBARA BENEDICT BUNKER, Ph.D.: Assistant Professor of Psychology, SUNY-Buffalo; Associate of NTL; Founding Member and Board Member, International Association of Applied Social Scientists.

DOUGLAS R. BUNKER, Ph.D.: Associate Professor of Policy Sciences, SUNY-Buffalo; Fellow, NTL Institute of Applied Behavioral Sciences.

MAGDA DENES-RADOMISLE, Ph.D.: Associate Clinical Professor of Psychology and Supervisor, Postdoctoral Program in Psychotherapy, Institute of Advanced Psychological Studies, Adelphi University; Supervisor, New York Institute for Gestalt Therapy.

CELIA DULFANO, C.S.W.: Director, Social Work Training Program in Alcoholism, New York State Department of Mental Hygiene.

ALBERT ELLIS, Ph.D.: Executive Director, Institute for Advanced Study in Rational Psychotherapy.

PETER HOGAN, M.D.: Assistant Clinical Professor of Psychiatry and Supervisor, Department of Group and Family Therapy, NYU-Bellevue Medical Center.

SEYMOUR R. KAPLAN, M.D.: Associate Professor of Psychiatry, Albert Einstein College of Medicine; Head, Social and Community Psychiatry, Department of Psychiatry, Montefiore Hospital and Medical Center.

SAMUEL B. KUTASH, Ph.D.: President, Association for Group Psychoanalysis and Process; President, HDP Associates, Inc.; Consultant in Group Process and Psychotherapy, Veterans Administration and Jersey City State College.

RACHEL M. LAUER, Ph.D.: Chief Psychologist, Bureau of Child Guidance, New York City School System; President-Elect, School Division, New York State Psychological Association; Vice President, New York Society for General Semantics.

ELIZABETH E. MINTZ, Ph.D.: Diplomate, American Board of Professional Psychology; Faculty Member, National Psychological Association for Psychoanalysis; Faculty Member, Workshop Institute for Living-Learning; Member, Executive Council, American Academy of Psychotherapy.

JOHN C. PIERRAKOS, M.D.: Director, Institute for Bio-Energetic Analysis; Member, American Psychiatric Association; Member, Association for the Scientific Study of Sex.

MAX ROSENBAUM, Ph.D.: In private practice; Editor, *Group Process;* Faculty, Institute of National Psychological Association for Psychoanalysis.

JAMES M. SACKS, Ph.D.: In private practice. Psychodrama Director, The Moreno Institute; faculty member at The Metropolitan Institute for Psychoanalytic Studies, and at Group Relations Ongoing Workshops.

EMANUEL K. SCHWARTZ, Ph.D., D.S. Sc.: Now deceased; formerly Dean and Director of Training, Postgraduate Center for Mental Health; Clinical Professor, Postdoctoral Program in Psychotherapy, Adelphi University; Adjunct Professor, Graduate School, New York University.

MARTIN SHEPARD, M.D.: In private practice; Director of Training, ANTHOS; Consulting Psychiatrist, New York City Department of Corrections (at Rikers Island).

LEONARD SIEGEL, M.D.: Director, Division of Family Therapy, Department of Psychiatry, Roosevelt Hospital, New York, N.Y.; Charter Member, The Council on Family Study and

Treatment; Member, The William Alanson White Psychoan-
alytic Society.
HYMAN SPOTNITZ, M.D., Med. Sc.D.: In private practice.
Fellow of the American Psychiatric Association, American
Group Psychotherapy Association, American Orthopsychiatric
Association, and the American Association for the Advance-
ment of Science.

Publications from the Postdoctoral
Program Conference Series

MODERN WOMAN: HER PSYCHOLOGY AND SEXUALI-
TY–George D. Goldman and Donald S. Milman

PSYCHOANALYTIC CONTRIBUTIONS TO COMMUNITY
PSYCHOLOGY–Donald S. Milman and George D. Goldman

INNOVATIONS IN PSYCHOTHERAPY–George D. Goldman
and Donald S. Milman

THE NEUROSIS OF OUR TIME: ACTING OUT–Donald S.
Milman and George D. Goldman

To Our Friends and Colleagues . . . In Memoriam

Asya Kadis
Jule Nydes
Emanuel K. Schwartz

INTRODUCTION

THE POSTDOCTORAL PROGRAM in Psychotherapy has, in its annual conference, focused on issues of current interest in the area of psychotherapy and psychoanalysis. Consistent with this tradition, this volume which arises from the conference, explores the area of group process, which is of much vital current concern.

The group psychotherapy movement originated, most probably, in the Emanuel Church Tuberculosis Class of Joseph H. Pratt in 1905. Julius Metzl, a police physician in Vienna developed a group counselling method for alcoholics in the late 1920's and in this same period Alfred Adler and his colleagues were working with group treatment methods in the Counselling Center for Parents and Children in Vienna. Metzl called his method Collective Counselling.

The terms *group therapy* and *group psychotherapy* were first used by Moreno in the early 1930's. Moreno, writing under the name of J. M. Levy, had published in 1914 a philosophical paper on group methods and in 1923 wrote about the *Stegreiftheatre,* a forerunner of psychodrama.

Despite those early beginnings, the group psychotherapy movement did not obtain a real impetus until and immediately after World War II. The Army and later the Veterans Administration, faced with tremendous professional understaffing and large numbers of psychiatric patients, did much to foster the development of the widespread use of groups for treatment purposes. The large numbers of group therapy oriented practitioners trained in the Veterans Administration and their success with this treatment modality contributed much to its spread to private practice. In its early days in general private practice in the 1950's groups were, for the most part, used as an adjunct to individual treatment. Concomitantly, Alexander Wolf and Emanuel K. Schwartz and their students pioneered in the utilization of groups for *group psycho-*

analysis where the group, by itself, had psychoanalytic goals and methods. Groups would be *open;* that is, the group would meet on a certain night or day, and would always continue at that time with some people terminating and new members joining the group. There would be *alternate sessions,* perhaps one other time a week without the therapist being present. For the most part, in this era, most therapists used a fairly similar model. This was one in which groups no longer were composed of such homogeneous populations as alcoholics, prisoners, soldiers or veterans. They became in private practice, heterogeneous, more of a microcosm of society.

Group psychoanalysis and the related analytically oriented groups used as adjuncts to individual therapy analysis of both transference and resistance and emphasize unconscious processes and intra-psychic conflict in their philosophy of treatment. To illustrate this in more detail let us magnify the above. The transferences are multiple, with the various group members often seen as different family members. Wolf, for example, described the group in familial terms and actively worked on brother and sister transferences as well as the traditional parental ones. The patient's distortions in perceiving people are quickly picked up by fellow group members and utilized as transference interpretations by the group therapist. Resistance is also readily available for analysis in a group situation. Group members, as well as the therapist, quite often react to a fellow group member's defenses. Intellectualizing, or avoiding the emotional interacting and reacting that traditionally characterize group interchanges are recurrently observed. Patients often begin to use phrases like *talking about* in contrast to *talking to* to indicate to fellow group members their defensive operations. The *real* meaning of various behaviors becomes the focus of the group's attention and superficial discussion is frowned upon. Members begin to learn, *in vivo,* how their behavior produces difficulties with other group members. Thus in group treatment this model serves to emphasize the patient and his *inner discontents* as the focus of the therapeutic process, following the tradition of psychoanalysis.

In the 1960's, therapists such as Elizabeth Mintz developed the practice of time extended groups. The Esalen Institute in California particularly stimulated by Fritz Perls and the Gestalt therapists, as well as William Schutz, began innovative and widely publicized new forms of group treatment. R. D. Laing in London began interesting new group living and group treatment methods in the so-called *blow-out centers.* Synonon, Daytop Village and other primarily drug oriented groups developed their very direct, confronting approach. Group methods had been applied to normal individuals as well as to patient populations and terms such as Encounter and Sensitivity Training became everyday words with newspapers, magazine articles, as well as books and movies popularizing them.

This above brief history does not completely clarify the issues relevant to the popularity and efficacy of group treatment, but does give us a perspective. To further understand the usefulness of group treatment, one must first begin to view it from both the analytic as well as the societal frame of reference.

The role of group treatment in the total analytic process is perhaps best understood when one sees the analytic treatment process as being concerned with: First, the identification of those parts of a person's behavior that are characteristic and yet maladaptive or what could be called, *What am I doing that is non-productive, anxiety producing, or uncomfortable for me?;* second, the exploration of the historical reasons for the origin and maintenance of such behavior; and finally, the opportunity for the individual to be freed from the necessity of repeating this pattern through the emotional re-experiencing of the original pattern in the present. Utilizing the alternatives that may be available, more effective behavior may be developed. From the above characterization one can more clearly see the place of group psychotherapy in the treatment process. Participation in the therapy group is probably the best way that the person can, with immediacy, vividness, and intensity, see himself as he behaves with others. The group catches the patient in the act of being himself and enables him to experience his humanness in action. The question of: *What am I doing that gets me into interpersonal difficulties etc.?* is answered in a beautifully effective manner, as the patient is confronted with himself with clarity and immediacy. Personality change takes place then, in part, through conscious volition with conscious awareness and control of the deviant behavior. The major changes take place, however, after analyzing the origins and working through alternative action patterns. The more formal individual psychoanalysis of transference and resistance precedes, is concurrent with, and follows the group experience.

In order to see the place of group treatment in today's society one should see it in the perspective of the origins of analysis. When Freud started treating patients in late nineteenth century Vienna, a crucial problem in his middle class Victorian patients was that of sexual repression. His treatment approach may have been excellent for those times and for its problems. In the mid-twentieth century, sexual freedom had replaced sexual repression and man has evolved a new set of difficulties: loneliness and alienation. The most commonly seen symptom-complex that therapists find is a character disorder, one that is usually more obsessive than hysterical. In our urbanized society man has gradually lost the close intimate contact of rural America where the family and the greater family unit were an integral part of the culture. As society became more industrialized, man evolved an assembly line-like attitude toward life as well as toward industrial production. People had their specific jobs and were only a small fragment of a large and all but unknown whole. With this fragmentation of job and life, people's contact with themselves and others diminished. Alienation rooted in his work situation encompassed man's alienation from his fellows as well as from himself. Michael Balint, for example, indicated the development of alienation as an almost universal complaint in the current patient population, which then became synonomous with grief, misery, anger, despair and feelings of being victimized. Alienation is also related to a sense of feeling sinful, guilty, and blamed for being defective and faulty. To understand alienation and its subsequent psychological consequences a better perspective is gained if one realizes that its roots are multi-determined. These roots could be found in man's aggressive nature and his conflict over this, or in the nature of his exposure to a society that is so constituted. Lastly, it could be understood in any one individual's case by understanding his personal familial dynamics. No matter what the explanation is, man's interpersonal interactions often leave him more isolated and alone. One finds that patients are often needful of more intense contacts and interactions than are present in the classical analytic situation which is, of course, dyadic. Thus more and more therapy moves toward multi-personal treatment and varieties of group process intervention are the treatments of choice in our alienated world.

Group process and group treatment cover so varied and divergent a range that this volume must, of necessity, be restricted. Social psychologists originally began the study of the groups, and the dynamics of small groups in particular that formed the base of present day group process study. The work of the National Training Laboratory in our present day helped make the transition from the theoretical to the applied, from group process to group treatment. This book, for the most part, emphasizes the latter, with some notable exceptions. Even in this latter emphasis we restrict ourselves to some of the more major technical approaches and only a few of the theoretical orientations. To understand the breadth of the group treatment approach one has to realize that the theoretical base could be, to name a few, humanistic, psychoanalytic, Gestalt, rational and learning theory. There are also varieties of groups that are self-initiated and/or self-help in orientation. These encompass divergent tasks from broad problems such as alcoholism to specific symptoms such as smoking. There are also wide varieties of populations to which the group movement is directed. Group encounter and sensitivity techniques have been employed with normal groups in settings as diverse as industry, schools and churches, for example. Techniques vary from role playing in psychodrama, to group games or experiments, to video tape playbacks, through to more usual verbal interchanges. The exchanges in the group may be focused on unconscious motivation or more superficially may serve as vehicles for didactic interaction. The experience and training of the group leader may vary widely in that he might be a psychoanalyst trained in both individual and group approaches or he could be a very minimally trained paraprofessional or self-appointed group leader. Styles of leadership also vary; from authoritarian to *laisse faire;* from trans-ference neutrality to the most intimate interaction; from sophisti-cated professional responsibility to lack of direction and irrespon-sibility; and from sophistication about group process to relative ignorance. Again illustrative of the breadth of the field are the following questions. At this point in its development group meth-ods have gone beyond the obvious therapeutic needs of the patient populations and one might ask, what needs do group process mo-dalities supply people beyond the more traditional group or even dyadic approaches? Further, with all these forms and varieties of encounter groups and others in the *human potential movement,* what are the forces operating within society at large that precipi-tated this particular phenomenon now?

There are many advantages that have been proposed for the group method over individual treatment approaches. Among some that have been offered are: 1) more persons can be reached at any one time by one therapist by group methods; 2) the goals that are set for individual treatment can be accomplished more easily, in-expensively, and effectively in the group; 3) the individual has more of an opportunity to question and realistically deal with au-thority; 4) there is an opportunity to model different moral and social roles; 5) there is an opportunity to experience and work through multiple transferences and 6) not only is a more real per-ception of the therapist possible but the group provides more op-portunities for gratification of needs both real and symbolic.

In summary, it appears that group process methods are pecu-liarly apt for our present day society. In the group situation the loneliness and alienation that characterize life today are replaced by a sense of trust, belonging and acceptance. In this atmosphere the individual's potential for insight and growth are enhanced and whether the method used is psychoanalytic, encounter, or non-verbal, they often serve effective functions that are difficult to meet in the traditional one to one therapeutic interaction. Family ther-apy, multi-familial therapy, couples therapy, and the other new group process concepts have expanded our horizons not only about techniques, but also about personal growth.

This volume covers this broad spectrum of what is being done and attempts both to evaluate a particular area and also put it in perspective with what has been and will be done.

The pages in this book, as in our other volumes in this series, do not follow the order of presentation of the original conference on which this volume is based, but are organized to make for greater clarity and cohesion. The book goes from the theoretical to the applied, from the general to the specific.

Following this general format the book begins with the late Emanuel K. Schwartz's paper on his, A CONCEPTUAL MODEL FOR PRACTICE and is followed by Dr. Max Rosenbaum's GROUP THEORY AND SENSITIVITY TRAINING. This theoretical section ends with Dr. Martin Shepard's views of the history of the group process field.

The next five chapters cover the area of different theoretical models that are used in group psychotherapy practices today. The first of these is Dr. Bunker's paper on his NTL APPROACH, followed by Dr. Barbara Benedict Bunker's paper on THE TRAVISTOCK APPROACH. Next is Dr. Albert Ellis' paper on his RATIONAL PSYCHOTHERAPY as it is applied to group process; this is followed by Dr. John C. Pierrakos' viewpoints of the BIO-ENERGETIC ANALYSIS being applied to group techniques. The last paper in this section is Dr. Magda Denes-Radomisli's GESTALT GROUP THERAPY: SENSE IN SENSITIVITY.

The next three chapters have to do with specific ways of using group techniques in new technical developments. These are Dr. Elizabeth E. Mintz's paper on MARATHONS. Dr. James Sacks' paper on THE PSYCHODRAMATIC APPROACH, and Dr. Leonard Siegel's and Ms. Celia Dulfano's paper on MULTIPLE MARITAL COUPLE GROUP THERAPY.

The next six chapters have to do with the specific adaptations of group psychotherapy for either a particular setting or a particular population group. These are Dr. Hyman Spotnitz's paper on GROUP PSYCHOTHERAPY WITH SCHIZOPHRENICS, followed by Dr. Brayboy's paper on BLACK AND WHITE GROUPS AND THERAPISTS, Dr. Akeret's paper on STORE FRONT GROUPS, Dr. Kaplan's paper, GROUP PROCESS IN

THE HOSPITAL SETTING, Dr. Lauer's paper on THE GROUP PROCESS TECHNIQUES IN THE SCHOOLS, and lastly, Dr. Kutash's paper on the GROUP PROCESS IN INDUSTRY AND PROFESSIONAL EDUCATION.

The final two chapters of the book have to do with the utilization of special techniques found particularly useful in group treatment. These are Dr. Peter Hogan's paper on the USE OF NONVERBAL TECHNIQUES, and Dr. Milton Berger's paper on VIDEO IN GROUPS.

ACKNOWLEDGMENTS

W E WOULD ALSO LIKE to give our thanks and appreciation to Elizabeth Zimmerman and Marge Burgaard, our secretaries for their help with running our conferences and in general making our lives at Adelphi both more pleasant and easier. In addition, for her general overall editorial assistance, we wish to thank Deborah Janis. And for her help with the workshop and conference, Lorelle Saretsky deserves a great deal of praise and gratitude which we most cordially give her.

During the time that elapsed between the conference and the publication of this book, the field of Psychotherapy and more specifically, we at the Adelphi University Postdoctoral Program, lost Emanuel K. Schwartz, a true pioneer and innovator in the group therapy field. We wish to take this opportunity to remember Manny as the fun-loving, warm, delightful man that he was, and for all the time he so unselfishly gave to the Adelphi Postdoctoral Program in Psychotherapy.

CONTENTS

GROUP PROCESS TODAY

CHAPTER I

PSYCHOANALYSIS IN GROUPS: A CONCEPTUAL MODEL FOR PRACTICE

Emanuel K. Schwartz

The late Emanuel K. Schwartz was a delightful human being, a brilliant thinker and teacher and a pioneer in the practice and theory of psychoanalysis in groups. This paper reflects all of these qualities directly. "Manny," a member of the Postdoctoral faculty, with his old friend and colleague Alexander Wolf, was one of the pioneers in group psychotherapy. It is his personal breadth and unique professional qualifications that we chose him to keynote our conference and this book.

Systematically and clearly, Doctor Schwartz first evolves his definition of analysis—a process characterized by unconscious processes, intra-psychic conflict, analysis of transference and analysis of resistance. Next, he outlines the other basic qualities and delimitations that he considers essential. One of his criteria, for example, is that it is essential in psychotherapy to make an initial diagnostic evaluation. From this the assessment of the repairability of the personality malfunctioning is made and the therapeutic purpose or goal of the relationship is established. In order to establish the context for his kind of group psychotherapy, his elaboration of the social contract between the patient and therapist is particularly meaningful. In this atmosphere one is aware of the organized, planned and thoughtful approach over time that is involved in the group process as envisioned by him.

Doctor Schwartz goes on to discuss four essential conditions for the presence of an analytic group therapy. To whet your appetite we will provide you with a sample of what follows by simply listing them: First of all, an analytic group must have at least three persons present, two of whom are patients. Second, multiple interaction among members facilitates both intra-psychic and interpersonal awareness. Third, there must also be continuous exploration of unconscious processes. And the last essential requirement is the acceptance of limits.

Dr. E. K. Schwartz teaches us lessons that are valuable for all therapists in this well planned and executed summary of his conceptual model for group psychoanalysis. He teaches us the rational scientific basis for his treatment tech-

*niques, hopefully influencing not only what we do, but also why and when we
do it. His paper left us with warm and pleasant memories of this delightful,
brilliant, dynamo of a man.*

D.S.M.

G.D.G.

I T IS DIFFICULT to provide a generally acceptable definition of
a psychoanalyst. There are some who believe that psychoanalysis is anything one asserts is psychoanalysis. Others say that
psychoanalysis is what a person does if he has been trained in a
psychoanalytic institute. There are still others who insist that only
if you are a member of the International Psychoanalytic Association you are a psychoanalyst. All too few professionals say that
a psychoanalyst is someone who identifies himself with certain
concepts about the nature of man and the human condition.

What are psychoanalytic concepts? Can we specify some? Is it
the use of the couch? Is it frustration and the silent analyst? Is it
a commitment to psychosexual development? Is it the belief in infantile sexuality? Is it the libido theory? Or Eros and Thanatos?
Is it the advocacy of the recall of the repressed; free association;
the understanding of dreams; defensive operations; inner conflicts;
unconscious motivation; psychic determinism; resistance; transference; ego, superego and id? Is psychoanalysis all of these, and
more? Is it the Oedipus complex, object relations, fetal psychology? It is not easy to reach an agreement as to what the essential
ingredients are.

In this connection a piece of as yet unpublished research may
be illuminating. E. D. Wittkower delivered his presidential address
before the American Academy of Psychoanalysis, April 29, 1971.
In it he reported some findings of an investigation he conducted
which may have bearing here.

Wittkower sent out two sets of questionnaires to psychoanalysts
in many countries of the world and to psychiatrists where there
were no psychoanalysts. Some were members of the International
Psychoanalytic Association; some were only known nationally;
some were practitioners in countries where there was no psychoanalysis and where even anti-analytic attitudes prevailed. He tried
to get from them an idea as to what concepts they would agree
upon as being generally requisite to psychoanalysis. I shall not

summarize the study but select some findings appropriate to our purpose.

Whether the respondents were orthodox analysts, deviant analysts or non-analysts there was almost universal agreement on the following three general concepts as belonging to psychoanalysis:

1. Unconscious processes
2. Intra-psychic conflict
3. Transference

Almost as well accepted as these three was the concept of resistance. Interestingly, only 8 percent of the respondents thought the death instinct was a necessary psychoanalytic assumption. On the other hand, 68 percent of them indicated that object relations, which according to Wittkower seems to be a new post-Freudian idea, was a necessary part of psychoanalysis. His findings also suggest that psychoanalysis in North America is waning. There are fewer candidates for training and less professional interest in psychoanalysis today in this country than in other parts of the western world. We might conjecture why this is so. Have we now entered a stage of anti-rational and existential despair? Freud is dead! Analysis is dead! Has the age turned against reason, history and tradition? But it is not my intention here to present a cultural analysis. I wish to discuss what I think psychoanalysis is, what mental health is, what therapy is, and specifically what group therapy is. The existence of unconscious processes is the hallmark of psychoanalytic psychology. The royal road to unconscious processes is dreams. Any therapy that claims to be analytic, whether in the individual or group setting, must work with unconscious processes as expressed through intrapsychic conflict, resistance, transference and dreams.

The mental health movement in the United States holds to some underlying assumptions that need to be explicated. John Seely (2), the sociologist, states that the mental health movement in this country is revolutionary in that it extends our basic democratic tenets by asserting that the human condition is knowable, changeable, controllable, and that each person is entitled to be regarded as an individual. As mental health workers these are the keystones of our practices.

In the field of mental health we work with individuals, children, adolescents and adults, with couples, with nuclear families, with extended families, with small groups, and with large groups. My fantasy is that one day there will be a mental health television program and like Big Brother, we shall do mass therapy. We will educate and reeducate by the millions. Of course that is a fantasy. Once upon a time, not so long ago, it also was a fantasy to work analytically with more than one person at a time. It was a revolution in my own life to sit in a group with eight or ten patients and to try to work with them analytically. Again it was revolutionary for me a few years ago when I went to England and visited for the first time an open-door mental hospital. I participated in groups running to 175 and 200 patients, with three or four adjunct therapists. Imagine the great hall of an old English manor house, with high ceilings and a gigantic fireplace. The patients sat circling around the room in rows, two or three deep, with former patients, recovered patients acting as the therapist's aides. What? A hundred or more persons being treated simultaneously in a group? It could not be done! But we were doing it. And it is being done, as for example in The Living Room of the Social Rehabilitation Clinic of the Postgraduate Center for Mental Health in New York. But these innovations are not my topic. I wish to restrict my presentation to psychoanalysis in groups with deals with eight to ten patients at a time.

What is therapy? What are its underlying conceptualizations? The practice of therapy involves certain parameters without which treatment seems to falter. First, we must do a diagnosis, an evaluation of the person. This is basic to what we do when we do therapy. We make a diagnostic assessment. Call it what you will. I do not like the word diagnosis although it has a remarkable origin. It is made up of two Greek stems meaning to know through and through. To get acquainted with, to know someone thoroughly, according to many contemporary therapists, is the equivalent of treatment. The knowing is the therapy, for some professionals.

Second, in doing psychotherapy we assume that it is possible to repair personality malfunctioning. This must be a shared assumption; one that the patient too must accept. It is part of a bilateral social contract. I have often defined psychotherapy as an interpersonal relationship between at least two persons, in which at least one is conscious of what is going on, hopefully the therapist. In his consciousness within the relationship he will attempt to help the patient with his disordered life.

Third, the patient must be cognizant of the fact that the relationship has a therapeutic purpose. "That is why you, the patient, are here. That is why you pay me with your good time and life and money. Moreover, you must be willing to subscribe to the idea that there is a psychological mode of functioning. We are going to work together not within an anthropological, historical or social context, but a psychological one." Of course it cannot be entirely separated from other human contexts. The therapist is a human being in relation to another human being, but as a psychotherapist he is a very special human being, in a very special kind of relationship to others. Of course the mother is a human being in relation to her child, but she is a very special kind of human being, called a mother, in a very special kind of relation to another very special human being, called the child.

The tendency to deny differences in knowledge and skill, in status, responsibility and authority befuddles considerably the nature of human transactions. Although it has been said that the therapist-patient relationship is not person-to-person, for one, it has always been thought of as person-to-person. But what kind of persons are involved, and for what kind of purposes? What kind of skills are needed? What is the fine print, the small writing at the bottom of the social contract called "In these transactions, I am therapist and you are patient." Does it say, you are the helpee who comes to me and cried, "Help me; coddle me; mother me; succor me; tell me what to do; relieve my pain." Does the social contract expressly state what you want from me and what I can or cannot do for you? Many therapeutic relationships founder on this point, that there is no honest, clear-cut statement of the stipulations, the conditions of the social contract. Part of that statement, as I have already said, must affirm that the patient is cognizant that this relationship is for therapeutic purposes and that there is a psychological mode of functioning in which the participants are going to involve themselves in the course of their work together.

Furthermore, there are certain overall criteria for good therapy, whether individual or group. One index is that it is a planful experience. Good mothering is planful, not haphazard and chancy. Teaching, too, must be planful; and so too therapy. It should be boldly directed and consciously pursued. In addition, the therapeutic relationship is continuously open to bilateral exploration, modification and change. Yet it is a relationship that persists over time. It has the quality of Bergson's durée. Significant change does not occur instantaneously. There is no such thing as instantaneous psychotherapy. One of the qualities of important, not shallow, human experiences whether emotional, cognitive, sexual or social, is that they are enduring activities. They are commitments over time. Man lives his life over time and therapy is a relationship that promises no instantaneous outcomes. It takes time.

Certainly we have a social and professional necessity to shorten therapy. That is very important. I hope, Adelphi will some day hold a conference on "How to Shorten Therapy." This is a very urgent problem. As we have more nationalized and group health services, delivery of such services will become more acute and complicated. For example, a certain patient will be allowed only ten sessions. How are we going to schedule them? Are we going to offer ten sessions back-to-back, in daily contiguity? Or are we going to hold the ten sessions weekly over ten weeks, or monthly over ten months? How can we best use the ten sessions which have been allotted? Experience over time will determine whether the ten sessions were used wisely or poorly, and for which patients.

So much for general concepts, the context in which I wish to present a discussion of my kind of group therapy.

What is group therapy? What is the kind of group therapy that I call *psychoanalysis in groups* (3)? I have already committed myself to certain concepts, and I have outlined for you something of my understanding of the human condition; that is, the ways human development, human motivation, human relationships are experienced. With such an armamentarium I do what most influencers do. I sponsor and facilitate certain kinds of activities and not others. You may not like my use of the word, but we need to be honest with one another. We are influencers. We are in an influencing profession, and we use every appropriate technique to influence the patient.

What do we do in group therapy? What are the conceptual bases for psychoanalytic group therapy? What are the foundation stones for doing this kind of work? There are, I believe, four essential, inescapable conditions for psychoanalytic group therapy. Together we could probably list an additional twenty-four, all of some value under certain circumstances, for instance, depending upon the personality of the professional who is leading the group, the make-up of the membership, and similar variables. But the four I am about to discuss are indispensable for analytic group therapy.

First, one can only do group therapy if there are at least three persons present. I do not believe that treatment in dyads is group therapy, as some claim. In my opinion there is no dyadic group therapy. Group therapy requires at least three persons only one of whom is a therapist. Group therapy presupposes the simultaneous presence of authority and peer vectors. Two therapists and one patient do not constitute a group therapy setting. It is individual therapy with co-therapists. A basic concept of group therapy is the simultaneous presence of vertical and horizontal vectors. In the dyad, in individual therapy the patient stands alone before the therapist in an authority-subordinate relationship. The patient has no peer. In the treatment group the patient has peers, persons who are present for the same purpose, with whom the patient can identify, and who represent the same force within the life of the group. For group therapy, then, there must be not less than three persons, two of whom are patients.

The implications of this concept are manifold. It tells us why we think group therapy has value. The group provides an opportunity to receive support also in the patient or peer vector. Such a condition is an antidote to the situation which unfortunately happens too often, where the therapist acts not as a benign authority but as a punishing or an indiscriminate and bad authority figure. In this way he repeats with the patient many of the experiences of his childhood, and the patient is retraumatized. For instance, a patient says to his individual therapist, "You know, you were angry with me last session." The therapist responds, "Who, me? I wonder why you had a need to see me as angry. I was not angry. You are projecting." What can a patient do in such a situation? The force of the assumption that all help, all reality, all knowledge, all truth stems from the authority figure, is strengthened. The patient is put in the position of having to submit. Like a good patient, he finally capitulates and says, "I must have projected it. I wonder why." And then some time later when he is alone, he looks deeply in his own heart and he knows how many times he had to satisfy the demand of an authority figure to submit, to take the blame. By now he has created for himself a host of rationalizations, obsessions and other mechanisms in order to cope.

In the group, however, this does not so easily come to pass. If a patient turns to the therapist and says, "You were angry with me last session!" and the therapist says, "Who, me?" several other members of the group will confirm the reality. "Yes, you!" It is not easy to communicate "I was not!" in the face of eight other pairs of eyes confirming the experience. The anchorages in reality are shared, and the opportunity therefore exists for the correction of the misuse of authority. The presence of more than one patient, peers, is an important neutralizer of the authority vector.

It is said the Talmud advises that if someone says you are drunk, you can shrug your shoulders. If two persons say you are drunk, stop and listen. But if three say you are drunk, lie down! The presence of multiple others is a neutralizer of the distortions not only of authority figures but also of peers. All of us, I, my family, my patients, my friends, and my colleagues, have difficulties with both authorities and peers. If I work out problems with authority figures in the dyad, I often still have problems with peers. One criticism of individual psychoanalysis has been that patients have often been analyzed so they can relate well to authority figures but are isolated from peers. There is less likelihood of working out their problems with peers in the dyad. The group then avoids this kind of isolation with a hopefully benign authority figure, experienced in reality or illusion. The quality of relating is different in the presence of another. The first inexorable ingredient for any kind of group therapy, then, is that there be at least three persons in the group, two of whom are patients.

I am reminded that once as a consultant I recommended to the staff that we try an experiment. It was a veterans hospital. We were considering the case of a poet who was some fifty years of age, and deeply depressed. Every form of treatment they had tried seemed to fail with him. I suggested that we try a group experience, not group therapy, but a group experience. I suggested that all the interns, all of them, simultaneously take him on as a patient. There were eight interns, three of them were women. They formed a group and had regular sessions with him, eight therapists and the one patient. What went on was like machine gun-fire and he parried all of it. This, too, did not work with him. It was an interesting experimental intervention, but it was not group therapy.

The second essential element for group therapy is that multiple interaction among members is facilitated. There is an emphasis on bi-personal and multi-personal psychology. In the group, interpersonal transactions are investigated for their real and illusory aspects. The traditional model of psychoanalysis, which has been jettisoned by most good psychotherapists, stressed therapy as a uni-personal experience. The analyst was not a participant, but a mirror; the analyst was not a person; he avoided involvement. The patient on the couch six times a week–Freud resented the Sabbath –had an experience in a kind of sensory deprivation. He verbalized in splendid isolation. The emphasis was upon the intrapsychic rather than the interpersonal.

In group treatment there is recognition of the simultaneous presence of intrapsychic and interpersonal processes. Even inner processes are seen as reactive. In the group, we look at the member's provocative role to which the other responded, perhaps with a transference reaction. Or one may react to another patient as if she were his bad mother, or treat still another as if he were the patient's older sister. But in examining the interaction we want to try to discover why the others triggered the particular responses. We look also at the provocative role which brings forth a certain kind of real or transferential reaction. We look also at the need to provoke the reaction. In transference there is not only a response pattern but also an implicit demand that the other respond reciprocally, familiarly. "If I react to you as if you were my older sister, I will do everything I can, seductively and manipulatively, to get you to respond as I expect." There is no value in behaving transferentially if the other does not confirm or fulfill the transference demand. In the classical model, transference is regarded mainly as an intrapsychic process, projective activity motivated subjectively, like the proverbial "arrow shot into the air."

The first ingredient of group therapy is the simultaneous presence of authority and peer figures. The second is the simultaneous presence of intrapsychic and interpersonal processes. We examine the interpersonal reaction as phenomonology, as manifest content and then seek what is latent in it, the intrapsychic. The third essential is the continuous exploration of unconscious processes, the intrapsychic, the latent, through the examination of free associations, slips of the tongue, resistances, acting-out, dreams and transferences. Human beings are more than as-if characters. There is more to a person than a cardboard facade. The profundity of a human being, what makes him human, lies often in the most creative aspects of his life, in his fantasies and dreams, in his unconscious processes. That is an important part of what helps make therapy work. It is grandiose for a therapist to believe that only the single contact a week with him is going to motivate the patient to modify his life. How do a few hours a week out of a total of 168 make such a difference? Therapy works in part because the patient incorporates the therapist and the treatment into his fantasy life, which in itself gives the experience duration, depth. When I listen to a patient's dreams, his free associations, I ask myself, among other things, Where am I in this? Where is the group? For the therapist and the therapy to be effective, to help patients to move, to change, to overcome resistances, to have the courage to try the new and the different, to try behavior they have never tried before, the therapist must be important to them, in a trusting meaningful way, in their terms. So patients incorporate the therapist and the treatment process into their fantasy life in an idiosyncratic way, depending upon their history, their psychodynamics, and their character structure.

The last essential requirement for any kind of good therapy is the acceptance of limits: limits on the therapist; limits on the patients; limits on the time they spend together. A question needs to be raised about marathon and endless, open-ended groups, for example. There must be some limits on how long therapy will go on.

Sometimes patients are in treatment for ten to twenty years. People may need treatment all of their lives, though not necessarily in the same group or with the same therapist.

There is some evidence that after three or four years the group loses value for the participants. There is a law of diminishing returns. If a therapist has a patient in the same group for three or four years, unless it is very exceptional and it has been demonstrated that the patient can still make significant changes, the matter should at least be examined, explored, questioned. Should the patient not be transferred to another group, another therapist?

Limits are necessary. There must be time limits; limits on what the therapist expects to do and the goals he sets for his patient; limits on the goals patients set for themselves; limits on the nature and extent of their interactions. Jacques Levy, a clinical psychologist trained at the Menninger Clinic, conceived and directed the original production of "Oh! Calcutta!" in New York. It is a show depicting how a group of actors can get undressed, walk around nude in front of an audience, and "make-like." It is a "make-like" experience in group sex. Levy (1) was the guest speaker at the American Group Psychotherapy Association national convention in Los Angeles, February 1971. He told about how he had to train the actors and actresses in "Oh! Calcutta!" to simulate sex. He had to forbid them to have actual, real contact with one another. Otherwise his objective that they be actors would not have been accomplished. He needed them to work as actors and never forget their roles. He produced the show on this premise and it became a hit. It still costs thirty or forty dollars to get front row seats. And yet it is all make-believe, pseudo-sex.

Levy gave his lecture on how to train a group of actors in simulated sex and then formulated some interesting hypotheses with regard to group therapy. He concluded that limits were necessary if the goals for which the group gathered were to be accomplished. "The group members had been able to maintain control and to exercise discipline. . . . It was possible to stop short of an orgy by setting up arbitrary limits only because they served an obvious aim definable outside the particular sensual exercise being performed."

Limitlessness is related to mindlessness and illusion, two antitherapeutic factors. The more explicit the limits, the more likely they will serve therapeutic ends, the more effective and efficient the process. Presentations like this one also need limits. So I shall close, again pointing out that I have been talking about my definitions of good group therapy. I am not putting down any other form of helping. But I am setting limits on what we call psychotherapy, group therapy, and particularly psychoanalysis in groups.

REFERENCES

1. Levy, J.: Responses to simulated erotic experiences. *International Journal of Group Psychotherapy, 21:*275-287, 1971.
2. Seely, J. R.: *The Americanization of the Unconscious.* New York, International Science Press, 1967.
3. Wolf, A., and Schwartz, E. K.: *Psychoanalysis in Groups.* New York, Grune & Stratton, 1962.

CHAPTER II

AN OVERVIEW OF GROUP PSYCHOTHERAPY AND THE PRESENT TREND

MAX ROSENBAUM

Dr. Max Rosenbaum, the editor of the journal, Group Process, *and former President of both the Association for Group Psychoanalysis and Group Process and the Eastern Group Psychotherapy Society, is one of the country's leading authorities on group psychotherapy. In this paper he integrates his wide range of knowledge in the social science, philosophy and current literature in order to give us his personal view of the affect of these forces on current trends in both psychotherapy and group psychotherapy. This erudite combination of cultural and social trends, external first hand familiarity with the pioneers in group treatment and extensive information from source material on psychotherapy and psychoanalytic theory is a perceptive commentary and overview of the group therapy field today.*

In this personal journey he begins with a criticism of therapists who do not write theoretical papers. He next takes the reader further along on this intimate trip with him, exploring the evolution of this treatment from the past to the present. In his diary-like beginning Doctor Rosenbaum touches on his reactions to many of the people who shaped his thinking in recent years. He found the book GAMES ANALYSTS PLAY *a parody and simplistic. In retrospect* THE ROOTS OF PSYCHOTHERAPY *which was a forerunner of experiential therapy was also seen by him in similar vein. His old friends Wolf and Schwartz over-reacted to this irrational trend in treatment, he explained to us confidentially. As befitting an elder statesman of the group treatment field, Dr. Rosenbaum twits psychotherapists for not understanding the philosophical implications of the work they are doing or for not reading original source material. He then proceeds to review the philosophies of Fogers, May, Fromm and Buber and to comment on the impact of their religious identifications and training on their work.*

Dr. Rosenbaum gives us a critical evaluation of encounter groups—where he feels the leaders impose normative behavior on people who participate in their groups and call for a revolution in psychotherapy through the experiencing of joy. He then makes an earnest and strong plea for all psychotherapists to combat

15

the irrational in psychotherapy today which he feels is leading up to fascism. This he proposes can be accomplished through the employment of rational, scientific and logical inquiry.

Dr. Rosenbaum beautifully integrates current social thinking as expressed by such divergent people as Vonnegut, Heller, R. D. Laing, Marcuse, Rieff, Brown and Charles Reich. In this his broad social analysis of our society as viewed by the young integrates for all to see our culture with its unsuitable alternatives, myths, and collective defenses.

In summary, Dr. Max Rosenbaum makes a plea for constructive utilization of our knowledge in a very personal essay that reveals the richness and breadth of his view of psychotherapy and our culture today. He calls for a systematic study of behavior within the framework of our culture and what is happening in it and to it. His thinking is provocative and exciting in this personal essay which is more than merely an overview of the group psychotherapy field.

D.S.M.
G.D.G.

M Y TOPIC IS AN OVERVIEW of group psychotherapy and where it is going, as I perceive it at this time. Previously I have discussed the responsibility of the psychotherapy practitioner for a therapeutic rationale (23). The points that I detailed are worth repeating.

There has been a tremendous surge in the field of group psychotherapy that has been in the nature of a geometric progression, as validated by the amount of articles published in the field. It has been my observation that the majority of articles are clinical articles. They are largely testimonial in nature and they are quite barren with reference to theory. There are some basic reasons for this. Many advocates of dynamic psychotherapy are unreal in their expectation of psychotherapy. As they work in intensive treatment process experiences they often become discouraged and frustrated. If their training is deficient and if in addition they are going through life experiences, either real or fantasied in nature, which are discouraging, this is bound to reflect in the type of work they do. More specifically, many therapists then find a need to look for short cut approaches to psychotherapy. Now, I want to clarify that I am not opposed to short cut approaches to psychotherapy— I am merely opposed to approaches which do not recognize that they are limited in nature and limited in their goals. I think the confusion often starts when psychotherapists are unaware of the implications of what they are doing.

One of the signs of Freud's great genius was the fact that he was able to set forth some body of theoretical knowledge. He speculated; he made many errors, and it is no significant discovery to find out that in many respects he probably was not a particularly good psychotherapist. At least, he was rather limited in the type of people he could work with. But, you remember, his original orientation and desire was to be a researcher. Essentially, he became a clinician because of financial reasons. The reader should be reminded of these facts because most psychotherapy practitioners, in my observation, read secondary sources. They don't read the original sources and consequently they make many significant errors when they describe Freud or his contributions.

During the past couple of years, one can observe in the professional literature articles or books which are often an effort to satirize what is described as classical psychotherapy. For example you have a book called *Games Analysts Play* (26). This book is an illustration of a book that makes an effort to parody dogma. In this respect it is helpful but this type of book is simplistic because what it pretends to do becomes unreal. Strong attention is paid to "true feelings" but there is no effort to note that "true feelings" while apparently easier to arrive at than "true thoughts" are not essentially truth. A book like the one described is a kind of attack against the conformity that is seen in traditional psychotherapy and yet the whole effort to explore *insight* becomes lost by the wayside. In the effort to rebel against what is perceived to be conformity some authors use phrases like "courage and risk taking" and yet there's a quality of confused thinking about their statements because there is no effort to describe a society which doesn't demand some degree of conformity from its inhabitants. Like promoters in a "get rich quick" business venture some of the current authors don't think through the deeper implications of encouraging people to take risks, without really thinking through what these risks might conceivably lead to. The type of book I've described, while I believe it to be bad and a reflection of a lot of the current climate of anti-theory and anti-intellect, is not as significant as some of the other distorted volumes that I want to comment upon. Currently, the writings of R. D. Laing emphasize that man should become joyful and ecstatic, living at a high pitch. All of this is a complaint against reality, a reality which is to be over-thrown.

Let me make clear that some 20 years ago I was amongst the forefront of a group of people in the greater New York area who made a strong effort to introduce new concepts of psychotherapy into what we felt was rapidly becoming a stagnant field of psycho-therapy and group psychotherapy in particular. At that time I was attracted to a book by two people from Atlanta, Georgia. The name of the book is *The Roots of Psychotherapy* and it was au-thored by Carl A. Whitaker and Thomas P. Malone (29). As I look back this year, the book, while interesting, was essentially rather simplistic. It did point out the importance of recognizing the therapist as an individual and it did point up the importance of the therapist's use of his own personality. It did attack the pre-vious, rather naive, concept of the analyst as a neutral screen. I think today we're far more sophisticated about this so-called neu-trality. For those of us who became enthused about the book it was a definition of something we had been doing, or thinking, or writing about for some years. At the same time, two psycho-analysts in the greater New York area became very exercised about the book and what they felt were its dangerous implications. These two people, Alexander Wolf and Emanuel K. Schwartz, asked the Eastern Group Psychotherapy Society for permission to give a series of lectures attacking what they felt was the dan-gerous trend of the book by Whitaker and Malone and later au-thored a series of articles which were incorporated in their writ-ings (30). Their articles attacked what they felt was irrational psychotherapy. In retrospect I believe that Wolf and Schwartz overreacted, or at least were "too subjective."* I could experience their concern that people who simply read books such as Whitaker and Malone wrote usually did not understand the fact that the ability to take certain new approaches with patients could only be based upon years of clinical experience, maturity and a kind of sensitivity on the part of the psychotherapists that we do not often find today. It is a worthy objective if someone wants to modify an

---

* Personal conversation, A. Wolf, 1971.

individual's behavior, but the unconscious forces at work cannot be denied–even if ignored.

One does not have to be a graduate of the New York Psycho-analytic Institute or worship Freud to understand that Freud's theoretical presentations require a good deal of training to understand and a good deal of thought to absorb. Many critics of Freud expose their own ignorance of the complexity of Freud's theories. Obviously, more simplistic interpretations of the problems of man's behavior are always attractive and today we find a kind of renaissance of people who have developed an interest in Jung and Adler. This is all to the good. It is a worthwhile task to evaluate and possibly synthesize different systems. However, it is important to read primary sources when we attempt to synthesize or combine different systems. I noted earlier many people read secondary sources. The great figures in the field of psychotherapy changed their minds and changed their thinking as they went along. As they matured they changed. Sometimes their writings are confusing; sometimes there is an absence of adequate translations. Essentially, what happens is that students and even experienced professionals begin to read secondary sources. So you find frozen into the literature of psychotherapy distortions of original writings and these distortions are frozen into a position where they are described as facts. This, of course, contributes to inaccuracy. For example, anyone who becomes interested in Alfred Adler should know that as early as 1914 he referred to the "creative power" of the individual. Later he began using expressions such as "self" rather than the "individual." It should be noted that his use of the concept of the self was also done on several minor occasions. It should also be noted that Adler, toward the end of his life, placed an increasing reliance on organic evaluation when describing man's problems. Therefore, the serious student has to follow the development of a system (2). Today we find writers, particularly those who write about women's liberation, who consistently distort Freud, particularly in the discussion of Freud's writing about the Oedipus complex. It is simpler, of course, to attack Freud for being anti-woman than to think through the theoretical implications of his writing. Freud, for example, did make it specifically clear that the superego is heir to the Oedipus complex. Based on his writings, it is clear that he was not hostile to women. He did state that men have firmer character structures than women and he gave a theoretic reason. He stated that this was due to the strong identification with the father on the part of the son achieved by the boy's fear of castration. While this is a concept that may be in error, it's a theoretic concept that has to be evaluated. Of course, it's easier to attack Freud as an individual than to come to grips with the theoretic implications of what I have just stated, and more specifically how these theoretic implications must be tested culturally in a sensible research fashion.

In a further development of the article I described earlier where I discussed theoretic rationale I noted the implications of what happens when psychotherapists don't understand the philosophical implications of the work that they are doing (24). I paid specific attention to the recent encounter therapy and the many encounter therapists who seem completely unaware of the enormous implications of what is being done. Let me summarize some points rather quickly. In this article I pointed out that there were basic philosophical issues involved. In the practice of the encounter therapies I pointed out that Freud was a logical positivist in his philosophical orientation. In Freud's *The New Introductory Lectures* (6) he stated in his chapter "The Philosophy of Life": ". . . the spirit and the mind are the subject of scientific investigation in exactly the same way as any non-human entities." Of course, this kind of sentence was bound to result in a good deal of negative response on the part of humanists as well as existentialists and accounted for much of the deep-seated antagonism that was to occur against psychoanalysis and, more specifically, classical psychoanalytic concepts. But the fact that this sort of sentence was written cannot deny Freud's perceptions because earlier in his book *Civilization and Its Discontents* (5) he stressed that aggression is part of man's instinctual nature. Essentially when you "cut the mustard" you recognize that Freud was a much greater realist than Rousseau, when he recognized that civilization is inseparable from man. Rousseau stated that man is by nature good and only civilization makes him bad. Today we recognize this as rather simplistic. But the basic philosophical argument between Rousseau and Hobbes continues–the entire question of whether man is basically good or bad; whether human nature is basically good or evil–and this argument is to be found in the schools of psychotherapy that currently attract a good deal of attention. For example, Carl Rogers is committed to the concept that man is basically good. His concept of unconditional regard makes sense, at least from the point of view of a man who originally was interested in theological training in the ministry. The Rogerian therapist accepts completely the client he is treating, since the individual is seen as someone who merely needs acceptance so that he becomes the really good person he is fundamentally. This also accounts for Rogers' enthusiasm for encounter groups since they are supposed to promote the basic goodness which resides within the individual. This point of view is not recent; as far as Rogers is concerned, the references are specific in the literature. As far back as early publications of Carl Rogers in 1931 and 1933 (21, 22), you will find expressions described in his clinical case histories which are quite unlike anything that Freud would ever have written, but they capture the picture of the man. Rogers wrote statements in his 1933 article such as: "John came from a slovenly home in which there was little or no discipline." A further quote describes this little boy, John. "He is truthful and dependable, although he is full of life and has to be handled with a firm and consistent hand." Or, in another case report in the same article, Bobby, another youngster, is described after placement in a foster home. "He has shown honesty and trustworthiness to a high degree" (22).

Now, my efforts certainly are not here to penalize people for the kind of reports that have been written earlier in their professional careers. I dare say I would not like to go back to some of the reports I have written twenty-five years ago. But what I'm trying to point out is that early in his background Rogers showed this kind of enthusiasm for the goodness of man and so essentially it would make sense that he would be enthusiastic for encounter groups, since encounter groups are supposed to promote the basic goodness which resides within the individual. One may argue that Freud was too pessimistic. More specifically, any psychologist who is unhappy with the "medical model" of emotional disorder, which of course is an entirely different issue, may seize upon Rogers' concepts as a way in which he can finally psychologize, as it were, his work. But the underlying concepts become blurred by over-enthusiasm. You don't have to seize upon Rogers' work if you are unhappy with the "medical model," but many psychologists will. Another humanist, such as Erich Fromm who was originally interested in the rabbinate, moved toward the direction of man's goodness, but it would seem to me that Fromm is more realistic, since he sees man as potentially good or evil. Currently we see Rollo May, who was a clergyman and who has this enormous enthusiasm about man's goodness. Martin Buber (4), who has influenced me greatly, described when he met Carl Rogers a third alternative to the problems of the evil or good man. Buber described the polarity of a man who is in need of personal direction so that he can move to the good or evil. Buber attempted to illustrate this point by discussing paranoid schizophrenics and Rogers stated "I would say there is no difference in the relationship that I form with a normal person, a schizophrenic, a paranoid. . . ." It seemed to me as I surveyed Rogers' work, that as he worked more with psychotics, particularly at Mendota State Hospital, he questioned this orientation somewhat but fundamentally his position remains the same.

Currently there is also a distortion by many psychotherapists. They destroy the concept of Freud—what Philip Rieff has called the "ethic of honesty." Freud noted that statements of love and friendship may in fact mask resentments or hatred. Earlier, great writers had noted this; specifically, writers such as Dostoievsky had formulated this concept in different terms. But many therapists, particularly in the encounter movement, unmask people and this becomes their great goal. And essentially what this does is undermine the relationships that exist between people. This kind of confrontation which simply rips away the defenses from people is not an uncovering technique but is more possibly a technique that could lead to a lot of brutality because you can be realistic with people and develop a trust relationship with them and not do it in any punitive and destructive fashion. Very relevant to this is the work of one researcher. Rotter (25), based on his research in the area of interpersonal trust, has stated recently ". . . The decline in trust over the last six years may not be surprising to many, but it appears to the author to indeed be precipitous, and should it continue, our society would be in serious trouble, if it is not so already."

I don't want to go any further in the larger philosophical implications because they are to be found in summarized form in my article. Essentially, many contemporary therapists, particularly those working with groups, when they write articles appear to be discussing human nature. They are discussing an image of man and they are venturing all kinds of opinions in the area of ethics, theology and philosophy, which to me often exposes a basic lack of knowledge, a basic weakness in their training. In the deeper sense, the image of man is not a fully formed model, but a dynamic, changing human being. Many psychotherapists, particularly those who work with encounter therapies, impose normative behavior on people who participate in their encounter meetings. Quite simply, their psychological framework is behavioristic. You can notice this, for example, if you read an article by Goldman and Brody, "An Analytic and a Behavioristic View of an Encounter Weekend" (8). Goldman returned from one of these encounter weekends and I don't think it's unfair to say that at the time he returned he was in a kind of state of shock from what he had observed there. I urged him to write about it and I must say he wrote a thoughtful article in which he described some of the implications of what he experienced in his encounter experience. But let us move further to what is going on.

The current threat to any scientific (and, mind you, I'm not saying there's any fully defined definition of science in the field of human behavior, but I think it's fair to say that it has to be a body of knowledge which hopefully we can pass on to the next generation of psychologists) inquiry concerning human behavior is a kind of call to a revolution in the field of psychotherapy through joy. This is most apparent in the work of the encounter therapists. You can also observe this in new books such as Charles Reich's *The Greening of America* (17). In the political area Reich's book is a kind of manifesto for an affluent, middle income, young people to face that society, in which we all live, is in its last death throes. Apparently, all we have to do is raise our voices in song and laughter, spend our days with other people in good fellowship and victory will come by default. The equivalent is the kind of "cop-out" for living that I observe in many of the encounter groups where we learn how to trust one another by falling back into one another's arms, or we link hands with one another, or we walk around with our eyes closed and all this, of course, is to teach us basic human relationships. To me this appears to be an effort to influence interpersonal competence, but it is not basic. Charles Reich in the area of the politics of joy rails against the monopolistic aspects of the capitalist society as well as the national power elite. He comes forth with a thoroughly revisionist theory of evolutionary strategy. In contrast to Charles Reich, I want to remind you that in striving for equality, blacks inevitably move the entire society to higher levels of moral sensibility–the struggle moves all of us to re-examine our roles as to what democracy is. When women ask for more flexible definitions of their sex roles they inescapably benefit men because they urge them to reevaluate the entire relationship of identity, sex roles and the relationship that exists between sexes. Reich, in his book *The Greening of America* challenges all this. He takes Bohemians or beatniks and makes them new messiahs, and so he defines it along his attack on Consciousness I, which we know under titles such as "the Puritan ethic," "rugged individualism," and "social Darwinism." "This is the creed of the farmer, of the owner of the small business, the immigrants, the many members of Congress, gangsters, Republicans, and just plain folks." Reich says that the release of Consciousness is drastically at variance with reality.

But of course Charles Reich isn't as bitter about Consciousness I because these are all about people who fall by the wayside, so now we go over to Consciousness II and these are the people whom Reich really goes after. The "business man" (new type), the "liberal intellectuals," the "educated professionals and technicians," the "middle class suburbanites," "labor-union leaders," "Gene McCarthy supporters," "blue collar workers with newly purchased homes," "old-line leftists and members of the Communist Party, USA." Classical examples of Consciousness II are the Kennedys and the editorial page of *The New York Times*. It is the consciousness of "liberalism," the consciousness largely appealed to by the Democratic Party, the "consciousness of reform." Charles Reich is very bitter about the Consciousness II man who believes in science, a nationality, a technology, an administration, a planning, an organization, meritocracy, and Reich is going to free this man. He's going to get him finally to be spontaneous about his emotions; to deny his yearnings. He is going to get him to leave off his denials of his yearnings for openness, spontaneity and play. And so Reich points out that people who live in Consciousness I or II have lost the joys of adventure in travel, sex, nature, physical activity, morality, bravery, worship, magic and mystery, awe, wonder and reverence, fear, dread, awareness of death, spontaneity, romance, dance, ceremony, ritual, mind expanding, drugs, wholeness, sensuality, bare feet, affection, community, solidarity, liberation, brotherhood, myth-making, transcendence (well, that's a long enough list). Now, what is the solution? The solution is Consciousness III. And this is where we tie in to where we are in psychotherapy. Reich says we begin by a liberation. We begin with a sense of self. We reject meritocracy. We reject these distinctions and rigid social categories. We look for authenticity in terms of personal relationships based on feeling and a community united by affection. We welcome music; we welcome psychedelic drugs because we want to heighten and create a new awareness of man, nature and human sensitivity. This is Eros; this is life. We value experience; we distrust science, analytic thought and logic, because we know from our gut and intuition. We are not bound by the meaningless bourgeoisie. We move from job to job as the spirit moves us. We do not place our lives in bondage to a career. The message is clear. American society is beyond hope. It will die and it will then be resurrected. Now, mind you, children–it's not Easter time, it's June of 1971 but the message is clear. So we live in a culture based on shame and degradation. We kill people in Vietnam. We tolerate poverty. We pollute the air. But there must be something a little good about our culture. We still manage, however difficult, to encourage some dissent. The majority of the people live at a material level way beyond anything their fathers ever dreamed of. We're trying arduously, with difficulties, to maintain a certain educational and social structure in this country. We do much of this based on Puritan values–the same Puritan values that Max Weber noted when he stated that the third gratification–stable life styles and rational thinking are useful and sometimes inevitable concomitants if people want to acquire wealth. Now Reich has merely reaffirmed the connection Max Weber questioned–value systems. But of course he hasn't told us what we use as a substitute. This is the same problem that we have with encounter therapists. How do we recognize this trust, this love, this authenticity and deny greed, hostility, murderous impulses? Can we truly escape into marathon groups that meet for weekends free from the realities of life relationship, of education planning, of budgets, of school budgets, of petitions to nominate new candidates. Can we really escape to a Carmel-type Esalen experience where people can drop out of life for a weekend and then have the feeling they can come back? Or do they in truth acquire a certain euphoria, a certain high? And do they find that this high wears off after a day or two, a week, a month at most? Who can argue against qualities of gentleness, idealism, being open, being real? But this doesn't mean that the respect for authenticity on this level should lead us to an anti-intellectualism. Behavioral scientists owe it to themselves as well as to the profession with which they identify to be able to discern between the intuitions of the left wing and the right wing. It seems to me that it can't be done without scientific inquiry and without some sort of logic and reasonable discussion. Now I come to why I think behavioral scientists have been reluctant to face the issue head on. Some months ago at a symposium, in which I discussed the field of psychotherapy and the encounter therapies and group therapy, one of the participants who apparently had been very much moved by the Esalen-type experience, got up at one point after listening to my comments and discussion and stated that I had accused him of being a Fascist. Now as far as I was aware I hadn't accused him of any such thing and the word had never crossed into my mouth or thought. But perhaps he was intuitive because for a month after that meeting I gave a lot of thought to his comment. I thought this is really where the issue is and this is why group psychotherapists, psychotherapists, psychiatrists, and social workers have been unable and unwilling to face the issue.

Essentially we are in the realm of fascism. I think it's about time that it be stated and stated clearly. Psychotherapists like to pride themselves on their sense of being accepting, real and unwilling to ignore all types of new inquiry. This is good–but think about it. The right wing, the far right, has always understood and has traditionally been the enemy of science. Hitler made his great step forward with his appeal to joy–the Nazi Youth Movement. Alfredo Rocco, a favorite philosopher of Italian Fascism, defined fascism as "feeling translated into action" (10). Rocco, one of the early intellectuals in the history of Italian Fascism, and one of the group that was acceptable to the middle-class and therefore instrumental in allaying their anxieties concerning Fascism, theorized about the nationalist-syndicalism base of Fascism. He stated: "Fascism rejects democratic theories of the State and proposes that society does not exist for the individual but the individual for society. . . ." Italian Fascists proselytized the myth of the leader–just, merciful and benevolent. Italians, thought Mussolini, should not try to understand Fascism but experience it. They should not think, they should feel. Fascism could replace truth, liberty, art and thought as well as Socialism and democracy. Now every one of us must be aware that a man is entitled to his retreat, his withdrawal. He is entitled to find his comforts wherever he wants to, but he must not forget that this is a withdrawal from the larger responsibility of dealing with the complexities of society and particularly complexities of psychotherapy. The complexities of psychotherapy will not be resolved by denying their irrationality and will only be coped with by a rational, scientific and logical inquiry. So at this time I would like to make the statement that the kind of absolute reliance on trust exercises, the kind of absolute reliance on feeling, the kind of absolute reliance on intuition with a complete denial of any sort of reasonable logical inquiry will finally undermine and defeat the field of psychotherapy, ultimately play into the hands of the far right as well as the hands of the far left, and, as far as I'm concerned, this leads to fascism. And it is about time that psychotherapists and behavioral scientists of all persuasions in their theoretical beliefs face the issue for what it is, confront the issue for what it is and take their position and make their stand.

Currently there is a major complication in the field of psycho-therapy. Young people react very strongly against a culture which confronts them with what they feel are unsuitable alternatives. Psychotherapy is attacked by writers who attack its very basis. The current bible of young people, Joseph Heller's *Catch 22* (9), captures beautifully the amoral quality of a military machine which destroys authenticity. Yossarian, in *Catch 22,* is asked to remain within a system and destroy and be destroyed himself, or to escape. Finally, he is faced with the existential dilemma of es-cape–the fear of being alone. He finally makes his decision when he realizes that he–if he remains within the military–becomes either the destroyer or the destroyed.

Another guru of young people is Kurt Vonnegut. He writes beautifully of the ways in which our culture destroys life, all the while justifying this in the name of morality, goodness, and ra-tional behavior (28). Vonnegut, of course, constantly notes the culture's denial of sexuality. We can go through all of the current writers, novelists, songwriters, and the theme is repeated. Even Ronald Laing can write poetry and find an audience. The message is repeated again and again–"the culture is mad" (15). The posi-tive in the individual can never fit into the insane society. And we, hopefully thoughtful, psychotherapists are not immune to a culture which despoils its environment, kills peasants in far-off lands, debases and brutalizes the young people of our great na-tion. A floundering "great society" even had to find a Dr. Spock as a scapegoat. After all, wasn't it *his* book that ruined our young people? The old adage applies–a demonstrable fact becomes the cause. I am reminded of the school district which hired a psychol-ogist and then decided that he was the cause of the students' un-happiness. After all, they reasoned, there were no unhappy adoles-cents until he came on the scene and identified them as being un-happy. Spock stated recently that the child-rearing concepts of Freud and educators such as John Dewey have "fortuitously pro-duced a crop of fearless children who are just what this country needs." Obviously he is not going to be the favorite of conserva-tives when he makes such statements–or for that matter even liberals, who feel "put off" by the provocations of over-excitable young adults. Further, Spock hopes that Charles Reich, author of

The Greening of America, will be right in his prediction that in some twenty to thirty years enough people will have adopted a simple life style and we shall have the greatest bloodless, non-violent revolution of all time (27).

It is my belief that certain subcultures of young adults glorify the sensory experience. As a result, the normal adolescent hunger for affective and apprehended experience is intensified. However, there is also a denial and rejection of thought and comprehended experience. Thus, adolescence becomes a prolonged experience, since the dependency conflicts are never worked through. Since sensory experiences are emphasized–drinking, drugs, etc., comprehension is excluded and there is no organization of experience and comprehension. Since thought is part of interpersonal relatedness, the individual who exists solely by sensory experience is delayed in maturation, becomes more anxious as he is isolated. Much of this is related to a confusion where the adolescent challenges the authority of the parents. But the adolescent often challenges the parent role and attempts to define for the parents their own parental role.

I won't want to cover three important writers for our field: Herbert Marcuse (16), Philip Rieff (19, 20), and Norman Brown (3), but their questions are serious ones, especially their perceptions of the culture as a myth and a collective defense. Their writings, I believe, should be required reading for all serious students of group process. All three writers emphasize the value of play as a way of the person being exposed to the feeling experience. My belief is that this finally leads to erotic demands as the basis for relationships–and I believe that this theme is fundamental to much of the new psychotherapies.

The conclusion that I have presented will confront psychotherapists with much conflict. Certainly it would be a major error to deny the contributions of the innovative and, hopefully, the creative. It is easy for experienced psychotherapists to become annoyed as they read or listen to simplistic answers to the emotional difficulties of people. The charismatic quality of some of the leaders of the "newer psychotherapies" are quite transparent to therapists who struggle with their ethical responsibilities to a science. It is easy to "turn off" what appears to be the wild ranting of inexperienced psychotherapists. There is a tendency to dismiss out of hand those psychotherapists who don't appear to understand fundamental concepts such as resistance and transference–as well as transference cures. Worse yet, there is a tendency to dismiss the comments of younger therapists as merely efforts to act out unresolved oedipal conflicts, masking the need to destroy the aging father-teacher. But we have a basic responsibility to younger therapists who will so easily follow the "pied pipers" of psychotherapy. As much as our efforts to encourage logical inquiry in the tradition of science will be repelled and attacked, we shall have to continue the struggle. After all, the desire for magic is not the exclusive wish of patients. Struggling psychotherapists also search for magic, however strongly they deny this. Let us not fall into the trap of setting up a heaven of experienced psychotherapists. Keep the lines of communication flowing, as well as the essential dialogue. It will be an increasingly difficult task but we have no alternative.

Finally, let me make these points. I do *not* accuse Carl Rogers of being a Fascist. I do maintain that over-eager acceptance of the encounter movement plays into the hands of those who oppose study–and these are the fascists. Therefore, someone like Rogers becomes the tool of the fascists. I do not oppose the integration of different points of view into the practice of group therapy. But I do believe that this is dependent upon proper training. An experienced therapist filters different approaches and constantly refines his techniques. This filtering happens after extensive training. My observation is that encounter therapists are alien to the systematic study of behavior. I don't happen to worship Freud, but I do admire his genius and contributions. And one of his most significant contributions was to remind professionals of their obligation to report upon their clinical experiences and codify this information for the advancement of the science of the study of human behavior.

Psychotherapists who work with groups are on the "firing line." They cannot escape the provocative insights of patients. They will be attacked by the far right and the far left, particularly as they point out that the individual should explore his own capacities and still remain non-accepting of a culture which needs reconstruction. We shall continue to be in an area where we can only count on our own resources. But this was the great struggle of Freud–a struggle which we continue to be engaged in.

Where does this leave those of us who have a major commitment to the science of human behavior? We are in great danger. We are confronted daily with a variety of alternatives to the systematic study of human growth, and most of these alternatives, if not all, prove to be quasi religious experiences.

It has been my observation that many intellectuals, if not the majority, are fearful of change and particularly change which involves their *own change*. In earlier writings I have referred to change as "becoming something different." This is the dictionary definition. One way to disarm the corrective power of intelligence is to engross it in solipsism. Today we witness psychoanalysts and psychotherapists who fall prey to the many varieties of subjective idealism as an alternative to systematic thought and conscientious study. How else to explain the attraction of Ronald D. Laing who, as recently as the February 1972 issue of *Esquire* magazine, where he consented to be interviewed and profiled, finally admitted that his behavior was a counter-reaction to his rigid Scotch Presbyterian background. At the time of his interview he stated that he was traveling to the Far East to observe the mystical experiences of that area–or perhaps to search for a new faith. It is interesting to note that Laing has found the same problems that confronted Ernest Jones, the pioneer psychoanalyst and biographer of Freud. But Laing is looking for answers in different geographic areas that aren't truly so new.

Ernest Jones (12) always had a deep interest in the psychological foundation of ethics. He professed to be an atheist and this appears to me to have been a product of his own unresolved relationship with his father and mother. He *did* distinguish between superstition and religion, which he felt was one of the means where man copes with guilt and fear. He remarked on "the flood of curves and statistics that threatens to suffocate the science of psychology." He was unhappy with those psychologists who display a "striking ignorance of the human mind" and who, because they lack creative powers, often make up for their deficiencies by inventing "objective methods . . . that are to make them independent of intuition" (14). Jones was sophisticated enough to know that as illusions born of ignorance are dispelled, humility before the unknown increases (13). However, I am uneasy about the substitutes that Jones offered. He daydreamed in his later years that in the future the analyst or medical psychologist, like the priest of ancient times, might serve as a source of practical wisdom and a stabilizing influence in this chaotic world. Thus the community would consult this figure before embarking on any important social or political enterprise. It would seem that the devout atheist, Ernest Jones, was not above founding his own religion. There is a tendency then for all of us, if we are not on guard, to make a religion out of a psychotherapeutic technique rather than face the pain of working with human behavior, particularly as we work with the intensive therapy group. Freud was always concerned about psychoanalysis becoming the handmaiden of psychiatry, submerged in medicine. But he sensed the larger danger involved when psychotherapy itself becomes an ethic. It is almost as if Freud's paper, "Thoughts for the Times on War and Death," first published in *Imago* in 1915, should be required reading at yearly intervals for all psychotherapists and especially those who work with groups (7). Freud, writing during the chaos and early years of World War I, never living to observe the monstrous atrocities that man could perpetrate upon his fellow man, noted the disillusionment that the individual experiences. To observe the individual's descent from "ethical nobility" is terrifying if we have not really mastered the fact of man's enormous propensity to absolute good or absolute evil. Recall again Freud's line in his paper, "Thoughts for the Times on War and Death," ". . . and the brutality in behavior shown by individuals, whom, as partakers in the highest form of human civilization, one would not have credited with such a thing." Yet Freud was not really surprised. Toward the end of his life when speaking with Theodor Reik about the Nazi regime in Germany and the blind instinctual cruelty of the Germans, whom he had thought more intelligent and capable of better judgment, he said (as quoted by Reik), " 'Look how impoverished the poet's imagination really is. Shakespeare, in a *Midsummer Night's Dream*, has a woman fall in love with a donkey. The audience wonders at that. And now, think of it, that a nation of sixty-five millions have. . . .' He completed the sentence with a wave of his hand . . ." (18). Theodor Reik again quotes Freud as noting, after listening to a young colleague lecture, and instead of examining a problem, merely present pretentious plans for the treatment of scientific questions, "Does reading menus fill your stomach?" Confronted as we are, all of us, by a world which asks for quick and simple answers to the most complex problems of living, we have to be on guard against taking on new roles and tasks for which we are not equipped and which will only result in failure.

The enormous potential of a group, and the intricacies and complexities of group process, defy comprehension. We are at best, only at the beginning. Like astronomers, we explore one galaxy and then find ourselves in larger and greater galaxies. Basic concepts such as transference and counter-transference have to be examined anew and refined more carefully. Small wonder then that out of our frustration we may move to enchantment with a variety of "gimmicks" which seem to promote a solution to the anxiety and despair of our patients and colleagues.

Let us then not be caught up in the newer religions that pose as modifications of psychotherapy. Let us renew our efforts to study man, especially in social interaction, but always with the knowledge that we are students of human behavior and not the high priests of a new religion called psychotherapy. Let us be open to new experiences and indeed welcome these experiences. But let us not be so over-eager that we dissipate the hard won struggles of our teachers and colleagues. The healthy skepticism that Freud wrote about may still serve as a worthwhile model. But the *study* of human behavior does not serve as a substitute for a *philosophy* of human behavior. We must continue to be clear as to our strengths and limitations and a periodic inventory of these strengths and weaknesses would be in everyone's self interest— and certainly those of us who profess to be students of human experience. Let us not turn the practice of psychotherapy into the myth of psychotherapy and establish the weak underpinnings of a new religion. We shall have to fight the Fascism that represses our intellectual inquiry and the kind of nihilism that promotes affective experience to the denial of all reason under the banner of experience.

Finally, a note of caution. We have been told that those who do not observe history and study the lessons of history are doomed to repeat history. In the 1920's, George Sylvester Viereck, a journalist and novelist, popularized the writings of Freud in America through Viereck's novels, books and particularly articles he wrote for the Hearst newspaper chain. He reached millions of readers and Freud was pleased to correspond with Viereck and to be interviewed by him. Viereck was a romantic who emphasized exotic and sensual themes and felt that since Freud's system emphasized Eros he could find a confirmation for his own beliefs. He liked Freud's views that man had a mania for authority. Therefore, if the authority of a priest was taken away, Viereck found a new authority in science—in this case psychoanalysis. He continued to find in psychoanalysis justification for his own views and Freud was apparently so pleased to have a sensitive exponent of psychoanalysis for the American public that he did not look carefully enough at his publicist. For by the 1930's Viereck was the leading and literate spokesman in America for the Nazi movement in Germany and Freud broke with Viereck, upset that Viereck had "debased" himself by his support of Nazism. What Viereck demonstrated in his writings was that while he understood psychoanalysis he was confused about ultimate end—about ethical and moral values. By committing himself to Eros he could ignore the question of permanent moral truths. His was a form of narcissism that could ignore the superego. As psychotherapists trained in the depth method of psychoanalysis we have the responsibility to look beyond the surface and this is our responsibility as we observe the current crazes in psychotherapy (11).

REFERENCES

1. Adler, A.: *The Practice of Individual Psychology*. New York, Harcourt, Brace and Company, 1929.

2. Ansbacher, H. L., and Ansbacher, R. R. (Eds.): *Superiority and Social Interest.* Evanston, Ill., Northwestern University Press, 1964.
3. Brown, N. O.: *Life Against Death.* New York, Vintage Books, 1959.
4. Buber, M.: In Friedman, M. (Ed.), *The Worlds of Existentialism.* New York, Random House, 1964.
5. Freud, S.: *Civilization and Its Discontents.* New York, Norton, 1930.
6. Freud, S.: *New Introductory Lectures on Psychoanalysis.* New York, Garden City Publishing Co., 1933.
7. Freud, S.: Thoughts for the times on war and death. *Collected Papers,* Vol. IV. London, Hogarth Press, 1949, pp. 288-317.
8. Goldman, G., and Brody, H.: An analytic and a behavioristic view of an encounter weekend. *J of Grp Psychoanalysis and Process, 3*(1): 101-120, 1970.
9. Heller, J.: *Catch 22.* New York, Simon & Schuster, 1961.
10. Hibburt, C.: *Benito Mussolini: A Biography.* London, Longmans, Green & Co., 1962.
11. Johnson, N. M.: Pro-Freud and pro-Nazi: the paradox of George S. Viereck. *Psychoanalytic Review, 58:*553-560, 1971.
12. Jones, E.: Some questions of ethics arising in relation to psychotherapy. *Dominion Medical Monthly, 35:*17-22, 1910.
13. Jones, E.: *What Is Psychoanalysis?* New York, International Universities Press, 1948.
14. Jones, E.: *Essays in Applied Psychoanalysis.* London, Hogarth Press, 1951, pp. 254-255.
15. Laing, R. D.: *The Divided Self.* Baltimore, Penguin Books, 1966.
16. Marcuse, H.: *Eros and Civilization.* New York, Vintage Books, 1962.
17. Reich, C. A.: *The Greening of America.* New York, Random House, 1970.
18. Reik, T.: *From Thirty Years with Freud.* New York, International Universities Press, 1940.
19. Rieff, P.: *Freud: The Mind of the Moralist.* New York, Doubleday, 1961.
20. Rieff, P.: *The Triumph of the Therapeutic.* New York, Harper & Row, 1966.
21. Rogers, C.: Measuring personality adjustment in children 9-13 years of age. *Teachers College Contributions to Education,* No. 458, 1931.
22. Rogers, C.: A good foster home: its achievements and limitations. *J of Ment Hygi, 17:*2140, 1933.
23. Rosenbaum, M.: The responsibility of the psychotherapy practitioner for a therapeutic rationale. *J of Grp Psychoanalysis & Process, 2:*5-17, Winter 1969-70.
24. Rosenbaum, M.: Responsibility of the therapist for a theoretic rationale. *Group Process, 3:*41-47, Winter 1970-1971.

25. Rotter, J.: Expectancies for interpersonal trust. *Amer Psychologist,* *26:*433-452, 1971.
26. Shepard, M., and Lee, M.: *Games Analysts Play.* New York, Putnam, 1970.
27. Spock, B.: Roche report. *Frontiers of Psychiatry,* May, 1971.
28. Vonnegut, K.: *The Sirens of Titan.* New York, Dell, 1959.
29. Whitaker, C. A., and Malone, T. P.: *The Roots of Psychotherapy.* New York, Blakiston Co., 1953.
30. Wolf, A., Schwartz, E. K., McCarty, G. J., and Goldberg, I. A.: *Beyond The Couch.* New York, Science House, 1970.

CHAPTER III

A PERSONALIZED DISCUSSION ABOUT GROUPS

MARTIN SHEPARD

In more recent years the popularity of encounter groups or the human potential movement has certainly increased both with the public and psychotherapists. Most therapists utilize some of their techniques in groups or groups in conjunction with individual therapy. As founder of one of the better known eastern "growth centers," Anthos, Dr. Shepard's ideas on group therapy provide a perspective of this new movement. In Dr. Shepard's conception of treatment group therapy has a prominent place. He views group therapy as being the most effective method of treatment and the treatment method of choice. With this point of view he makes a particular case for the utility of groups and why he feels you can accomplish the same objective, and more, within the group setting. He outlines those issues which he feels impede therapeutic progress and those aspects of the therapists and of groups that implement human development.

This paper is more than solely a plea for the utility of group therapy. It is a statement of a very personal philosophy of life and treatment delivered in a quite personal style for a formal professional meeting. It outlines some of the aspects of group therapy that Dr. Shepard feels are useful to him. As such, it is his personal odyssey of his psychiatric training with a detailing of those experiences that he feels have molded his present stance. He indicates his various professional experiences with different people and their effect and influence on him. Although he begins with psychoanalytic training as the foundation for his later professional evolution, his attitude towards this branch of therapy is more negatively critical than positive. The utility of the therapists' personal disclosure in therapy is exemplified by his experience with Albert Ellis. The further influence of Fritz Perls, Schutz and Esalen are indicated both in terms of specific techniques that he utilizes and more broadly as general philosophic and personal attitudes that have affected his style of psychotherapy.

Dr. Shepard's presentation, and even his question and answer format, is a very individualistic one as is his approach to group treatment. As he presents it, it may seem patently easy and even exciting to follow in his footsteps. A word of warning may be in order; individualistic approaches developed over many years of experience seem easy to adapt and implement. The beginning group therapist should be aware that this seemingly easy therapeutic action does not generate overnight, nor is it easily acquired by everyone practicing in the field. Letting it "all hang out" and "doing your own thing" can only be seen or done in the perspective of good professional training and background so that what follows is truly psychotherapeutic and not acting out.

D.S.M.

G.D.G.

I SHOULD LIKE TO GIVE YOU a bit of my own background and invite your questions so that we might discuss, more intelligently, group process according to your interests.

I am a physician and a psychiatrist. And I have had experience in running groups ever since the second year of my residency training.

When I finished my psychiatric residency, I decided that I had an obligation to obtain psychoanalytic training, for I had been helped enormously by an analyst. I felt like the analysts had the secret of secrets. And I had to learn that secret in order to best help others.

However, the biggest secret I learned in the course of that training was that the analysts were made of the same clay as other mortals–that they were as presumptuous, arrogant, blind, competitive, uptight, and as capable of being tin-gods, as all of the non-analytic therapists I had seen in the course of my training.

And I began to realize that my own successful analysis was the result not of magic, but of a meeting between one particular female therapist and one particular patient–namely myself. This first analyst of mine was truly humble. She was aware of her ignorance, comfortable in not knowing the future, and therefore able to tolerate the unknown. Her openness to the unknown–her relative lack of prejudgments and presuppositions–coupled with my basic counterphobic philosophy, was what accounted for the good "analytic" result in my case.

With this as a brief introduction to myself as a person and therapist I would like to now continue my presentation by answering audience questions.

Q: You say your "counterphobic philosophy" contributed to your own successful analysis. Just what does that mean?

A: Counter-phobia means going against your fears. When I discovered that I feared confronting some issue–be it dining in a restaurant by myself, living alone, breaking off with a girl friend, being honest with people, speaking to strangers who attracted me –I would attempt that which I was afraid of. Most often, I discovered in the process that the only thing I had to fear was fear itself. I found that I had been imposing restrictions on my behavior that were unnecessary–restrictions rooted in childhood superstition and social conditioning. I began to appreciate options in living that I never dared see, much less take. I began to know what freedom was about.

My counterphobic style accounted for a very different type of psychoanalysis than others that I came to see. Some people are so well analyzed that they can give you exquisite reasons for why they do what they do. They appreciate the influence of their mothers, grandmothers, maids, fathers, sisters and neighbors in contributing to their "neurosis." Of course, they are just as limited after this type of analysis as they were before–just as "neurotic." Except that now they "understand" the reasons for it.

In any event, the important thing, for the moment, is that I have been through the mill of analytic training. That began in 1964. And while it was most useful, I also felt that there must be some way to speed up the therapeutic process–that for me consumed over four years of three times a week and four times a week visits. That too, led to my increasing interest in groups.

From 1966 through 1968 I was actively involved politically, being one of the founders of the "dump Johnson" movement–a worthy but misguided attempt to end the Vietnam War. Following Robert Kennedy's assassination, I returned to psychoanalytic studies and in addition immersed myself in the new wave of nonanalytic group therapies.

I studied Marathon encounter techniques with Albert Ellis, and found him to be a refreshingly honest and rational therapist. Someone in one of his groups could ask him the most personal question and he would answer it without hesitation.

"Dr. Ellis, have you been intimate with other women since living with your current girl friend?"

Ellis would answer such questions fully and unashamedly. He

too would eventually pose the question "Why do you ask?" to his questioner, just as an analyst might. But you *know* that he wasn't hiding behind his counter question.

Sitting in his group I saw how much more effective his responses were. People opened up much more readily. They were willing to share more of themselves as Ellis was willing to share himself. And secrets considered "shameful," that might wait months before emerging on the analyst's couch, would come out within hours.

I studied with Bill Schutz, of Esalen fame, when he and some of my group leaders he trained came East in the winter of '68. With him I came to appreciate non-verbal approaches as a means of gaining greater awareness of self. And the importance of risk-taking. And the very great value of having a person "act out" his fantasies in order to grow, change, and move on to other things— as opposed to incessantly talking them out.

I worked with Fritz Perls, the great psychiatric genius of our time and the inventor of Gestalt Therapy. Fritz himself, born and educated in Europe, was trained and certified as a Freudian psychoanalyst. After fleeing the Nazis, he headed the South African Psychoanalytic Institute. Perls came to realize three levels of "explanatoriness"–of talk. They were "chicken shit, bull shit and elephant shit." He came to appreciate that most psychopathology was the result of not owning parts of yourself and, instead, projecting them outwards.

Fritz went on to develop a therapy that gave people an opportunity to re-own their projections, by having them act out parts and characters in their dreams and play act people they felt were causing them difficulty.

It was an exciting time for me. I was discovering therapies and therapists that I never knew existed. My training had made me aware of Freud and some of the neo-Freudians, of electro-shock and the chemotherapies, of decent environments and occupational therapies, but had not prepared me for this. I soon realized that I, and the other "well trained" establishment analyst/therapists, were phenomenally ignorant. We were learning more and more about less and less, until at the end of analytic schooling, we knew practically everything about absolutely nothing.

There was a whole world out there of other approaches to life, harmony, self-fulfillment, integrity, and health that the analytic establishment knew nothing about. There was Yoga, meditation, Rolfing, Gestalt, Sensory awareness, Bio-energetics, nude therapy, Rational-emotive therapy, Synanon. And just as I embarked on analytic training in order to become as good a therapist as I could be, I now studied all of these other approaches.

Esalen, of course, was the center for the study of these varied approaches. What a marvelously experimental, open-minded place it was. They would try any approach if it seemed to further human understanding. But I was not prepared to relocate in California. So, along with some others, I helped establish Anthos–an Esalen-like center in New York.

Q: What is the purpose of a group?

A: The goal of any group, I would think, is that people who are confused, lost or lonely get together for the purpose of sharing things with others–breaking out of their isolation and loneliness –to end their state of confusion, or to become enlightened. In one way or another, all of those elements are probably operating in every participant. So that's the general goal.

People in groups always share stories. That gets accomplished very quickly. In terms of getting some overview or enlightenment about what people do with each other–the ways they interact with one another–any observant participant can't help but get something out of that, too. In terms of confusion, the thing that usually ends confusion about "who am I, how am I doing, how am I affecting other people," is FEEDBACK. And a lot of people give that. "I think you're doing this." "I think you're pompous." "I think you're a manipulator."

Q: What is Gestalt Therapy about?

A: In simplest terms, Gestalt Therapy is Psychodrama without a supporting cast. You play everybody–all parts. And it's based on the idea that everything that exists in the world you deal with is, in a sense, a *projection;* and that people are projectors par excellence. For a third of our existence we are indisputably projecting. For our dreams are all projections–images we've created in our mind's eyes that spring from within ourselves. Attitudes you see in other people are often projections. Not that there isn't such a thing as "reality"–things that come from other people–but certainly when you're dealing with problems people have–with psychopathology–much of this is projection.

People who always fear being attacked by other people and walk around like timid little mice have usually disowned part of their aggressiveness. So the *other* person–out *there*–they're the angry aggressive person and *not* me. Other people are irritated and angry all the time. They go to a movie where the hero and heroine are kissing and they have this "aw shit–I don't want to watch that love stuff" reaction. Well, they're cutting off a certain amount of their softness and tenderness. The professional old-maids who spy on young girls and their dates and condemn their "immorality," disown and project onto others their sexuality. Or take the bullies you read about or see here in America or England who beat up young men with long hair for being "faggots" after projecting their disowned homosexuality onto them.

So the idea of "cure" (although I don't think that Fritz Perls, the father of Gestalt Therapy, would use the word cure. He talked about making people "whole," "bringing their parts together," "being centered") is to capture these split off parts. To own them. To acknowledge them as part of yourself and take responsibility for them instead of projecting these attitudes onto others.

There are a number of ways to work with Gestalt, which we could discuss. Essentially all of these ways involve providing some sort of gimmick by means of which people can recapture their projections. Perls himself used the gimmick of an empty chair and a "hot seat," and worked with dreams quite heavily, because dreams are the clearest instance of projection. In working with a dream, you relate it in the present tense, and then start to be–give voice to–all of the characters and things in your dream. You can be a landscape ("I am hot, arid and dried out"), a monster, an attaché case ("Hard on the outside and empty within")–anything at all that you dream about. And between the hot seat and the empty chair, you can have encounters between these various "beings." It's very hard to blame anybody for something in your dreams, since you've made it all up. When you're dealing with an interpersonal situation there is always the possibility of saying "so and so *is* really that way." Then you lose a chance to get into the "Aha!" phenomenon–where, when giving a voice to some character or thing, you suddenly appreciate "THIS IS ME."

Q: Can you say something about inactive leadership in a group– as, for example, a Tavistock group?

A: If you become a group leader, you will find it hard to resist the feeling that you have to *do* things for people, that it is up to you to set things in motion. I feel that way frequently, and I've watched enough other group leaders to know that they share this feeling.

You will have the feeling that you must get a process going, that you have to push people, that you must be therapeutic. You want to give people an honest return on their group dollar. You'll start to think "I'm paid to be the leader and damn it, I'm supposed to lead. Otherwise I'm not earning my money. Just to sit around, listen, and say nothing doesn't validate all of my training. That could be done as readily by any housewife or cleaning woman." Now my maid doesn't have my degrees or my training, and so it's unlikely that people will seek her out as a guru. Yet she's most sympathetic and a good listener to boot. So the above thought is undoubtedly true.

With all of these factors working against you, plus your desire to share your insights with those attending your group, it requires a great deal of discipline to stay out of things. Yet if you can relax sufficiently so as to stay completely out of it, something will evolve on its own. And it will be interesting more often than not.

One thing that will happen is that the group participants will become particularly aware of their desire to be led plus their reluctance to allow anybody to lead them. And you will find out rather quickly who the natural leaders and followers are. And you will have an opportunity to witness the social roles and games that people adopt against an unstructured situation.

I can assure you that it is very different to sit in a room and not do anything as opposed to leaving the room entirely. In my private group practice I leave the room after an hour and a half and let the group meet without me for another hour and a half. And people do different things then. For one, nobody is play acting to win the authority's favor because the authority isn't there. Lots of other people who are intimidated by the leader, suddenly find they can take a much greater part in things. But most importantly, people begin to realize that they can help themselves and others even without a "wise-man" being present–i.e. that the wise man exists in themselves.

But being in the room and inactive shifts the focus. Somehow, whatever the mystique is that people invest in you, carries over so that your presence accomplishes something even as you do absolutely nothing. One safe thing in doing absolutely nothing is that you don't hurt anybody. It's rather ego-shattering to realize that a lot of good things can happen without your doing anything, yet in the end, people of course have to help themselves.

Q: One thing I noticed about non-directive groups is that they don't seem to have any rules. In other types of groups I've been acutely aware of rules.

A: There are always rules underlying all groups–even non-directive ones. HONESTY is a good example. And WE SHOULD ALL BE OPEN WITH EACH OTHER. WE SHOULD ALWAYS SAY WHAT WE FEEL. YOU HAVE TO BE SPONTANEOUS. These are all implicit rules. THE LEADER SHOULD BE RESPECTED. Everybody's got that one. Even if they fight against it in a negative way. It's still a rule that they're relating to. And depending on the group you're in, the rules very quickly establish themselves.

If you are doing Albert Ellis' type of Rational-Emotive group, people don't stay with the rule of WHAT THEY'RE FEELING NOW, but BRING IN PROBLEMS FROM THE OUTSIDE. And that's what the group works with all the time. That's the rule, although it's not explicitly stated. But it's equally obvious that that is what the system lends itself to. There are other rules for other groups. In a Gestalt group the rule is YOU ARE A PROJECTOR. EVERYTHING THAT HAPPENS IS A PROJECTION, AND YOU HAVE TO OWN THIS AS A PART OF

YOURSELF. Another Gestalt rule is that you keep relating only to the leader and yourself. But the rule of a non-directive group is that EVERYBODY ELSE HAS TO DO THE WORK. THE THERAPIST DOESN'T HAVE TO DO ANYTHING.

I get bored by a rule that goes on too often, and so I enjoy switching rules just· so that people can't get used to expecting things. But that's also a rule.

Q: I've always experienced inactive leaders as supportive—just by virtue of their being in the room.

A: Right. And everybody senses you as supportive in running this type of group. Because you haven't antagonized anyone—you haven't put anybody down.

Theoretically I think you should be able to be helpful to people even if you're antagonistic to them. Supposedly, if someone stays with you long enough, is willing to tolerate your dislike of them, your contempt for them, they can get something out of it. But the actuality is that it usually doesn't happen this way. They don't often stay long enough. By doing absolutely nothing, some people may get restless and say, "To hell with this. I'm paying all this dough and I expect something to happen. I expect to be cured." On the other hand, you're sure of not hitting a person hard and turning him off from whatever supernatural powers—witch doctor powers—he has given *you* in order to help *himself.* That quality of faith that helps people feel better, or that feeling that the God-like therapist thinks well of me. After all, he smiles. He's pleasant. He seems to listen. You know, the therapist can be thinking of his accounts, his latest golf score, or God knows what. But the group members don't necessarily know that and (laughter)—in spite of your laughter that does have a curative effect.

Q: Do you care about the opinions of any of your fellow profes-sionals?

A: Yes. A few.

Q: Who?

A: I care about Fritz Perls' opinions. He was a crusty old man, content to accept most every aspect of his personality—be it his pissiness, conceit, or whatever. He referred to himself proudly as a "dirty old man" and his sexual exploits are legendary. Fritz once claimed that he could tell more about a woman from the way she kissed than he could by interviewing her in a fifty minute analytic hour.

And I believe him.

Q: But Fritz is dead now. How about your contemporaries?

A: I care about what Ronald Laing, the Scot psychiatrist, thinks. For like myself, he recognizes that personal stability is best maintained by living out and living through one's "madness."

He knows that there are people throughout the world (most therapists included) who try to *invalidate* the experience of the "madman"–so threatened are they by the experience, the awareness, the slice of reality that the "madness" presents. So they try to "psychoanalyze" his experience away. Or they place him in hospitals. And with talk, drugs, or occupational diversions they hope to make him "normal"–not realizing that the pressure he underwent in *acting* normal was what drove him "mad" in the first place.

Q: Anyone else?

A: Thomas Szasz.

Q: Who's he?

A: A maverick Freudian analyst who has written extensively on the myth of mental illness. He knows that most of what passes for "sickness" (*neurosis* and most *psychosis*), are, in actuality, life styles that differ from the norm. No one has yet–or is ever likely to in my opinion–demonstrated a biological basis for these "mental illnesses," the way that one can show a relationship between the influenza virus and the flu or between a tubercle bacillus and tuberculosis. Neither has anyone demonstrated organic lesions for most "mental illness" as one can demonstrate lesions in cancer patients, for instance, where the etiological factor is unknown.

Szasz identifies "patients" as I would. A man becomes a patient not by virtue of his "sickness," but rather because he either accepts the label–the *role*–of patient or because it is forced upon him by a society that is troubled by or hostile to his life style. For a "patient" to exist, however, you must have another person about willing to play the role of "therapist." That is to say, the doctor must be willing to view this unusual life style as a *sickness* that he then might be able to *cure*.

I refuse to enter into that phony game. I will not allow a "patient" to hide behind and excuse his behavior on the basis of his "sickness." I would rather have him accept his behavior as an authentic experience–without apology and without shame.

The philosophy behind Anthos epitomizes these ideas. *Psychotherapy* is not considered *therapy* at all. Rather, we conceive of therapy as being nothing more than part of one's educational process. Our present system of education–from the first grade through the university–teaches people how to relate to geography, history, spelling and arithmetic. Yet it is rare to find any program that teaches people about how they relate to themselves and others. The group at Anthos, offered to the general public (not "patients," mind you), address themselves to that educational deficit. These groups are experimental/experiental laboratories where participants have an opportunity to know themselves and others better and in which they can try out, act out, and adopt new patterns of interaction.

And when you strip the traditional therapies of their theoretical double talk and technical bullshit, that is all that they really offer –that is, when they work effectively.

Q: Are there specific types of groups you would advise for certain categories of patients? And are there certain gimmicks you would use for particular problems in a group?

A: In talks I have given to professional societies I am frequently asked whether or not there are specific techniques to use in dealing with particular problems. My answer is that there is no way of preselecting such tactics. Not that some professionals don't try that. Indeed, they do. But I feel that such attempts are either well intentioned folly or rationalizations of orthodoxy.

For me, the really good therapist is much like the good artist. In art school one studies technique after technique. You learn perspective, landscape, figure drawing, abstraction. You practice working in various media: oils, watercolors, tempera, charcoal, ink, woodblock, etching. You attempt to understand all of the "rules" for working in each of these modalities. And in the end, if you are any good at all, you throw out all the rules and work instinctively. Perhaps it would be more appropriate to say that you go *beyond* the rules. What comes out of you then is YOU, tempered and refined and broadened by all you have studied and then "forgotten."

In the same way the gifted therapist exposes himself to all of the psychological disciplines he can and then acts instinctively–assuming that his organism will pull out of his vast experiences that response to his "patient" that makes the most sense.

I've come to feel that when you strip "psychotherapy" (including analysis) of all of its technical jargon, what it comes down to is one person commenting upon the life of another and authentically sharing that other's experiences. If these comments make sense, and if the sharing with and acceptance of the other is sincere, then the client and patient and student and other profits from his or her experience.

From what I've said about the essence of "therapy" (making sound comments and sound contact) you should not be surprised that I consider individual psychotherapy an anachronism–a holdover from the past. I've come to feel that it is outmoded, unnecessary, extremely expensive, ridiculously "private," and limited –inasmuch as the "patient" only gets the limited feedback and comments of *one* person–the "therapist." Whereas in a group, other people might have useful comments to make and experiences to share.

My style is unpredictable when I work with people. It is intuitive, and I will do what I feel most like doing. By and large I listen as attentively as I am able and make comments about what I see happening. I rarely pull my punches. Some people respect and appreciate this. Others consider this crude and cruel. I don't consider myself to be especially cruel.

Q: Is there anything more you can say about your own particular style of leading groups?

A: Lately, I have originated a new wrinkle in therapy. "Hat Therapy," I call it. And I employ "Hat Therapy" regularly in my groups. The hat becomes a gimmick that focuses attention on the fact that people are ultimately responsible for themselves and capable of fulfilling their own needs.

The more I see in my professional capacity, the more I become aware of the fact that people suffer from either not clearly knowing what they want or, more likely, not daring to ask for what they know they want. For they don't want to appear foolish, deviant, awkward, ignorant, or wanting.

Too many people come to see a psychotherapist in the hope of being magically cured, believing that some magical words on their therapist's part–some great interpretation–will cure them. Hat Therapy simply represents an attempt to place responsibility for cure back where it belongs–not with the "therapist" but with the "patient."

I will start a group session by explaining to those present exactly what I've just explained to you. Then I will pass somebody my tennis hat.

"When you get the hat, your job is simply to get in touch with what you really want RIGHT NOW . . . and *ask* for it," I will say. "Whether it be help with a problem, a kiss on the cheek, or a desire to have somebody lick your left buttock. Whatever it is that you really want to do or express–be it mundane or dramatic, serious or silly, proper or perverse–try to do it. While you may not get what you ask for, you stand a much better chance of fulfilling yourself if you make your wishes, thoughts, dilemmas, and desires known. And when you've finished using the hat–finished getting what you want whether it takes ten seconds or two hours–you are responsible for passing the hat to someone else."

So that is the stage I set for Hat Therapy. And that is the essential message I have to teach. Of course, I will comment freely about what I see happening in myself and others along the way.

More often than not, people, with the support and encouragement of the group, meet their needs. Eventually, hopefully, they come to realize that they don't need my hat to ask for what they want–and moreover that they can do just as well asking for what they want outside of the group–in the "real world," so to speak.

They learn that there *are* people in the world who will help them if they ask, who will date them if they ask, whom they can confront with their grievances if they dare. What I look for as a therapist and what I comment on is, more often than not, how they *fail* to follow through on this process. I expose the pseudo-wishes and the self-deceptions; the lack of daring and the failure of self-responsibility.

CHAPTER IV

SOCIAL PROCESS AWARENESS TRAINING: AN NTL APPROACH

Douglas R. Bunker

The NTL method of group interaction is one that has an extensive history and influence on the group process scene in this country. Despite the recent burgeoning interest and participation in T, sensitivity, encounter, and marathon groups, the relationship and debt to the NTL leadership is not always clearly perceived nor understood by many group workers. This is particularly evident in some of the applications of T groups and sensitivity groups where the direct inheritance is to NTL, but wherein the application is irrelevant to the entire laboratory method and its theoretical and technical elements. At times this "wild" misapplication of T group concepts has led to an unfortunate misunderstanding of the very extensive and carefully constructed research literature compiled by the NTL proponents. In a more positive sense, the laboratory method has been the catalyst for the interest in and extensive use of groups in a variety of settings; probably is directly responsible for the development of time extended groups such as the marathon and was almost as immediately effective as a generator of the encounter movement. Unfortunately, their extensive literature on group process and the research on these processes is not utilized frequently enough by practitioners in group therapy.

Dr. Douglas Bunker's analysis of the NTL method is both conceptually relevant to an understanding of the NTL process and to an awareness of its similarities and differences to other approaches. Although Doctor Bunker modestly indicates that his assessment is primarily a perception of the NTL approach as viewed from his particular stance, it is an evaluation that has a great deal of generalizability to others within that "school" of thought. His clarity in presenting the outlines of the method as he views it also enables us to see its relevance historically and theoretically to other group methods presently extant. The description of the importance of group development and its contrast to groups that focus on the individual is also pertinent to an understanding of the location of the laboratory training method in regard to other perspectives. Obviously, the multiple variations and developments from Doctor Bunker's model cannot be described in a paper of this scope nor would it be possible to cover its possible difference from and similarities to all the other methods of personal growth through group methods.

D.S.M.
G.D.G.

51

THE FINE PRINT ON THE LABEL

TITLES OF SERIOUSLY INTENDED PAPERS, as all labels on packages offered to the public, should describe their contents accurately, instruct consumers about suitable conditions for use, and warn of dangers if any, from mis-application.*

First, a minor disclaimer relating to the sub-title. Though I have been invited to participate here as an expositor of the "NTL Approach," I cannot presume to represent the NTL Institute of Applied Behavioral Science as an organization, nor to encompass the variety of group process approaches practiced at one time or another under NTL's auspices. Indeed, I have chosen to present a construction of the NTL approach which, though historically authentic, may now be distinctly under-represented and even obscured by the variety of other activities and orientations of the Institute. In this I am deliberately atavistic, seeking to sort out the core of the laboratory approach from the accretions of often uncritical eclecticism.

Secondly, in a field characterized by richly connotative language, new, unclearly bounded concepts often represented by old words, and a seeming preference for imprecision, I believe it necessary to point out the denotative content of my title. It is intended to delimit and contrast, revealing that my subject is *awareness* rather than "sensitivity, growth, or encounter"; that the emphasis is upon *social* rather than *intrapsychic* processes, states, or capacities; and that the mode of activity to be explored is toward the

---

* There is, upon reflection, a touch of irony in this obsessiveness about titles and labels in a paper dealing with the recently emerged group experience industry. No field is in greater need of a terminological purgative. Existing labels have no consistent meanings. Purveyors of group experience workshops are often almost evasively inexplicit in their announcements, employing a jargon that may be richly evocative within certain sub-cultures, but that does not translate clearly into even "bare bones" understanding of what to expect either in terms of processes or of learning outcomes. This condition makes it very difficult for the public to discriminate between offerings, and almost impossible for them to participate knowledgably in the negotiation of a psychological contract with those responsible for the design and conduct of the group experience. The clarification of labels might well serve to sharpen the practitioner's thinking about purposes and means as well as to help resolve the ethical issues surrounding the merchandising of the group experience.

training end of that much contended continuum from training to therapy.

A LABORATORY APPROACH

The central concept in the NTL tradition is the training (learning) laboratory, a multigroup residential conference composed typically of previously unacquainted members who devote themselves to the study of experienced social relationships as they develop both within and between groups. The notion of a laboratory suggests that the primary activity is inquiry and experimentation. The subject matter consists of the emergent social processes among members, which though they occur under the controlled and unfamiliar conditions of the laboratory are assumed to be somewhat representative of the patterns of behavior which might occur in natural groupings in other settings. Members are both subjects and scientists, faced on the one hand with the operational problems of how to get on with one another toward the realization of individual and common ends, and on the other with the scientific problems of how to make sense of what they are doing to and with one another. In the latter set of tasks they are aided by a professional usually referred to as a "trainer."

The notion of the member as a scientist-subject is a unique emphasis of this conception of experiential learning. Though usually translated into the participant-observer analogue, the implicit characterization of the member as "scientist" keeps vivid the intellectual component of the experience as well as the emotional and relational aspects. This usually happens without being trapped by scientistic formalism or the polarization of affective and cognitive concerns. Members become adept at moving back and forth between intense involvement and relatively objective observation and data organization. Benne describes the way these functions converge:

> . . . the uses of data interpretations in a T Group are not alone to verify or disverify hypotheses formed independently of (but relevant to) the value choices or actions of the group or to make post hoc sense of historic events in group life. Interpretations serve also to clarify and guide the current choices of action policies and of procedures in and by the group. It is only as interpretations are translated into action policies and tried out by the group that they are effec-

tively tested, corrected, and qualified in the minds and experiences of T Group members (1).

It is not only as passive observers that members are encouraged to model scientific concerns. Active experimentation in which members openly, voluntarily, and provisionally manipulate group conditions or individual behavior is also legitimate. Though such efforts are sometimes congruent with the pursuit of group goals, they may also be indulged by the group as an individual's effort to try new role alternatives. As a group gets on with its work, almost all members come to participate in the generation and analysis of data for explicating processes and assessing consequences of behavior. The group's acceptance of responsibility for the content of work and for the norms, procedures, and role differentiations required to pursue the selected task is crucial to this mode of operation.

An emphasis upon group development as the context of learning opportunities means that the traditional form of a training laboratory is more time consuming than some alternative forms. While other purposes may be served by weekend workshops; marathons, and other brief training designs; at least two and preferably three weeks are required to experience the group development cycle which occurs in a human relations training laboratory of the form I advocate. Given market pressures toward shorter programs and the proliferation of group experience offerings which are represented as equivalents, this orthodoxy might seem self-defeating. Indeed, the empirical supports for this contention are meager (see Bunker and Knowles) (3), but a case can be made on the following grounds.

Re-educative learning about social processes requires both personal emotional investment and support for the cognitive exploration of experience. In most of our daily experience these modes of operation are separate and even mutually impeding. For most of us analysis, observation, and intellectual understanding are associated with detachment and external observations, while emotional intensity and commitment tend to preclude objectivity almost by definition. It is this separation of action and participation from reflection and observation that blocks adaptive re-orientation for most people in most daily situations. The laboratory is designed to create conditions under which the fusion of these two modes of action can lead to improved understanding of social processes in which one is involved, increased capacity for adaptive adjustments in behavior, and more differentiated flexible, and accepting concepts of self and of others.

Usual descriptions of these essential conditions include (1) the creation of a supportive environment to reduce anxiety and to facilitate moderate risk taking, (2) the development of norms to support the exchange of reactions and the construction of a responsive social environment, and (3) the provision of models and methods of inquiry. The first two of these elements are related not only to individual affective readiness and cognitive preparation, but also to progress in group development: the determination of the conditions for membership, the development of a common language system and a minimally common set of working assumptions, and the accumulation of a body of behavioral data about the group to which all have access. Such developments can be encouraged and aided but they cannot be engineered or contrived. Thus they are time consuming. It is the essence of the laboratory method that they emerge naturalistically, by group direction and are used as the context within which interpersonal transactions may be explored and cast in relief. To seek to accelerate them by gimmickry is to alter not only their path but their fundamental nature.

Two other conditions are required for effective T Group learning: internal and external experiential validity. Successful learning is associated with both.

Internal validity is defined as a sense of realness participants experience in the situation. Situations and relationships which are marked by high internal experiential validity are those in which they can experience themselves and others as uncontrived and whole, in which the context is credible, and in which the task commitments are accepted as congruent with personal interests, i.e., are individually "owned," not externally imposed. Low internal experiential validity is associated with the perception of the situation as unreal and with reluctance to make an emotional investment in the situation. Internal validity may be influenced by the degree of congruence between the member's preliminary information and the nature of the training situation he discovers, by his perceptions of the competence and commitment of the staff, by his level of free-floating anxiety, by the availability of member opportunities to influence the situation, and by the length of time in the situation. Internal validity tends to increase when one makes a commitment of a substantial block of working and living time to a situation, and is thus faced with the necessity of coping with the situation without the prospect that if one withdraws it will shortly pass. The experience of internal validity varies across persons and over time, but can be viewed as a multiplicative function across a group.

In order for any group to function as a learning group the internal validity level must rise above some empirically undefined threshold. I suggest that the group's experience of internal validity is reduced by trainer control and by an overkill of facilitating technologies intended to accelerate selected processes.

External experiential validity is defined in terms of the sense of continuity between the training situation and other settings in which members operate. Where this sense of continuity is established, the relevance of the experience is reinforced and the hopes and plans for transfer of training are rendered more realistic. Training situations marked by high external validity are those in which the participant can discern common elements with relationships and task settings elsewhere in his experience. A high level of external validity does not preclude the recognition of a sharp contrast between the character of the laboratory setting and other domains. Such contrasts may, when understood, be the foundation for perceiving fundamental similarities and identifying salient dimensions for comparison. External validity develops through time as the group experiences progressive stages of development, as opportunities for moving back and forth between the living out of events and the analysis of these processes are repeated enough to develop a sense of the generalizability of process concepts, and as attention is devoted explicitly to the practice of transferable skills and planning for application of learnings. An important motiva-

TABLE I

ELEMENTS OF LABORATORY TRAINING FOR SOCIAL PROCESS AWARENESS

Methods	*Necessary Conditions*
1. Make assumptions and images about self, others, and groups explicit, test them against other views, and check out alternative ways of viewing experience.	Situation contrasted sharply enough with the familiar and routine to challenge the validity of our implicit assumptions about self and others.
2. *Behave openly,* presenting not what one wants people to believe but what one feels and believes about one's self, the group and group events.	Mutual trust founded upon suspension of evaluative sets and establishment of a norm of confidentiality within the group.
3. Take risks in *sharing reactions* to the behavior of one another in ways that will permit each to understand the consequences of behavior for specific others and for the group.	Acceptance of mutual responsibility for one another's learning. Presentation of reactions in ways that will minimize threat to self esteem and permit the use of the information by the receiver to make appropriate behavior changes.
4. Confronted by new and more adequate information about the consequences of behavior, explore alternative ways of behaving. *Experiment.* Extend behavioral range and repetoire.	Group support for experimentation based upon willingness to suspend expectations based upon one's past performance in the group or one's back home role and status, and also upon cooperation in reflecting back the relative effectiveness of alternative patterns.
5. Make sense of experience by *Building Cognitive Models.* Individually and as a group members try to conceptualize experience. This involves raising questions in the group, expressing hypotheses and collectively gathering data about them, objectifying experience to see continuities over time and across groups.	Access to multiple observations from differing perspectives. Explication of conceptual systems which provide frameworks for understanding group process and individual experience.

6. Observant Participation is at once a condition, a consequence, and a method of laboratory training. It is easy enough to observe with objectivity from the side lines or to act with meaningful intent in the thick of action, but combining the two is a considerable achievement toward which guided practice is helpful.

tional increment is available in the realization of high external experiental validity.

Where the training situation is so structured and managed as to lead participants to seek to substitute the "immanent reality" of the training experience for the sense of reality once vested in one's relational history, and to assert that only the training situation is "authentic" while the world is "phony," there is a high risk that learning will be aborted. External validity cannot be developed adequately in short or even week-long workshops. It is partly contingent upon the parallel development of internal experiential validity and partly upon specific structured attention to the link between phenomena in the training situation and in the outside world. There is some evidence that transferable learning outcomes are directly facilitated by designs which devote time to the planning and practice of specific applications "back home" (3).

The quality of work in a training laboratory is highly variable. Some, both trainers and trainees, lacking imagination, preparation, or motivation, perform trivial experiments with matching results. Others do what for them are very important studies of how they may best reduce the discrepancy between the intentions and effects of their behavior in groups. There tends to be a contagion effect of serious, well directed work. Solid progress by one or a few stimulates serious efforts by others. In terms introduced herein, such leading efforts increase the internal experiential validity of the laboratory setting.

The essential operating methods and the required conditions for this model of training are outlined in Table I. Though these may overlap with methods and assumptions associated with other small group training methods, other aspects of the structural design of the program may differ. Further divergence may be noted in the goals of various approaches.

GOALS AND OUTCOMES OF LABORATORY EDUCATION

The object of process awareness training is not to learn *about* social processes abstractly, but to learn to understand concrete interactional situations in which one is a participant. *Awareness* is construed to mean not only conscious access and attention to information about particular social events, but cognitive reorientation in which the learner acquires new recognition cues, new concepts to permit the differentiated and enriched apprehension of people in social transactions, and an appreciation of the systemic interdependence of social processes. The utility and applicability of this augmented capacity to understand is also learned in training laboratories which provide opportunities for *practice* in diagnosing social situations and in making corrective behavioral adjustments to influence group behavior toward an approximate realization of individual or group goals. The concept of awareness also includes increased consciousness of the multiple consequences of one's own and other's actions.

Practice in the monitoring of these effects while one is in an action mode, coping with a dynamic interaction process, shapes *perceptual and behavioral skills* by an interactive process. The enhancement of these skills in maintaining and managing relationships, adjusting behavior to changing task and social demands, and in sending and receiving in face to face communications constitutes a second goal of laboratory training.

A third goal of process awareness training is to increase intellectual comprehension of a kind that is both operationally facilitating and generalizable. Through T Group experiences, supported by application planning, inter-group exercises, skill-practice, paired consultations, and other designs for learning, participants experience and come to increase, both understanding and coping skills in dealing with the phenomena of group formation and development, decision making, pairing and asymmetrical attraction, leadership and task coordination, conflict management bargaining, role definition and influence. It is not that everyone learns precisely the same thing, but that these aspects of group experience are typically encountered and explicitly addressed in the typical laboratory.

The fourth category of learning goals are those identified by Warren Bennis as "meta-goals" or "values" (2). These are general orientations to action which inhere in the laboratory culture and are acquired through indirect and informal induction. Bennis' list includes:

1. Expanded consciousness and the recognition of choice.
2. A spirit of inquiry.
3. Authenticity in interpersonal relations.
4. A collaborative conception of the authority relationship.

I submit that it is appropriate that these values not become the object of explicit persuasion or sanction in a laboratory. It is better that they be acquired by internalization to the degree that they are found meaningful and valid. If they are modeled in the design and conduct of the laboratory, they may be detected and independently appraised. The laboratory staff should not engage in the direct promulgation of value-orientations, but should create conditions and model behavior the value implications of which may be independently discovered and appraised by each member of the community.

INDIVIDUAL LEARNING AND GROUP DEVELOPMENT

The issue of individual vs. group orientations in the conduct of learning and therapy groups is a worn, often overdrawn, and largely fruitless controversy. If it seems necessary to place NTL training approaches within this framework, they belong toward the group oriented end. The early development of laboratory re-educative methods closely paralleled the emergence of the social science sub-discipline of group dynamics. And yet it distorts our perspective to treat group and individual orientations as polar opposites. Rather, as we have indicated in an earlier section, the developing group provides the context for individual learning about self and social process. In traditional NTL workshops, the processes of group formation are given explicit attention, and the content of individual work and of trainer interventions are rooted in the developmental tasks with which the group is concerned at any given time. Learning activities are typically structured in terms of the relational issues which develop between two or more people, or between individuals and the group. Typically these issues will be subject to interpretation in terms of their portent for group level work. This does not mean that work is depersonalized or that group development concerns pre-empt individual work, but that this work is given meaning within the context of immediate, here and now relationships, emerging group history, and interpersonal and group consequences. It is the continuity and contextuality of group process that gives the laboratory its internal experiential validity.

This approach tends to treat more heavily than some other kinds of group work such issues as membership, coalition formation, social influence, conformity, interpersonal perception, and group decision making.

TRAINER ROLES AND INTERVENTION STYLES

In this age of the escalation of charisma, the role model of the laboratory trainer may seem quite prosaic in contrast to that of the group guru. One central component of the trainer role is the inquirer function. The trainer facilitates learning by framing questions, defining dilemmas, guiding the collection of data, and helping to collate and interpret observations and reactions. He does this informally usually without resorting to instrumentation. The trainer typically seeks to model the process of inquiry and at the same time avoid pre-empting that function, for his purpose is to induce others to share his explorations.

A second component of this role is analagous to the function of a national park ranger on a nature tour.* His task is to point out important and interesting phenomena which others might at first not recognize. In this he operates with a richer conceptual apparatus for understanding group and social processes than most participants initially possess. This is not mere labeling, but involves the directing of attention and the training of others in the use of recognition cues.

A no less important third component of the trainer role is his function as a member of the group. Though he cannot be, at least in the beginning, quite like other members, he can acquire a role in which he can begin to share responsibility with other members for the direction of group effort, for the facilitation of group work, and for the maintenance and development of satisfying and effective interpersonal relations. There is no uniformity with regard to this element, since some NTL trainers maintain the professional role as scrupulously as the stereotypical Tavistock consultant, while others try rather actively to meet the conditions for group membership from the outset. There is an interesting question here concerned with the facilitating effect of mutuality. I am uncertain as to whether this is an important factor, but in my own experience learning is aided when the group is able to deal with the trainer as a person as well as in terms of his role. This does not deny either his unique resources or responsibility, but it makes them both more accessible and more subject to critical review.

---

* This metaphor was first suggested to me by Roger Harrison.

This aspect of the trainer's role is also relevant to the issue of group control vs. trainer programming. The maintenance of the group's collective responsibility to manage its affairs and to program its own work within laboratory boundaries and design constraints is more consonant with the laboratory approach.

CODA

There are a number of people in contemporary society who are not interested in "encounter" *qua* "encounter," in "consciousness expansion" for its own sake, or in any of the other varieties of existential excursions in groups. Many of these people, though "square" from the perspective of the encounter movement and unlikely to ever volunteer for a group experience as a route to "personal growth," increased "inner harmony," "wholeness," or "spontaneity," could be more effective in their various action roles and more able to participate creatively in solving problems, promoting social change, and inventing new institutions if they could increase understanding of social processes and develop additional operating skills. The laboratory approach to training for social process awareness is uniquely suited to the achievement of these ends. It should be distinguished as a re-educative technique from the proliferating variety of other group approaches now offered, for it differs fundamentally from most of them in goal orientations, methods, and learning outcomes.

REFERENCES

1. Benne, K. D.: From polarization to paradox. In Bradford, L., Gibb, J. R., and Benne, K. D. (Eds.): *T-Group Theory and Laboratory Method.* New York, Wiley, 1964.
2. Bennis, W. G.: Goals and meta-goals of laboratory training. *Human Relations Training News, 6*(3):1-4, 1962 (NTL Institute for Applied Behavioral Science, Washington, D.C.).
3. Bunker, D. R., and Knowles, E. S.: Comparison of behavioral changes resulting from human relations training laboratories of different lengths. *J Applied Behavioral Science, 3*(4):505-523, 1967.

CHAPTER V

THE TAVISTOCK APPROACH TO THE STUDY OF GROUP PROCESS: REACTIONS OF A PRIVATE INVESTIGATOR

BARBARA BENEDICT BUNKER

The Tavistock method of group investigation has been in effect for a fairly extensive period of time; yet, the details of the method are relatively obscure to American practitioners of group therapy. One wonders whether this is a function of distance—this method developed essentially in England—or that there are other reasons. Perhaps there are some cultural forces at work. One major reason for the lack of emphasis on this approach in this country may lie in its primary focus on its training aspects. However, the focus on training or education is not antithetical to the American mental health scene. The emphasis here is on the practical and pragmatic in the mental health field and the Bion, Rice Tavistock approach is not in essence a therapeutic technique. But since it focuses on group process is that not essential for our understanding of groups and also mandatory in treatment by the group method? The answer to this may shed some light on some of the shortcomings of the American group therapeutic scene.

Dr. Barbara Bunker's familiarity with the Tavistock method and her extensive background in the NTL tradition makes her ideally suited to communicate an understanding of this approach. For from her background at NTL she has evolved a conception of the fundamental importance of group dynamics and their relevance in the methods devoted to change through group process. Her ability to see the role of training separate from therapeutic pragmatism is particularly useful in providing us with a perspective on the utility of the Tavistock approach. Her analysis of the elements of this approach is also an excellent synthesis for we can clearly see its relevance to other threads of group techniques that exist in this country. When one completes her excellent paper one is familiar with the

The comments of Murray Levine, David Singer, and Edward Klein on an earlier version of this manuscript are gratefully acknowledged.

basics of this approach as well as its general ramification. And although the experience of a Tavistock study group may still be lacking it no longer seems so foreign to us nor a possible participation in a training session so anxiety laden.

D.S.M.
G.D.G.

I N THE LATE 40's and early 50's two simultaneous but quite independent developments in new methods of studying groups and their processes emerged. In England, W. R. Bion and A. K. Rice were associated with a "training group" which was conducted at the Tavistock Clinic over a two year period (1947-1948). In the United States, an intergroup relations workshop held in 1946 in Connecticut by Kurt Lewin and his students developed a training method which led to the establishment of the National Training Laboratory for Group Development (now NTL-Institute). The first formal program in "sensitivity training" was sponsored by NTL in Bethel, Maine, in 1947.

Despite concurrent origins, the history of these two developments has been divergent. After its initial experiment in 1947, the Tavistock Clinic dropped training groups in favor of a concentration on the development of group therapy. The training group was not revived until 1957 when the first full scale Group Relations Conference was sponsored by the Tavistock Institute and the University of Leicester. This conference emphasized the study of group process in the small group. Subsequently numerous conferences were held in England until in 1965 the Washington School of Psychiatry, Yale University, and the Tavistock Institute sponsored the first Human Relations Conference in this country at Mt. Holyoke. Since then the number of conferences sponsored by the A. K. Rice Institute of the Washington School of Psychiatry and other groups has increased annually.

While these developments were proceeding in England, NTL Institute had been actively engaged in the sensitivity training business since 1947. The cultural milieu in which each of these group training methods arose shaped its development. In America NTL was early associated with social psychology and with the adult education movement. (The therapeutic milieu of the Tavistock Clinic likewise effected what was focused upon in its style of group training.) NTL training events (laboratories) of the 50's emphasized three elements: 1. the study of group processes in "sensitivity training groups," 2. skill training (individual learning and change), 3. theory. In the early 60's non-verbal techniques came more and more to the fore in sensitivity group training. The emphasis on the "study of the group" was replaced by an emphasis on personal growth and interpersonal competence. That is, the emphasis was on individual learning which clients found personally satisfying (congruent with the adult education tradition) rather than on the study of group processes. Thus, when the Tavistock Human Relations Conference with its emphasis on group process was introduced into the American scene in 1965, many professionals whose careers were shaped in the early 60's found the group process emphasis new and exciting while older professionals saw it as a return to an emphasis within NTL of the early 50's.

This paper is written from the point of view of one who has roots in the sensitivity training group tradition as it is embodied by the NTL Institute but who has over the last few years been an active participant, staff member, and sponsor of events in the Tavistock tradition. Its purpose is to describe the Tavistock method of studying small group process, to clarify differences between this method and another major method (sensitivity training) and to point out the benefits of this training method as well as some of its limitations.

INITIAL IMPRESSIONS

My first contact with the Tavistock approach to the study of group process was in 1968 when I required students in a course I was teaching to observe several sessions of a Tavistock Study Group. (For clarity, all subsequent references to "Study Group" should be understood as in the Tavistock model and references to "Sensitivity Training Group" as the NTL model.) Having decided that it would be a useful experience for the students, I felt I could do no less than attend myself. We sat mesmerized through several sessions. After each session the study group "consultant" sat down with the observers for a discussion. The outrage of the student observers from my course as they accused the consultant of being "arbitrary, obscure, unfeeling, mechanical and incompetent" is a still vivid memory. Had they been in the Study Group, I am sure some one of them would have referred to him as "the insultant" (meaning the consultant), in a slip which has been made on more than one occasion in a Tavistock Study Group.

Strong reactions to the consultant are, in fact, not atypical of the early sessions of such groups. In this case, they were heightened by an entirely different expectation of the consultant's role which originated in the student's Sensitivity Training Group background. As our discussions with the consultant progressed, we began to understand these behind-the-screen reactions as extensions of the process in the Study Group which we had observed. The issues which arose appeared at first to be simple products of individual action. However, the irritating insistence of the consultant that behavior is a group product and his relentless focus on group level phenomena finally compelled attention. We saw that not only is behavior susceptible to group level interpretation but what is learned is quite different than what is learned from an analysis of individual or interpersonal behavior.

A COMPARISON OF OBJECTIVES

When one begins to compare the Study Group (Tavistock) with the Sensitivity Training Group (NTL) it becomes apparent that the objectives of each type of training are different.

In the Tavistock Study Group the objective is to study group process and to learn about forces which retard group development. Anxiety and the way the group organizes to defend against it is often a focal part of the initial learning. As the group progresses in this early stage of development, issues of authority and the desire of members not to take responsibility for themselves in the group arise. Another way of describing this phase is to speak of the need of members to establish their membership, to feel included, to feel they can trust the group. Still another is to speak of the process of establishing norms which will support the kind of work that members wish to do. However described, this early period is an essential precursor to the *middle phase* of group life. In this phase self-disclosure, feedback, and mutual give and take occur. Finally, of course, there is an ending phase in which the group has to deal with its own death. In the Study Group a great deal of attention is given to the beginning phase of the group. In short most of the Study Group's life and learning may be in this phase; the middle phase which is more like a Sensitivity Training Group may never be reached.

In the contemporary Sensitivity Training Group the objective is likely to be the development of interpersonal competence or some version of a contract for increased interpersonal awareness and feedback from others. A Sensitivity Group trainer may wish to move through the early stages of development as quickly as possible into the middle phase of group life where this objective can be met. In this situation he would not be as interested in studying the transference to him as an authority as in trying to move through or break that transference so that the group could proceed. His effectiveness as a trainer could be partially assessed by how well he was able to facilitate the group's dealing with conscious or unconscious feelings about him and by how well he helped them move toward authentic interpersonal work. Nonverbal techniques have been a major innovation for facilitating this latter process. With the carefully calibrated use of non-verbal techniques it is possible to instrument the development of the group so that members gradually get to know each other, self-disclose, and respond to each other with feedback in a relatively short period of time. Such groups can be quite effective at increasing interpersonal learning when trained by a competent and experienced person. It is important to point out, however, that they frequently, though not necessarily, remain *leader dependent* groups and as such are subject to all the tyrannies and benefits of such a relationship.

The learning focus of the Tavistock Study Group is complementary to the learning focus of the Sensitivity Training Group. The Study Group provides a rich opportunity to understand the impact of group process on individual action and to sharpen and clarify the covert issues of group life. An understanding of these issues is essential to the understanding of small groups. It is particularly important for persons who are using an instrumented method of group development through the use of non-verbal techniques to comprehend group level processes. Every intervention by a trainer involves a choice which may focus the group on intrapsychic issues, interpersonal issues, or group issues. The decision among these levels is often crucial. If the real problem is a group level issue and the trainer is trying to deal with it by focusing the work interpersonally, the work will take on a hollow tone which can only be remedied by a shift to the appropriate level. Only when all levels are part of one's repertoire can one adequately make decisions. Since the Study Group and the Sensitivity Training Group lead to different types of learning, each has a contribution to make to the understanding of small groups.

THE SMALL GROUP CONFERENCE ON HUMAN RELATIONS

The Tavistock Study Group is usually embedded in a learning system known as The Small Group Conference on Human Relations. The conference or workshop as it is sometimes called has several distinct elements which are often though not always included in a single conference. The *Study Group* is in many ways the heart of the conference. In this group 10 to 12 persons meet regularly with the services of a consultant to study their own behavior as it happens. The consultant is present with the specific task of facilitating the learning. "Only the staff roles and the staff relationships are defined. No rules are laid down for members. They are free to make their own" (7). The *Large Group* includes the total conference membership and several consultants. Its task is to provide an arena for the study of behavior in a group larger than can form a face-to-face group. The *Intergroup Exercise* is an event in which members study processes involved in relationships between and among groups. There are at least two forms of this exercise which structure the consultant relationship to the exercise differently. So powerful is this exercise that there have been workshops which focus on it alone. *Application Groups* meet to consider the relevance of the conference learning to real world working situations. They use various methods, case study, discussion, etc. The consultant role in this group is to discuss with members the transfer of conference insights to back home settings. *Lectures* are part of many conferences. In these the staff deliver themselves of conceptual schemes or cognitive material which they believe will increase learning. This same function may also be filled by staff-led *Discussion Groups* during the conference.

For those who come to a Tavistock conference with little

knowledge of the training method, the initial experience can be quite bewildering. At least four factors contribute to the difficulties which members may have in using the conference environment productively for their own learning. First, the group experiences are unstructured; that is, they are determined by the group. In group relations conferences the assignment to groups and meeting times are established by the staff. At the intergroup event only the time boundaries are established: members must form their own groups, their own intergroup events, and learn how to learn in that setting. Thus individuals are confronted by a complex learning task from the outset. Second, most members bring with them expectations about what the experience will be and what they will learn. If the member is widely read or has good informants, his expectations may be realistic and within his reach. As often, expectations are unrealistic either through misinformation or the distortion of personal desire or both. Expectations which are not congruent with the primary task of the conference are disconfirmed. When this happens the member must re-orient himself to the reality which is present and decide how to use the experience. Another factor which may add to initial uncertainty is the focus on covert processes. For members whose frame of reference is nonanalytic the transition to this view may take some adjustment. Finally, the consultant role, separate, defined, non-reinforcing, leaves members without the usual cues about what behavior is acceptable and pleasing. This in turn increases uncertainty and anxiety. (At the same time it is important to recognize that uncertainty and anxiety are necessary catalysts for the emergence of the covert processes which these groups study. The gentle balance of "enough but not too much" is a conference design consideration whose parameters are relatively unexplored.)

DISTINCTIVE CHARACTERISTICS

Three characteristics are important to the Tavistock approach. They will be mentioned briefly and then discussed in more detail. First, there is the emphasis on the process of the total group. Individual behavior is interpreted in the light of its meaning in the whole group. Second, the "consultant" has a specified role from which he does not deviate. This role lacks the more nurturant or helping kinds of behavior which are associated with the "trainer role." Third, there is an emphasis on member responsibility and on freedom to learn or not to learn in the workshop context. Of course, the Tavistock conference is not the only place where these notions are salient or available. Many of us work within the framework of some of these notions. It is true, however, that for learning purposes, a Tavistock conference is an excellent way to understand more fully how these issues affect us.

In turning to a discussion of the emphasis on group process, it should be recognized that there are a number of approaches to group process. One can observe the group from the point of view of its problem solving adequacy, one can observe decision making, one can examine the adequacy of role taking behavior in light of the task of be accomplished. These modes of observation focus primarily on task functioning. In the Study Group, however, there is a unique opportunity to look at the psychological functioning of the group. Although there is no single theoretical orientation among Tavistock consultants, they do tend to rely move or less heavily on the concepts of W. R. Bion. Bion treats the group as an entity which has a life of its own. "With enormous skill and subtlety, it uses its members to carry out its needs. The behavior of any member at any moment is the sum of two forces: a) his own needs, history and habitual behavior patterns, and b) the needs of the group being expressed through him. Whatever the group is talking about, the group is always talking about the group. It is only necessary to decode the symbols" (3). The two major concepts suggested by Bion which help us to make this translation are "the work group" and "the basic assumption group" (1). Groups can be described as having two faces, two aspects of functioning. When a group is operating in the *work group* mode, it is pursuing its real task effectively and singlemindedly. Structures and plans are congruent with goals to which members are actively committed. It behaves, in short, like a mature and rational being. Thus, in the Study Group when the group is effectively studying its own behavior it is operating in the work group mode. The *basic assumption* mode of group functioning is one way of understanding the ineffective and self-contradictory behavior which occurs in all groups. Bion describes three types of assumptions which can motivate behavior in a group where they are present. "When living in the basic assumption world the group ignores other purposes and goals and abandons intellectual work" (4). It acts as though its work task is to try to find leadership who will gratify very powerful and very primitive shared group needs. For example, when the group is operating in a *dependency* basic assumption mode, members behave as though they have no resources, skills or capacity to function. The search is for a leader who can protect and guide them. If the designated leader or consultant can be maneuvered into such a role, it is assumed he will solve all their difficulties. If he refuses they may turn in anger and frustration toward other members or snuggle up to each other in a warm groupiness which gives a temporary sense of comfort and security (8). These operations are, of course, basically defensive against the work task which requires independence, responsibility and risk on the part of members.

When rage or fear arise in a basic assumption group the frustration which results cannot be tolerated. Basic assumption groups, like children, are not good tolerators of delayed gratification. This may lead to the second type of assumption activity which Bion calls *fight-flight*. Attack or full scale flight offers an immediate way to reduce frustration. It also offers a compellingly interesting detour around the work task. Just as a mature individual gradually comes to understand and direct his own childishness so also mature groups can learn to use basic assumption life in the service of the work task.

A third basic assumption mode is called *pairing* or *fusion*. In this mode the group dotingly supports the development of an intimate relationship between two of its members. An optimistic and hopeful note pervades, as if somehow this pair might create a new leader who will solve the old problems of being and doing. Consultant comments about the defensive nature of this activity are met with outrage and righteous indignation. After all, are not the members now engaged in the task of creating deep and meaningful relationships and is not such a task ipso facto justified?

The answer to the question is "It depends what the primary task of the group is." For the Study Group the primary task is the study of the group's "here and now" behavior. The consultant's job is to interpret what is happening in the group. Hence, his comments often focus on the covert (basic assumption) processes. He may also help the group clarify issues of boundary control and maintenance e.g. the difference between sentience and the work task (6).

This brings us to the second important characteristic of Tavistock training, the consultant role. The consultant is a model of dedication to the work task. He states as clearly and as competently as he can what the group is doing. He does not deal with individual behavior, dispense reinforcements, impose sanctions or act in the traditionally helpful manner. There is here a clear parallel to the role of the classical psychoanalyst. The role frustrates the dependency needs of the members. Its impersonality provokes transference reactions and regressive behavior which can then be studied. "The consultant also provides boundaries for the group to explore by being punctual, formally attired, and remaining in role throughout the course of the group. In certain areas, his behavior is delimited (time, dress, role). The members must define for themselves whether or not they will accept the same boundaries on their own behavior, and explore what the implications are of acceptance and rejection" (5).

Two important types of interaction between consultant and group members should be mentioned. The first involves the reactions of members to the consultant role as traditionally defined and to the person who fills that role. In the early hours of Study Group life members tend to deny all knowledge that persons can perform roles. They may ignore the fact that a person is certainly sitting with them being their consultant and treat him as though he is only a role, a robot or mechanical device from whom all interventions flow; or they may pretend the role is nonexistent and try to seduce him into personal interactions with individual members. These behaviors are, of course, covert ways of trying to avoid the issue of authority resident in the group. As this issue is addressed, however, members increasingly deal with the consultant, a person-in-role, whose interventions can be evaluated for their usefulness to the group in doing its work task. The acumen of the comments, the deftness of their phrasing as well as their timing are all germane to the consultant's effectiveness.

The second interaction involves the effect the consultant has on the phenomena which occur in the group. While it is true that there are phenomena which are common to most groups, it is not true that all groups manifest identically cast or equally intense issues. It is interesting to consider whether when a consultant makes repeated interventions which, for example, focus the group on reactions to him he is simply pointing to latent issues which are being resisted or whether he is by reinforcement helping to create the very phenomenon to which he points. Insofar as the latter is true, there needs to be intensive investigation of the nature of the interaction between members and consultant.

A third emphasis which pervades Tavistock training is a refreshing clarity about individual responsibility. The consultant has certain responsibilities but they do not include responsibility for providing a good experience for a group member or ensuring his learning. The human tendency to assume many constraints based on prior experience is often examined by members who discover that in fact the restraints upon their behavior come from themselves and not from the consultant. There is an accompanying emphasis on the responsibility of members for the consequences of their behavior. Members are free to learn or not to learn, to calibrate their own learning process, to come or to leave, to make their own evaluations of what is occurring, how the consultant is doing, etc. This freedom is not earned by members. It is always available but only slowly taken. It is the gradual recognition of individual freedom which moves members into being able to address the work task maturely and permits the group to move from the early defensive phases of group life to the more rewarding middle phase.

ISSUES RAISED BY THE TAVISTOCK METHOD OF STUDY GROUP TRAINING

Finally we turn to two issues which deserve both further thought and thoughtful research.

The most intriguing question of small group training is: "What is learned?" At present we have only the most rudimentary descriptions of the process of experiential learning and little illuminating research. The declared task of the Study Group is to learn about group process through the study of its own behavior. A question which is frequently asked is "Can't I read about it somewhere? Is it really necessary to go to one of these conferences?" The reply that is usually given is to say that one certainly can read a great deal about group process. Reading is instructive and will describe many of the concepts which can be applied in the experiential setting. What one can't get from books, however, is instruction in the skill of recognizing group process issues at the time when they are happening. It is assumed in this learning model that if a concept is learned as it happens, the learner will recognize the same psychological process when it occurs again in another group. Reading may inform one about what the concepts are, but it does not teach one to recognize them. Experiential learning teaches recognition which is a skill which must be practiced. So far as I know, no one has adequately tested this proposition. Another assumption made by this model is that understanding group dynamics leads to more effective individual behavior in groups. Thus the well-trained person is a better leader and/or a better member because of the improved functioning which results from training. Although there is some interesting research literature on this issue in the T-group tradition (2) there is none that I am aware of in the Tavistock tradition.

There is a second type of learning which goes on at conferences and workshops which should be mentioned. This is personal learning. From the point of view of the primary task of the conference what an individual may learn about himself is serendipitous. When it happens it is applauded but no effort is made to ensure personal learning. The informal oral tradition of these events, however, does put some emphasis on this type of learning. It is often said by conference "regulars" that the best way to learn is to decide what you want to learn about and then act in that role. For example, several years ago some members at a Mt. Holyoke conference decided to mount a revolution against the staff. This event, of course, provided an enormous amount of data for the whole conference. In addition the leaders of the movement learned some things about revolutionary leadership which might have been learned had they taken similar action back home. Their jobs, however, might not have survived their learning. Conferences are relatively safe environments in which to pursue personal learning objectives. Similarly, members may choose not to join a group in an intergroup exercise in order to understand more fully what being outside is like or they may withdraw in a group to experience themselves as silent members, and so on. The available projects are endless and promise considerable personal learning.

Who is a candidate for this type of learning? Potentially, the learning has wide applicability and therefore it is not relevance which limits the potential client population. If there is a limitation it comes from the method and assumptions of this particular model of training. First, a person should be stable emotionally before participating in this kind of training. A certain amount of anxiety is essential to the learning process and over-anxious persons often become too anxious to learn. Second, one needs to be reasonably bright to profit from the experience. The form of analysis is quite sophisticated and requires intellectual alertness to reap its benefits. Third, one should be able to accept the value of understanding covert processes. People who don't live in a world which acknowledges the covert (and many people don't) may not judge this experience as at all valuable.

The final issue which deserves attention is whether the specific culture which develops around a training method sets expectations and influences behavior in such a way that what is studied is culture specific and generalizability to real world situations is reduced. Taking an example from the Sensitivity Training movement, there is currently controversy and concern over concepts like the routinization of affect. That is, the pressures which group members may feel to meet some covert norm of acceptable affective involvement in the group. In some Sensitivity Training Groups, for example, members may feel that they are not members in good standing until they have "had their scene." Insofar as they behave to meet novel normative expectations their behavior is not typical of real world reactions and what they learn is less relevant to the world outside the group.

Tavistock consultants pride themselves (I think accurately) on being attuned to the development of such norms in the Study Group and committed to their exposure for study. There are, however, covert norms which affect behavior in the Tavistock culture as a whole which seem to me to require more consideration. A brief description of the culture will assist the elaboration of this point.

There is a very strong informal social system among Tavistock consultants in America. The group is still small enough that most of them know each other, work together periodically, and are concerned with decisions about the organization of this training enterprise. They are friends, competitors, inheritors of a tradition.

At many conferences one finds members who arc aficionados of the Tavistock conference. Their experiences are numerous; they appear to know their way around and more important, to know how to learn in the environment. They *may be* consultant-hopefuls; they *are* almost always the socialization leaders for the new generation of Study Group members. Their orthodoxy and the catechism which the novice learns is about the contract, the consultant's role, what he will and won't do, his centrality in issues of authority, boundaries, etc.

The expectations which are built up are strong. For example, a very competent and experienced member at a recent workshop reacted with outrage to the behavior of one of the staff. It seems that this consultant, when she entered the Study Group said "Hi" and sat down. Now in orthodox logic, Tavistock consultants do not greet the group, they sit down and go to work. Therefore if a consultant behaves "out of role" one is free to examine the effects of that behavior as it affects staff competency. It is not clear however whether this reaction which comes at least in part from cultural expectations will produce learning applicable to another culture.

In any social system the strengths and nature of the expectations which are built up do affect behavior. The question is what is the effect of the Tavistock culture on what is experienced and learned at a workshop? Is it possible that the more ritualized the expectations of staff and members, the less applicable these learnings may be to other real world settings? If in fact some behavior, some reactions are controlled by cultural expectations that are Tavy-specific, one would not necessarily expect the same reactions and behavior in the outside culture. Insofar as this is true, what is learned is culture-specific and not generalizable.

It should be clear that this question is raised as an issue for study not as some kind of wholesale rejection of this style of training. This is a subtle, complex and fascinating issue which resides in all forms of training: clinical, group and others. It merits more consideration than we have given it.

REFERENCES

1. Bion, W. R.: *Experiences in Groups*. New York, Basic Books, 1959.
2. Campbell, J. P. and Dunnette, M. D.: Effectiveness of t-group experiences in managerial training and development. *Psychological Bulletin, 70:*73-108, 1968.
3. Kahn, M.: Proposal to NTL Institute. 1971 (mimeo), p. 1.
4. Klein, E. B. and Astrachan, B. M.: Learning in groups. *Journal of Applied Behavioral Science* (in press), p. 8.
5. *Ibid.*, p. 9.
6. Miller, E. J. and Rice, A. K.: *Systems of Organization*. London, Tavistock Publications, 1967.
7. Rice, A. K.: *Learning for Leadership*. London, Tavistock Publications, 1965, p. 25.
8. Rioch, M. J.: The work of Wilfred Bion on groups. *Psychiatry, 33:*56-66, 1970.

CHAPTER VI

RATIONALITY AND IRRATIONALITY IN THE GROUP THERAPY PROCESS

ALBERT ELLIS

Dr. Albert Ellis, the originator of rational-emotive therapy, has written extensively about his approach to therapy. In this paper he adds some additional material to his already extensive review of the topic. In the early days of his development his techniques seemed much more restrictive than they are at this time. Almost all of the major technical therapeutic innovations of the past two decades have been incorporated in the procedures employed by Ellis and his coworkers.

For those who tended to view his approach, narrowly, as a totally cognitive one, they will be impressed with the flexibility and breadth of his vision. The incorporation of some of the techniques from the area of behavior modification seem to be logical extensions of Ellis' initial position. However, the utilization of technical tools such as non-verbal exercises, group therapy marathons, and personal encountering seem initially less than "rational" additions to his therapeutic armamentarium. However, what seems like a contradiction at first is admirably cognitively integrated into the Ellis system and consistent with his approach. It is neither a dilution of his conceptual theory nor a diffuse eclecticism. His basic notions of what makes people function and malfunction remain the same as does his ultimate goal in therapy and the road to its achievement.

The extension of rational therapy into the area of group therapy and the extensive use of group methods does not also seem initially to be a logical outgrowth of the rational method. But as indicated before, Doctor Ellis does make an excellent case for their utility in his frame of reference. In defining these issues for himself he presents an excellent analysis of some of the positive attributes of group process as tools for growth that are also applicable to other theoretical orientations as well. His comments about what he views as some of the errors in many group approaches are also instructive in indicating the pitfalls in some differing methods. They are important elements to consider no matter what your personal orientation may be. Thus, as usual, one may not always agree with Doctor Ellis in his theory of personality nor in his techniques

78

for change, but since he is so clear in his presentation of his frame of reference, the differences between his system and others', he is always instructive and one usually learns from hearing his ideas.

D.S.M.
G.D.G.

THE GROUP THERAPY PROCESS obviously aids both rationality and irrationality; but practitioners and theorists rarely explicitly delineate exactly how it is instrumental in both these respects. Although I have previously tried to clarify some of the rational and irrational goals and methods of group psychotherapy (6, 10, 11, 14), I shall now try to be even more precise in this regard.

First let me say something about the rationality of all psychotherapeutic procedures. All therapists whom I have ever known or heard about appear to have basically rational goals for themselves and their clients; and it may well be impossible for them to remain alive and to be therapists without their consciously or unconsciously working for such goals. For *rational,* as the dictionary defines the term, simply means "1. of, based on, or derived from reasoning: as, *rational powers;* 2. able to reason; reasoning: as an infant is not yet *rational;* 3. showing reason; not foolish or silly; sensible; as a *rational* argument." Applied to human life and health, a rational procedure is one that enables the individual 1. to stay alive; 2. to avoid getting into needless difficulties with others and with the inanimate world around him; 3. to achieve sufficient satisfactions to make his existence worth the effort of continuing it; and 4. preferably to maximize his pleasures, gains, and gratifications and to minimize his pains, losses, and discomforts.

Rational, of course, does not not mean unemotional. For in the last analysis the goal of reasonable and sensible procedures is some form of hedonism or pleasure-seeking; and pleasure without emotion is almost unthinkable. What we call emotional*ism,* or *over*-reacting to external and internal stimuli in an exceptionally emotional way, is often irrational: because it easily leads to short-range rather than long-range hedonism (that is, striving only for the pleasure of the moment rather than of now *and* the future); to a dysfunctional narrowing of experience; to considerable amounts of needless pain; and to various other self-defeating (and antisocial) results. Reason, when it is properly employed in the service of human living and enjoying, does not necessarily constrict but enhances emotion. On the one hand, it abets such feelings as joy, love, creative involvement, and sensory pleasure; and, on the other hand, it minimizes or eliminates such feelings as overweening anxiety, depression, guilt, and hostility, and leaves the individual much more available time and energy to devote to enjoyable emoting.

To think and behave rationally, therefore, means to stop defeating yourself (and, by extension, the members of your social group), to plan your life so that you have more intense and growth-enhancing experiences, and to have a goddamned ball in spite of the many noxious stimuli and life conditions which inevitably tend to impinge on you. If there is any kind of therapist who does not try to help his clients achieve these goals, and hence to be simultaneously more rational and emotional, I do not know where he is to be found.

More specifically, psychotherapy tends to combat irrational thinking, inappropriate emoting, and dysfunctional behavior. When such self-defeating conduct becomes habitual we usually label it emotional disturbance. According to my way of looking at this kind of disturbance, it largely stems from and is concomitant with the individual's disordered or inefficient value system. For, along with such cognitive-oriented therapists as George Kelly (22), Eric Berne (2), Aaron T. Beck (1), E. Lakin Phillips (25), and Abraham Low (24), I hold that human beings are primarily evaluating creatures and that they woefully sabotage themselves emotionally by dogmatically and devoutly holding to several central irrational beliefs or philosophies (6-9, 12, 13, 17-20).

Still more concretely, I have recently summarized the major forms of human disturbance under the heading of childish demandingness (16). *Demandingness* or *dictating* seems to be, in fact, the essence of virtually all of what we normally call emotional upsetness. While the less disturbed individual strongly *desires* what he wants and makes himself appropriately sorry or annoyed if his desires are unfulfilled, the more disturbed person dogmatically *demands, insists, commands,* or *dictates* that his desires be granted and makes himself inappropriately anxious, depressed, or hostile when they are not. The emotionally malfunctioning individual foolishly and unrealistically makes three major kinds of demands: (1) that he do consistently well and receive the approval of virtually all the people whom he makes significant in his life; (2) that others treat him with fairness, consideration, and sometimes love; and (3) that the world be an easy and gratifying place in which to live.

Since all three of these demands are irrational, and simply do not accord with reality, it is largely the therapist's task to show his clients exactly how they display, and are rigidly sticking to, their demandingness; how they can give up their childishly dictating that they, others, and the world be pretty perfect; and how they can finally acquire a thoroughly reality-centered, rational philosophy of life so that after therapy has ended they will only rarely sink back to their old self-defeating, disturbed ways. Effective psychotherapy, in other words, teaches–and I mean teaches–the individual that he is insisting, in something of a two-year-old manner, that he be pretty perfect and that the universe revolve around him, when, in actual fact, he is incredibly fallible and the universe is completely impartial to him, doesn't give a shit about him, and in all probability never will. Even the relatively few individuals in the world who truly seem to love him–such as his family and his close friends–do so with unabashed intermittancy. By far most of the time, they are hung up with their own problems and desires, and are amazingly indifferent to or inconsiderate of him; only occasionally, do they actively concentrate on abetting his wants and pleasures; and some of the time they are literally unkind, nasty, hostile, and cruel. As for the vast majority of the people in the world, they hardly know he exists–and care exceptionally little whether he does or not.

Psychotherapy, then, would better largely be some form of helping the individual grow up, accept reality, and become more tolerant of himself and others. It may accomplish these rational goals in a large variety of ways, virtually all of which may be subsumed under three major headings. For man, as I have indicated in several previous books and papers (6, 13), is a cognitive, emotive, and behaving creature; and he almost invariably learns, unlearns, and relearns through these three major interacting modalities. Consequently, psychotherapeutic processes—whether or not the therapist is conscious of this fact—normally include perceptual-cognitive, emotive-evocative, and behavioral-motorial techniques. Thus, even old-style nondirective Rogerian methods (28) employ behavioristic reinforcement methods by putting their "Uh-huh's" in the proper places when their clients do what they think is the right thing; and even orthodox behavior therapists, such as Wolpe (29) direct their clients into highly cognitive-imaginative byways and relate to them emotionally, as Lazarus has shown in his book, *Behavior Therapy and Beyond* (23).

Rational therapeutic goals, consequently, can be achieved by many methods which at first blush seem to be either nonrational or antirational. In my own brand of rational-emotive therapy, for example, I largely work on the assumption that for the individual to achieve an elegant change in his personality structure, he'd better significantly modify some of his deepseated and longstanding cognitions and beliefs. But I realize that such philosophic restructuring, though most efficiently brought about by philosophic discourse and didactic dialogue or group discussion, at times is instituted or abetted by several kinds of emotive-evocative methods (such as direct confrontation, the use of dramatic language, role-playing, directive risk-taking, personal encountering, and supportiveness) and by many varieties of behavioristic-motorial methods (such as desensitization, self-reinforcement schedules, graduated in vivo active homework assignments, behavioral rehearsal, modeling, assertion training, and operant conditioning).

The question is: What, especially in terms of group therapeutic processes, are some of the most rational and irrational goals and procedures? Let me try to answer this question by first discussing what I consider to be irrational processes.

Irrational group therapy goals have two major aspects. Either (1) the group leader or facilitator believes that rationality is undesirable and he deliberately strives for nonrational or irrational goals; or (2) the group leader believes that rationality is desirable but that it can be best achieved, at least at times, in nonrational ways.

It is difficult to think of a clearcut example of the first form of irrationality in group therapy. Many group leaders ostensibly talk against rationality and are exceptionally anti-intellectual in their approaches (21). But most of the time they are actually pursuing rational goals, albeit in somewhat "irrational ways." Thus, the premise of anti-intellectualism is that human beings are too intellectual for their own good—that is, to live "humanly" and undefeatingly. And the premise of those therapists (and nontherapist group facilitators) who stoutly fight cognitive or rational kinds of problem solving is that these methods dehumanize, inhibit, or de-emotionalize people, and that they thereby render them less experiencing and less enjoying. Consequently, such group leaders implicitly if not explicitly seem to believe in the minimizing of severe disturbance and the maximizing of self-actualization; hence they are, at least in my sense of the term, positing and working for highly rational goals.

Occasionally, this does not seem to be true. To encourage a person, for example, to become more self-disciplined is usually to be efficient and rational, since discipline will normally help him, ultimately if not immediately, to function well and to enjoy himself more. But to encourage him, as several religious sects do, to become disciplined for the sake of discipline itself, or to control himself now in order that he may be happier in some hypothetical kind of heaven, does not appear to me to be sane or rational—in fact, it seems to me to be taking a reasonable view to unreasonable extremes, and hence to be essentially irrational. Similarly, to encourage a person to be emotional for the sake of emoting, or mystical for the sake of merely being mystical, or experiencing just because it is presumably good for him to experience is, I think, to lead him up the garden path and to present him with a dubiously worthwhile goal. I, for one, do not want to live *merely* for the sake of living; and I do not want to experience or to emote *only* because I define experiencing and emoting as good or worthwhile occurrences. I am still prejudiced enough about both short-range and long-range pleasure to believe that I'd better live largely (though

not *only*) to enjoy, and that similarly I'd better experience and
emote mainly because, in some immediate or ultimate way, I will
also enjoy, feel satisfied, have some kind of a goddamned ball. I believe, moreover–though I may prove to be wrong about this–
that if most humans most of the time do not survive in order to
enjoy, they will tend to lose their reason or motive for survival,
and the human race will consequently die out. This would not, in
my estimation, be necessarily horrible or awful; but it would be
damned inconvenient and unpleasing!

Some therapeutic goals, consequently, seem to be at least partly
irrational–or life and joy defeating. When an encounter therapist
tries to induce his group member to become permanently more
hostile to others; when a Zen Buddhist oriented therapist endeavors to help his client reach nirvana, or the state of perfect
blessedness achieved by the extinction of individual existence and
by the absorption of the soul into the supreme spirit, or by the extinction of all desires and passions; when an orthodox Christian
therapist strives to help an individual deliberately suffer earthly
woes and deprivations so that he will presumably enter and be
happier in a heavenly afterlife; I believe that these kinds of group
facilitators are pursuing irrational rather than rational goals, and
that it would be nice if they and the rest of us were honestly aware
of this aspect of their therapeutic endeavors. Fortunately, I have
never met many therapists who follow this extreme bent; but they
do exist, and I am personally opposed to their philosophies and
their methods.

On the other hand, I think that there are a great number of
modern therapists who have pretty rational goals–in fact, much
the same as I and my associates have–but who utilize exceptionally illogical or irrational ways of trying to achieve these goals.
And I am not, mind you, talking about nonrational or irrational
therapeutic techniques. As stated and implied above, I have no
hesitation utilizing, in RET group (or individual) therapy, nonrational, nonverbal, and noncognitive methods–as long as I consciously do so for rational ends. Thus, as a group and marathon
facilitator, I may employ emotional support, friendship, touching,

behavior desensitization, activity homework assignments, and a host of other nonrational procedures.

Not that these techniques are absolutely or entirely nonverbal and noncognitive; for the human being almost invariably adds, in his head, verbal and cognitive elements, to any supposedly nonverbal and highly emotive action that he takes. Thus, if I direct Joe, a group member, to pat Josephine, another group member, on the shoulder or to express warm feelings to her in other ways, he is cognitively signalling himself various messages while he is behaving in this manner, and she is cerebrally cogitating, and sometimes most actively, while he behaves "nonverbally" toward her. It is nonetheless true that certain group therapies are at least relatively nonrational, nonverbal, and noncognitive, and that as a rational-emotive therapist I would not hesitate to employ most of them.

Many therapeutic methods, however, tend to bring about irrational, self-defeating results, or at the very least to be quite inefficient (considering the amount of time and effort that goes into utilizing them) in bringing about effective results. Consequently, I would deem these partly or largely irrational group processes. There are many examples which quickly come to mind in this respect, including these:

1. Pure sensitivity training or ultra-nondirective procedures encourage group members to mull around endlessly in their own emotional juices, to become unduly upset (partly about the inefficiency of the procedures themselves), and to emote rather than to motivate themselves to behavioral change.

2. Encounter facilitators often are hung up on the compulsive experiencing and expression of *all* feelings, indiscriminately, including violently hostile and disruptive feelings, and abet rather than discourage needless hating of themselves and others by group members.

3. Overly-physical measures, such as gouging massage, slapping, kicking, biting, pummeling, wrestling, head-standing, often lead (a) to injury of oneself or others and (b) to the fostering of cruel and inhuman, oneupmanship attitudes.

4. Many group leaders, partly because they are not trained as psychotherapists, stick almost exclusively to physical and non-verbal methods and compulsively avoid any kinds of problem-solving which would much more directly and effectively help most of their group members.

5. Over-emphasis on relating procedures, which are again common on many traditional encounter groups, foolishly divert the participants into believing (a) that they can solve their deep emotional problems very easily; (b) that temporarily feeling better is equivalent to truly getting better; (c) that they truly do *direly need* (rather than merely *strongly desire*) others to love or approve them and that they are worthless slobs without such human support; and (d) that they are now worthwhile *because* the group leader or some group members seem to love them.

6. Some achievement-oriented groups (such as those commonly held for business executives) instill or abet the tragically superficial and often pernicious philosophy that the group member *is* a louse and can *not* possibly accept himself if he does not outstandingly succeed in the world.

7. Many problem-solving groups mainly emphasize practical, one-level solutions to personal and other problems and fail to touch, evaluate, or try to change the group member's basic disturbance-creating philosophy of life.

8. Some groups over-emphasize sexual blocks and difficulties and spend so much time and energy, on the part of the leader and the members, presumably working on these blockings that they ignore the fact that (a) they are usually a small part of the individual's basic disturbances and (b) they tend to stem more from rather than to create deepseated emotional difficulties.

9. Many encounter-type groups are so replete with clever games, exercises, diversions, pleasure-giving pastimes, and other gimmicks that the personality of the group members, and their fundamental value systems which underlie this personality, get lost in the shuffle.

10. An increasing number of groups emphasize magical, mystical, religious-oriented experiences that strongly imply that reason and science cannot help the individual and that there is some su-

pernatural and fairly easily achieved solution to his serious problems.

11. Some group leaders over-emphasize positive thinking, pollyannaish imagining, and other forms of autosuggestion which have palliative value but which give very inelegant solutions to serious issues.

12. There are a good many groups which condemn the members severely for their acts, particularly when they do not follow the group procedures. Not a few members are actually harmed by this kind of group blaming.

13. Some groups unrealistically arrange situations where the individual finds it almost impossible to fail, instead of examining and attacking his perfectionistic attitudes toward failing; and consequently they poorly prepare him to live in the real world where a good amount of failure is virtually inevitable.

14. Many analytically oriented groups are so preoccupied with the member's presumably unconscious thoughts and feelings that they sadly neglect his easily available, and often more important, conscious and preconscious thinking and emoting.

15. Some group leaders are so consistently and vehemently anti-intellectual that they help subvert normal reasoning processes and encourage the individual to surrender his most unique and important human powers: namely the power to think deeply and to think about his thinking. Consequently, his problem-solving abilities are sabotaged rather than enhanced and his emotions tend to become more inappropriate and uncontrollable.

16. Many group processes are so woefully inefficient that the members needlessly suffer for long periods of time before they improve, they become disenchanted with the entire therapeutic process, and they are thereafter given a good excuse to avoid effective therapy.

I could continue listing some of the irrational methods almost endlessly; but I would then have no remaining space for some of the chief rational aspects of group therapy! Let me therefore, with no further ado, get around to rationality in the group process. As you might expect, I tie these up with a rational system of psychotherapy—namely, rational-emotive therapy—which I created around the middle of the 1950's and which I and my associates have been practicing, in individual and group form, ever since.

Rational-emotive therapy (or RET, for short) very specifically posits that clients would better have rational goals–notably those of staying alive and enjoying themselves in both a short-range and a long-range manner–and that they'd better achieve them by vigorously using the logico-empirical scientific method. It assumes that so-called emotional disturbance is created when the individual, at point C, has a dysfunctional emotional Consequence: for example, feelings of anxiety, guilt, depression, or hostility; or defenses against these feelings, such as avoidance, rationalization, and projection; or needlessly self-defeating behavior, such as procrastination, inertia, or overeating; or psychosomatic symptoms, such as ulcers, high blood pressure, or heart palpitations. This Consequence, at point C, is usually preceded, at point A, by an Activating Event, Activating Experience, or Activating Environmental Situation.

Whereas most disturbed individuals, and perhaps most psychotherapists, believe that C is caused by A, or that Activating Events in the person's life make him feel poor emotional Consequences, RET believes that this is false: that C is really caused, almost invariably, by B. And what is B? The individual's Belief System. At point B, he tends to have first a rational Belief (rB), or appropriate negative assessment of A and its probable consequences. Thus, if A is a noxious Event or Experience–such as someone's rejecting him, he first signals himself something like: "How unfortunate! I wish I weren't rejected, but it looks like I am. I don't like that. What an inconvenience!" If he stuck rigorously to this rational Belief, he would feel, at point C, the Consequences of sorrow, regret, disappointment, annoyance, and irritation; and these feelings would all be appropriate, since he can empirically prove that it *is* unfortunate and inconvenient for him to be rejected, and that therefore it is appropriate for him to feel displeased and sorry about this rejection. Moreover, his feelings, at point C, would usefully motivate him (1) to seek to overcome this present rejection; (2) to look for other acceptances; and (3) to arrange his life so that in the future he is more likely to be accepted than rejected, and thereby be less inconvenienced. If he made himself happy about or indifferent to his being rejected, that would be pretty inappropriate: since he would then refuse to work against this and other rejections and would tend to become more disadvantaged.

The disturbed individual, however, also tends to have a highly irrational Belief (iB) or exaggerated, unrealistic, and inappropriate assessment of A and its probable consequences. Thus, if he gets rejected, at point A, he additionally signals himself (along with his rational Belief): "Isn't it *awful* that I was rejected! I *can't stand* it! I'll *always* keep getting rejected! What a turd I am for being rejected!" And then he feels, at point C, very anxious, depressed, and often hostile.

His irrational Belief is *not* related or relatable to empirical reality; and it is frequently also quite illogical or inconsistent. For several reasons:

1. It is hardly *awful* for him to be rejected, because *awful,* when honestly defined, means (a) very inconvenient or obnoxious and (b) *more than* very inconvenient or obnoxious. But nothing, of course, can really be *more than* 100 percent disadvantageous—as he probably believes, and *feels,* it *awfully* is. *Awful* also really means *full of awe;* and it is hardly full of awe that he has been rejected; it merely *is.* Awful furthermore means that because it is quite inconvenient for him to be rejected, he *should* not, *must* not be rejected. But, of course, there is scientifically no reason whatsoever that what is inconvenient to him should not or must not exist —especially when it *does* exist! By terming rejection *awful* he really is demanding, dictating that there be a law of the universe which insists that when *he* is very inconvenienced, *his* state of frustration simply must not be. Well, how the hell can he ever prove the existence of such a law?

2. By claiming that he *can't stand* being rejected, he means (a) that he can't tolerate it–but, of course, he can. He means (b) that he will probably die now that he is rejected–but, of course, he won't. He means (c) that he cannot ever, in all his years to come, possibly be in the least happy about anything now that he has been rejected–but, of course, he can be. He *can't stand* being rejected, in the final analysis, only because he *thinks* he can't stand it, and because he *defines himself* as a baby who cannot stand it. Shit, he can't!

3. By contending that he'll *always* keep getting rejected again now that he has been rejected *this time,* the disturbed individual is making a wholly unprovable statement. For no matter how many times he gets rejected, these past and present events never indicate that he must *always* be turned down in the future. There is just about no way he can prove total and inevitable rejection— no matter how devoutly he believes this unvalidateable hypotheses.

4. The disturbed person's contention that he is a turd, a worthless individual, because he is rejected is a silly, empirically unprovable abstraction for several reasons: (a) An individual is much too complex an entity to be given a total or global rating, and consequently *he* cannot possibly be worthless even though some of his behavior is ineffectual. (b) The contention that an individual is worthless is an allegation that because he acts badly, and is presumably rejected for his poor performance, he deserves to be punished and damned for this performance. But no matter how poorly he behaves or may behave in the future, he is never *damnable* by any empirical assessment but only by a hypothesized, and quite unprovable, theological postulate. (c) If an individual, rather than his specific behavior, is rateable the purpose of the rating is presumably to help him change his performances for the better in the future. But rating *him* as worthless, when he acts ineffectually, implies that he can *never* possibly improve his deeds. Consequently, such a rating tends to encourage him to make a self-fulfilling, self-downing prophesy, which will hinder rather than abet his future performances.

No matter how irrational the disturbed person's Belief System is, at point B, it will almost always have significant behavioral results. And the kinds of Beliefs that I have just delineated will inevitably lead to self-defeating, and hence in my definition of the term, irrational consequences. The main therapeutic tack, therefore, for the individual to take is to go on to point D, which consists of Disputing his irrational Beliefs (iB's). Thus, he could ask himself, at D, "Why is it awful that I was rejected?" and answer: "It isn't; it's merely unfortunate." He can ask, "Where is the evidence that I can't stand being rejected?" and reply: "There is no such evidence." He can ask, "Why must I always keep getting rejected, just because I now was refused?" and answer: "There is no reason why this rejection must lead to subsequent ones." And he can ask, "What makes me a turd for being rejected," and respond: "Nothing does! There are no human shits! I am merely a person who unfortunately got rejected and might continue to be in the future. Tough!"

When a group process is highly rational, it first selects sane and disturbance-undoing goals, and then it goes about trying to achieve these in logical, empirical, efficient ways. In rational-emotive therapy and similar cognitive-behavioral types of group therapy, the leader encourages rational processes in many ways, including the following:

1. The leader and several of the more sophisticated group members collaborate to teach the individual who brings up an emotional problem how to accept grim reality, when it occurs at point A, and to try to change it by concerted, determined effort instead of magically expecting it to evaporate by whining demands.

2. The group shows the troubled member (a) what he is specifically thinking at point B to create his inappropriate feelings and behavior, (b) how his muddled thoughts are causing his destructive feelings, and (c) how to logically parse these thoughts, how to empirically challenge and attack them, and how to persist at trying to modify them. Where less rationally-oriented groups emphasize feelings and insight, rationally-centered ones stress disputing irrational Beliefs until they are surrendered.

3. The group, under the leader's clearcut direction, is philosophically and cognitively centered, but it tends to use a wide variety of evocative-emotive and motorial-behavioral techniques in order to foster and abet cognitive change. It is rational in the sense that a business enterprise is rational: that is, ready to employ almost any method that truly works to encourage core attitudinal change.

4. The group leader–such as the RET group leader–is unusually active, probing, and challenging. He utilizes the group process partly to foster suggestions, comments, and hypotheses by other group members, which in turn spark him to focus on important issues that he might otherwise neglect, to present premises which he may check on and add to, to reinforce some of his main

points, and to allow him at times to stand on the emotive and intellectual shoulders of other group members and thereby augment
his therapeutic effectiveness.

5. The group rationally utilizes action within the group session
and preferably gives group members activity-oriented homework
assignments to be performed outside the session. Thus, it may as-
sign a group member to look for a new job, date a girl he is afraid
to date, or deliberately visit his mother-in-law, whom he may de-
test. Such homework assignments are often more effectively given
and followed up when given by a group than by an individual
therapist.

6. The group, in using evocative-emotive and motorial-behavioral techniques, does not naively accept the members' expressions but specifically probes for and emphasizes their cognitive
correlates. Thus, it looks for the actual behaviors which substantiate the individual's verbal expressions; and if, for example, he is
denying that he has hostile feelings it provides a laboratory where
the emotional, gestural, and behavioral aspects of these feelings
may directly be observed and questioned. Moreover, when such
feelings are revealed and authentically expressed, the rationally-
oriented group shows the member exactly what he is telling himself to create them, how he is cognitively sustaining them, and
what he can do to minimize or eliminate them if they are self-defeating. In this manner, it goes much deeper into the expression
of and understanding of feelings than the group which does not
emphasize rational analysis and change.

7. The rationally-oriented group provides each member with
several important kinds of feedback from other group members:
(a) It shows him that he is similarly troubled and has the same
kind of irrational ideas as many or most other group members.
(b) It gives him honest observations and feelings from other
group members in regard to how he comes across to them, how
he relates, what they think he can do to improve his human relationships, etc. (c) It provides a forum in which the group member may engage in psychodramatic, role-playing exercises with
other members, and hence learn assertion-training, social practice,
and other kinds of social skills. (d) It sometimes offers the individual social participation, and valuable feedback, outside the im-

mediate group situation, and thereby helps him relate and learn significant things about himself. (e) It particularly offers him other individuals who, both inside and outside the immediate group therapy situation, show him what his irrational thinking is, indicate how he can Dispute and challenge it, give him practice in Disputing, and encourage him to keep thinking in a more rational manner about himself and the world. (f) By teaching him how to be something of a therapist to the other group members, the rationally-oriented group gives him conscious and unconscious practice in seeing some of his own irrationalities and talking himself out of these self-defeating ideas. For in actively confronting others' crooked thinking, he is practically forced, by a unique feedback method, to confront and challenge his own. (g) When he questions and disputes other group members' irrationalities, the individual is observed and corrected by the leader and the remaining members of the group, and he is nicely shown what his *wrong* challenges are, how he can correct them, and how he can think his way through to more appropriate challenges that would be good for the group members and also good for himself.

8. In a rationally-oriented group, the member is able to observe the progress, and especially the philosophic progress, of other group members and thereby to see (a) that treatment can be effective, (b) that he can similarly change, (c) that there are specific things he can learn by which to help himself, and (d) that therapy is hardly magic but almost always consists of persistent hard ideational and active work.

9. In a group, the individual is offered a wider range of possible solutions than he would normally be offered in individual therapy. Out of ten or twelve people present at a given group session, one person may finally zero in on his central problem (after several others, including the leader, have failed) and another person may offer an elegant solution to it (after several lower-level solutions have hitherto been offered). Where a single individual, including a single therapist, may well give up on a difficult issue (or person), several group members may collectively persist and may finally prove to be quite helpful.

10. In almost every group process, the individual's revealing intimate problems to a group of people may in itself be therapeu-

tic. In RET group sessions, the client is encouraged and sometimes practically forced to disclose many ordinarily hidden feelings and ideas and thereby to see that nothing is really so shameful as he previously thought it was. The therapist and other group members specifically try to show an inhibited person that nothing awful will happen if he does honestly speak up; that once he has spoken up he usually feels better; and that even if he were excoriated and laughed at, that would be unfortunate and frustrating but would not truly be ego-downing or catastrophic—unless he *defined* his experience as being so.

11. A rationally-oriented group therapy process includes considerable educational and didactic material, such as explanations, information giving, and the discussion of various problem-solving techniques. Teaching, as John Dewey (4) and Jean Piaget (27) have shown, is more effective when the individual actively enters the teaching-discussing-doing process than when he is mainly a passive recipient. Group therapy, consequently, is an excellent means for the teaching of emotional education; and it is so effective in this respect that at the Institute for Advanced Study in Rational Psychotherapy in New York City we operate a private school, The Living School, where normal children are taught the elements of emotional education in the course of group counseling sessions and during regular classroom group work.

12. Severely disturbed individuals hold on to their irrational ideas and inappropriate feelings so rigidly and determinedly that they usually require persistent and consistent intervention. In RET group procedures, we usually hold sessions of two and a quarter hours, followed by an aftergroup session of an hour or so; and we also hold regular twelve-hour minithons and twenty-four hour marathon weekends of rational encounter, in the course of which massive efforts can be made to intrude on the negative thinking and acting of the group members.

In many ways, such as those just listed, group processes can include a great many rationally-oriented and rationally-executed procedures. These procedures incisively and intensively reveal and assail the troubled group member's irrational premises and illogical deductions and help him reconsider and reconstruct his basic self-destructive philosophies. Groups are so effective in this respect that they are frequently employed by leading cognitive therapists–such as Berne (2), Corsini (3), Dreikurs (5), Ellis (6, 13, 15), Ellis and Harper (18, 19), Lazarus (23), Low (24), and Phillips and Wiener (26).

To conclude: man is unusually prone to self-defeating thinking and inappropriate emoting and behaving. But he can significantly change his cognitions, emotions, and behavior if he clearly understands exactly what he thinks and does to create his so-called emotional upsets. He can do this by exerting the choice, which he uniquely has as a human being, to think and act differently; and he can be appreciably helped to do so in the course of active-directive, rationally-oriented group psychotherapy.

REFERENCES

1. Beck, A. T.: *Depression.* New York, Harper and Hoeber, 1967.
2. Berne, E.: *Games People Play.* New York, Grove Press, 1964.
3. Corsini, R. J., with Cardono, S.: *Role Playing in Psychotherapy: a Manual.* Chicago, Aldine, 1966.
4. Dewey, J.: *Human Nature and Conduct.* New York, Modern Library, 1930.
5. Dreikurs, R., and Grey, L.: *Logical Consequences: a Handbook of Discipline.* New York, Meredith, 1968.
6. Ellis, A.: *Reason and Emotion in Psychotherapy.* New York, Lyle Stuart, 1962.
7. Ellis, A.: *Homosexuality: Its Causes and Cure.* New York, Lyle Stuart, 1965.
8. Ellis, A.: What *really* causes therapeutic change? *Voices, 4*(2):90-97, 1968.
9. Ellis, A.: *Is Objectivism a Religion?* New York, Lyle Stuart, 1968.
10. Ellis, A.: A weekend of rational encounter. In Burton, A. (Ed.): *Encounter.* San Francisco, Joseey-Bass, 1969, pp. 112-127.
11. Ellis, A.: Helping people get better rather than merely feel better. In Blau, T. (Chmn.): *The Necessary and Sufficient Conditions for Change in Psychotherapy.* Conference sponsored by the Division of Psychotherapy of the American Psychological Association and the University of South Florida, Tampa, January 10, 1969.
12. Ellis, A.: Rational-emotive therapy. *Journal of Contemporary Psychotherapy, 1*:82-90, 1969.
13. Ellis, A.: *Reason and Growth: Verbatim Case Experiences in Rational-Emotive Therapy.* San Francisco, Science and Behavior Books, 1971.
14. Ellis, A.: The group as an agent in facilitating change toward rational

thinking and appropriate emoting. Paper presented at a conference on group processes, University of West Virginia at Morgantown, April 3, 1971.

15. Ellis, A.: *Emotional Education*. New York, Julian Press, 1972.
16. Ellis, A.: Rational-emotive psychotherapy. In Corsini, R. (Ed.): *Current Psychotherapies*. Itasca, Illinois, Peacock, 1972.
17. Ellis, A., and Gullo, J. M.: *Murder and Assassination*. New York, Lyle Stuart, 1971.
18. Ellis, A., and Harper, R. A. H.: *A Guide to Successful Marriage*. Hollywood, Wilshire Books, 1970.
19. Ellis, A., and Harper, R. A. H.: *A Guide to Rational Living*. Hollywood, Wilshire Books, 1971.
20. Ellis, A., Wolfe, J. L., and Moseley, S.: *How to Prevent Your Child from Becoming a Neurotic Adult*. New York, Crown Publishers, 1966.
21. Howard, J.: *Please Touch*. New York, Dell, 1971.
22. Kelly, G.: *The Psychology of Personal Constructs*. New York, Norton, 1955.
23. Lazarus, A. A.: *Behavior Therapy and Beyond*. New York, McGraw-Hill, 1971.
24. Low, A. A.: *Mental Health Through Will-Training*. Boston, Christopher Publishing Company, 1952.
25. Phillips, E. L.: *Psychotherapy*. Englewood Cliffs, N.J., Prentice-Hall, 1956.
26. Phillips, E. L., and Wiener, D. N.: *Short-Term Psychotherapy and Structured Behavior Change*. New York, McGraw-Hill, 1966.
27. Piaget, J.: *Science of Education and the Psychology of the Child*. New York, Orion Press, 1970.
28. Rogers, C. R.: *Client-Centered Therapy*. Boston, Houghton Mifflin, 1951.
29. Wolpe, J.: *Psychotherapy of Reciprocal Inhibition*. Stanford, Stanford University Press, 1958.

CHAPTER VII

OBSERVATIONS AND TECHNIQUES IN BIOENERGETIC GROUP THERAPY

JOHN C. PIERRAKOS

John C. Pierrakos, a psychiatrist trained in the bioenergetic school of Alexander Lowen, has applied these techniques and principles to group methods of treatment. Following the initial teachings of Wilhelm Reich, Lowen and Pierrakos feel that in order for an individual to achieve "unity" he would have to become more aware of his body and integrate the physical functions with the emotional and mental aspects of himself. In this very practical, clear, and direct paper we are given detailed descriptions of their theory and its very specific applications to a group situation.

Initially Doctor Pierrakos places his approach in its historical perspective, outlining the bioenergetic approach. Basically a physical approach it considers the expression of feelings through the avenue of movement, musculature and other physical acts such as breathing. In a group situation all participants evaluate each other's flexibility and blocking and the correspondence or lack of correspondence their physical and emotional states. In his approach the participant first "cleans up" or expresses his negative and destructive feelings and then can regress and experience his early life deprivations. The consistent emphasis for each patient is on the integration of the physical with the emotional. Touching and physical contact between therapist and patient and among patients is encouraged as a diagnostic as well as a therapeutic tool. The interdependence of group members upon one another is stressed on many levels from sharing observations and reactions to sharing living and breathing space.

Doctor Pierrakos outlines several group techniques in detail which he feels increase the energy levels of the group and bring to full view the muscular blockings that have to be worked out, since these are the counterparts of the neurotic complexes. One such technique involves the group in forming a wheel with the participants feet at the center, the bodies as spokes, and the head on the rim. (Body portions within the wheel may be reversed.) The group members breath in unison, touch one another and then releasing tension feelings beginning with angry affect and ending with tender affect.

Dr. John C. Pierrakos in this clear exposition of the bioenergetic school's approach to group treatment methods has vividly shown his readers his approach to group psychotherapy. His experience indicates that this approach can precipitate powerful emotional responses among group members and, therefore, concludes his paper with a note of caution warning that these techniques should not be employed by the untrained, or those not knowing their blocks and bodies. But for those experienced in the bio-energetic approach there seems to be a resultant feeling of fusion, unity and knowledge of self and others, that promises a new dimension to group treatment methods.

D.S.M.

G.D.G.

HISTORICAL PERSPECTIVE

GROUP THERAPY is an evolutionary process developed from individual therapy. The group has to be looked upon as an organism that has a life of its own and a movement leading to heightened experiences. This is possible only when there is development in the identity and the feelings of the individual members.

In the evolutionary development of organisms, the evolution progresses from the unicellular organisms to organization; from the amoeba to the mammalians. In the development of man and his culture, group living and group experiences progress to the focusing of the importance of the individual and his personality. In man, primitive living grouped around tribal experiences develops also into individuality which characterizes civilization. The great religions of humanity make specific issue of the responsibility of each human being for his acts, thoughts and decisions. In the United States, through the development and expansion of industrialization, there has been a progressive cutting-off of the individual from the roots of his creativity and normal life. This has created mass production, mass culture and a mass individual.

The work of Wilhelm Reich pointed out the importance of the preservation of the natural state for the growth of the individual. The work of Alexander Lowen amplified Reich's work, pointing out that the only way to find unity would be to go back to the physical body and integrate the physical functions with the emotional and mental aspects of man. Also, Lowen pointed out the importance of the individual as opposed to mass living, mass production and mass philosophy. A movement has developed in the United States called the "human potential movement" coming from a group of psychologists, psychiatrists and many experi-

menters. This movement was a reaction to the rigidity of therapeutic techniques which could not catch up with the needs and the
numbers of people in need of help; and emphasized the discovery
of new experiences, feelings and attitudes of the individual through
group interaction and encounter of the basic feelings.

UNITARY ASPECT OF THE BIOENERGETIC APPROACH

However, it is in the field of bioenergetics where all the aspects
of man are dealt with simultaneously; the physical, the emotional
and the mental. This approach works through the direct and indirect involvement of the body in the therapeutic situation. The
physical organism is exposed to the examination and perception
of the therapist, as well as, of all the group participants. Great
emphasis is placed upon the expression of the body, its motility,
its harmony of parts and its relationship and appropriateness to
the expression in the face. The person's movements are very important in giving a clue to his aggression or passivity; to his acceptance or denial of life. By having the body exposed (women
work in leotards, men in shorts), there is a direct contact with the
therapist and the other participants; thus, it increases the feeling
of security and acceptance through physical contact.

The work is based on the principle of psychosomatic identity;
that is to say, whatever occurs in the mind, occurs in the body
simultaneously. This principle was developed by Wilhelm Reich
and gave an impetus to the specific study of the energetic processes of man. When the problem is looked upon both as a physical,
emotional and intellectual unity, it adds a new dimension to the
therapeutic process. Because of this unitary approach, it is many
times possible to shorten the time necessary to reach the deeper
emotions by proceeding through the physical root while simultaneously working on a psychological and a mental level.

BASIC EXPRESSIONS OF MAN

The physical approach considers first the natural functions of
life such as moving, breathing and expressing feelings.

Breathing is the bellows of life. It is a pulsatory phenomena
similar to the expansion and contraction of the heart. It can produce energy to invest in emotions or can create blockage to the

movement of feelings. A child who is in panic draws in his breathing, raises the shoulders and stops the feelings by restraining the breathing, thus making it possible to survive the onslaught of painful emotions. A person who is happy breathes deeply and fully, thus accentuating the perception of feeling which he enjoys experiencing. In the bioenergetic approach, the breathing is examined meticulously in terms of the inspiratory and expiratory phases, the length, the frequency and how the respiratory movement progresses or is arrested throughout the abdomen and chest.

The next thing that is examined is the motility of the organism; whether the movements are voluntary, purposeful and limited or whether the involuntary aspect of the movement is allowed. The way a person stands on the ground indicates his position to the earth; if his knees are locked back and his pelvis retracted or pushed forward, he expresses his lack of grounding and a displacement of the center of gravity from the small of the back to the thighs or the calves or the shoulders. It is interesting to note that unless a person is grounded and has good contact with his legs and the soil, he is like a tree, top-heavy but with no roots, vulnerable to the slightest wind of life.

The ability of a person to be flexible and express feelings on a wide scale while at the same time able to integrate his feelings in an adult level gives him a tremendous strength and resourcefulness. In bioenergetics, the emphasis is not placed upon explosiveness of feelings or rigidity (as an expression of strength), but in the ability of the person to play different tunes in the instrument of life, his body.

When a person is brought up in an atmosphere of anxiety, fear and restriction of the natural movements, the organism protects his integrity by developing voluntary and involuntary resistances which are simultaneously somatized in the skeleto-muscular complex, creating a bunching up and rigidity of the muscular structures, thus prohibiting a free flow of feelings, emotions and movement. When the repression and suppression of the emotions are carried on for a long period of time, the corresponding muscular blocks become also chronic and impeding upon the movements of life; thus, expressing on a deeper level, the negative attitude, for no muscular block means anything else but "NO" to life.

OBSERVING THE REACTIONS OF THE PARTICIPANTS

In approaching this problem in a group situation, the participants evaluate each other's flexibility, blocking and expression and reacting to this accordingly; becoming, thus aware of their own physical and emotional state. Very many movements are mobilized and made available to express the positive and the negative reactions; for the person who cannot say "NO" is unable to say "YES." He has no choice.

A basic approach to the work is to focus the feelings at each member and each person takes full responsibility for his feelings instead of acting them out on other people. This is observed very carefully by the group and when the person is blaming, complaining or accusing, his attention is called to this. On other occasions, a person is asked to act irrationally, to let go in an irrational manner all his feelings in expressions of aggression, passivity, etc. This, however, is tied up eventually to the adult level instead of acting them out on an infantile level as the final expression of emotion. The group observes constantly the connectedness or disconnectedness between the content and the appropriate or inappropriate way it expresses the thoughts. For instance, if a participant wants to call his boss and he expresses this with a dead-pan face and a flat voice, the other members of the group imitate him and ask him whether he really means it; trying to prod him to connect his emotions with their expression.

One important principle in the group work is that the negative feelings and attitudes of it be constantly dealt with and cleaned up before any positive expression of emotion is encouraged. When a participant first cleans up the negative and destructive feelings, his hatred and his rage, he then can ask for help and many times go into the childhood level and call for his mother so he can make connections with his deprivating experiences historically. The therapist as well as the group members can touch each other, if this is a spontaneous expression of their feelings. Emphasis is placed into creating a feeling of unity in the body which defocuses the person from his genitals and overt, acting out sexual behavior. Many times, one member of the group works with another by laying his hands, feeling the tenseness of the other person and thus, perhaps perceiving his own tensions, his own chronic spasticities. The physical work is constantly integrated with spontaneous reactions and behavior on a verbal level. It is important to note that each person is taught to recognize the basic personality and character structure *on a physical level of each participant:* on the physical, the emotional and the mind level. Therefore, the basic resistances of each participant is recognized openly, pointed out and kept in mind for future reference when the irrational arises and is then easily understood to be the projection of the neurotic complex of the total personality.

A basic rule in the work is the full acceptance of the negative and the irrational with no blame. It is essential that each participant will have the right to express his negative, destructive feelings if he recognizes them as being irrational and out of place. The therapist does not allow other members of the group to use this information for ammunition against him. It is important to note that each participant has voluntary and involuntary resistances. The work at the beginning is done with the voluntary aspect and integrating this with the personality. The involuntary resistances emerge slowly as the character is pointed out by the therapist or the members of the group. This prevents the acting out of rivalries, resentments and destructive reactions in the group situation most of the time.

THE ENERGETIC ASPECT OF THE GROUP: THE PRINCIPLE OF MUTUALITY

When a group of people gather together, they effect each other deeply, not only through their verbal and emotional expressions but also through the organismic energies surrounding the bodies. A person has an energy field within and around his organism. When we are in proximity, we are touching each other's energy fields. One person's energy field can affect the energy fields of the entire group. If a person holds back with his negative feelings and refuses to express himself freely, his energy field becomes altered, that is, slows down and tends to stop the energy fields of the other people in his proximity. On the other hand, if a participant expresses his poignant emotions fully, there is a resonance effect on the energy fields of the rest of the group. For instance, if a person expresses deep feelings of anguish and crying, many of the participants may start sobbing, especially if they can identify with such feelings.

We are constantly interdependent upon each other and the living and breathing space of each member is shared by the rest of the group. However, eventual development of a human being depends upon his assuming full responsibility of his body, his mind and his feelings and whether he will allow himself to fuse with another human being according to the principle of mutuality. Mutuality means that there is a fusion of two different aspects of people in a comprehensive whole. *Mutuality is the movement towards unification.* For mutuality to occur, there must be an expansive energetic movement of one person towards another, of one group member towards the other members. There must be two "YES" currents moving closer to one another. It is important to note here that for a person to develop, he should be able to increase his quantitative level of energy which then can lead to the experience of removing the neurotic complex and allowing the experience of pleasure. The ability to sustain more and more pleasure and a richer life has to be obtained gradually through the principle of mutuality. The person has to accept pleasure and say "YES" when "YES" is offered. A person who is deeply alienated from himself will deny the possibility of expansion and therefore, of mutuality and he will remain safe and separated in his isolated ways. The developing process in each participant depends upon his ability to become aware of his previously hidden destructive side. The weeds have to be removed from the garden so that the flowers can grow and the most important thing is the lack of awareness of the existence of the weeds. The splitting of the emotions within a person must reappear as a division and splitting between that person and the group or the society in which he lives. In a group, it is important to note that by using the reactions against another member of the group, one can arrive at an accurate measure of the personal reactions of each individual adult member. Therefore, the group must be carried out in an atmosphere of revealing and dropping down the mask which covers up each individual. This should be accomplished in an atmosphere of full acceptance with no criticism. In summary, after very many of the negative, destructive attitudes of each group member has been worked out, there should be an integration and focusing upon what the individual really wants consciously. This is usually a wish for development and an opening up of the capacity to experience pleasure. In the subsequent stages of the group work, an attempt to integrate the individual to the group and to society is carried on by utilizing the physical techniques described above and the character analytic approach, as well as, acting out of irrationalities purposefully. In each group session, there is a great deal of physical work incorporated in the group techniques which will be very hard for me to describe in this article. However, there are certain techniques that can be extremely useful in working with the body. They are simple, they increase the energy level of the group and they bring in full view the muscular blocking that has to be worked out which is the counterpart of the neurotic complex. These processes tend to fuse energetically the group and further the principle of mutuality.

SOME SPECIFIC ENERGETIC TECHNIQUES LEADING TO MUTUALITY

Some of these processes which I have found to be useful are the following:

1. For example, if a group composed of 14 people is arranged in *mandala* or wheel position with the feet of the participants forming a small circle towards the center with the head radiating outward, many things can be worked out. The therapist should be at the hub so that he can observe every participant as each one begins to breathe heavily: thus, he notices where they are blocked physically and where the energetic movements in the body are not stable. This wheel which is formed by contact of the feet and hands, in effect becomes a cyclotron of energy which spins the movement around the circle in a counterclockwise fashion. By deep breathing that is specifically regulated by the group leader, a great many reactions start occurring in such a group. Events such as tremors, vibrations in the feet and stiffness in different parts of the body can be thoroughly observed. The movement of energy creates an overcharge at the weak points of each individual, so that his muscular blocks put pressure on them and stimu-

lates awareness of his inadequacies or his blocked movements. On the other side, it builds energy levels in weak individuals such as schizoid structures and makes it possible for them to express feelings much stronger than they are able to do in a single situation with the therapist.

2. When the group as a whole starts breathing in unison, many amazing phenomena make their appearance. Often, people holding the crying and anger for years erupt into a deep sobbing. This has to be followed carefully and graduated so that there will not be any adverse reactions, which may throw any of the participants into panic. I have found out that by the continuous breathing that is composed of short expiratory movements and a long expiratory movement accompanied by the voice when expressions of negativity are first taken up, such as, *No,* the group starts to cleanse itself as a whole. It accepts its negative and destructive tendencies, thus making room for better reactions to appear.

Actually, the group is similar to an orchestral ensemble of many instruments: the leader is the conductor. He regulates the pitch, the tone and the rapidity of the emotions by decreasing or increasing the breathing, or by stopping the movement completely; on the other hand, he may also accelerate it. It is, therefore, important to bear in mind that by first releasing the negative movements it is possible to proceed safely into the expression of tender feelings. I have worked out a scheme which is useful and safe:

3. The people in the group should be placed in the circle with the leader in the center, feet pointing toward the middle, heads in the direction of the periphery. Approximately fourteen people is the best size for a group, alternating men and women in the position of the circle. First, several intervals of two to three minutes of deep breathing should be initiated. This should be accompanied by deep sighing. Then the breathing is accelerated and the participants are requested to flex their ankles and push on their heels; thus, a vibratory movement is created which unifies them all. At the same time they are asked to move their heads from side to side and express the feeling of *No.* This, after several intervals of breathing of two or three minutes, of stopping and then working through the blocks individually, is carried on to a temper tantrum;

fists are clenched; the participants pound the floor with both fists and feet, moving from side to side with loud screams of *NO!* These episodes are not allowed to continue more than one or two minutes but they are repeated successively. It is important to note that in each interval the group leader must observe carefully the reactions of every participant. He must see the body exposed or half nude in order to observe where each person is blocked and if the block, for example, is in back of the neck, his helper who is on the outside must proceed to release the block until the entire group can proceed to a deeper emotion. There are many amazing experiences which occur in the mandala position, such as deep crying, sobbing, anger and temper tantrums which appear to be genuine expressions of the rage within a person's body and soul.

4. Another position that furthers the soft movements is to place the fourteen participants with the head facing towards the center and feet outward. In this position they again start breathing: they can raise their hands toward the hub of the wheel, touch each other, express tender feelings, smack their lips, cry mama and ask for her to come. Very deep experiences result as the breathing deepens and the people call for Mother or call for help. The deep sobbing appears, strong vibrations stream through the body, heart breaking cries of emotions which have been held in for years and years come to the surface. At the end, the participants are asked to turn towards each other and hold one another, looking at each other in this lying down position of the wheel, without making any demands or expecting anything from one another except to make contact. During this time sobbing and crying also occurs on a much deeper level in many of the couples. The circle or wheel is ended all the time with the participants standing in a circle and facing the center. They follow the group leader's instructions.

The basic idea is that after the person has gone through experiences of early childhood in the temper tantrum position and the *No,* the crying and the lesser position of protest, now he is able to stand on his feet and ground himself with the life energy movements of the adult person. In this position, therefore, the participants are instructed to spread their feet approximately one and one half feet apart, heels out, hands on waists, breathing and allowing once more the vibratory movements to flow through their bodies. The circle is maintained through touch of the feet. In this position again negative expressions are taken such as "NO," "I won't" and others. Also, in this position and at this stage, they are asked to vocalize with long expiratory phases. The vocalization builds an aspect of resonance and feeling in the whole group. Finally, the phenomena of resonance leads to harmony and it is really amazing that the vocalization takes a form of singing. It is very difficult to explain this phenomenon but it does occur so often and my observation of the energy field is the impression that during these experiences the energy field of each participant becomes greatly excited, fuses with the energy field of his neighbor and creates a dynamic, powerful movement which runs through the whole and then the entire group; luminating the entire energy field which is emitted in the form of light and movement. This makes the participant feel like one individual while at the same time he is part of the group. The emphasis on this group work is in the individual experience of each participant. It is only through individual experiences that he can participate in the group. It is only if he develops his personal feelings, bodily awareness and sensations, and his own breathing that he is able to share his energies with the participants of the group. Therefore, the principle of mutuality, creative movement, fusion and unification which occurs within each person, is extended to the whole group.

I want also to add a word of caution. These techniques can be utilized safely only when a person is able to read the structure of the participant and have the awareness to see his blocks and attempt to release them by specific methods developed in bioenergetics. These techniques should never be done by people who are not fully aware of their own blocks and their own bodies because it may throw some of the participants into panic reactions. So, when the group is carried successfully there is a feeling of fusion and unity, a consciousness which develops out of this experience. This happens because there is no part of the individual which is excluded, denied or cut off from the experience of each person with himself and with the group.

CHAPTER VIII

GESTALT GROUP THERAPY: SENSE IN SENSITIVITY

Magda Denes-Radomisli

Dr. Magda Denes, a faculty member of the Adelphi doctoral and postdoctoral program, is a regular contributor to our conferences and books because of her expertise as a psychoanalyst trained in Existential and Gestalt psychology. In her very effective and direct style, she utilizes this expertise in a careful evaluation of the encounter movement and evolves a very enlightening critique of it in this paper. She then proceeds to provide us her alternative to the encounter group, Gestalt group therapy, which she feels gives "the most complete and efficacious technical translation available today of Existential therapeutic technique into practice."

In a delightfully witty, open, and penetratingly critical discussion, Magda Denes describes the encounter movement as the most significant socio-political movement of our time. In the first half of the paper she explores its premises of being rooted in humanism and existentialism. She argues that the encounter movement's utilization of these two fields is illusory based upon apparent similarities. Shared vocabulary, apparent adoption of the Existentialist conception of the importance of person to person relatedness, and the utilization of the existential techniques of phenomenological observation are the attempts that failed, in Doctor Denes' opinion, to make these group techniques valid therapeutically or technically. In her paper Doctor Denes utilizes a fund of research sources to substantiate her erudite condemnation of the place of the encounter movement in today's culture. She ultimately sees it as a socio-political force symptomatic of the failure of our society to have met the psychic challenges that its technology imposed. She warns us that in her opinion they represent a crypto-fascist force. Doctor Denes then goes on to outline an alternate therapeutic set of constructs and techniques as she describes the Gestalt therapy applications to group treatment as putting sense in Sensitivity and encounter in Encounter. In a clearly understandable presentation she first characterizes Existential Analytic work in terms of the particular open, respectful dialogue between patient and analyst and the one to one relatedness between these two even in group treatment, which she feels is facilitated by Gestalt techniques. And in the remaining part of her paper she highlights the similarity and differences between Existentialism and Gestalt theories.

This paper is characterized in the main by broad scholarly analysis and in addition, by adept and effective emotional involvement of reader. In it Doctor

Denes succeeds in getting us to think and feel more deeply and critically about the encounter movement and its possible dangers. Thus, unlike some critics she is not solely an iconoclast, but provides with constructional and viable alternatives as well.

D.S.M.
G.D.G.

CARL ROGERS HAS SAID that the Encounter Movement is the most significant social movement of our time. I would like to alter that statement somewhat to suit my vision and say that I see Encounter as the most significant socio-political movement of our time. Significance and benefit are naturally not synonymous words.

The Encounter Culture (and I am including here Sensitivity Training, T-Groups, Awareness Groups, Growth Center Groups and so on) admits to be atheoretical but on the whole, presents its Image as primarily Existential and Humanistic.

It is the reality of this image that I propose to examine in the first half of my paper.

Existentialism to my mind is most especially a point of view, a stance of relatedness to reality, a manner of appraisal of life and its events. It is a philosophy in the literal sense in that it represents "a system of principles for guidance in practical affairs."

Unfortunately, Existentialism in America has been grossly misrepresented and misunderstood. This is partly traceable to the fact that a large proportion of Existential texts are translated from foreign languages in nearly incomprehensible terms and partly traceable to the fact that the literary works of the modern Existential writers, notably Sartre and Camus, have been taken as pure philosophy rather than as what they are, literary works that of necessity exaggerate philosophy into drama.

Existentialism, then, is not the esoteric concern of Teutonic minds and most definitely not the nihilistic cavorting of a lunatic fringe. It is an intricate discipline whose intricacy dictates a certain degree of abstraction in its communication, but whose proper subject matter is the individual, the Single Being and his personal significance, the private predicament, the unique destiny, the concrete and specific Existence in the World.

Historically, Existentialism, whether in philosophy or art or literature has always flourished in times of crisis. This is understand-

able for several reasons. First, since Existentialism as I said earlier is a mode of relatedness to reality, it takes hold at those moments of cultural upheaval when the traditionally prescribed
modes of relatedness to reality have failed and can no longer offer
security. Second, since a major tenet of Existentialism is to regard
the Individual as always in the process of becoming, that is, as
from moment to moment choosing his Being, the individual, from
an Existential standpoint is always potentially in crisis. A philosophy then, for which crisis is an opportunity rather than a disaster,
is obviously a helpful philosophy in times of crisis. Third, since
Existentialism is more than anything an attitude that moves from
the general to the specific, from the abstract to the concrete, from
the hypothetical to the phenomenal, it provides criteria for meaning and authenticity in life that are relatively independent from
cultural prescriptions (counter or otherwise) although of course
not independent of the possibilities the cultural provides. Indeed,
Existentialism, when adequately understood does provide a life-
view, a style of apperception of the World and of the Self, that
fulfills a profound lack in the contemporary American intellectual-
emotional climate.

I emphasize "adequately understood" because it is my contention that Encountering reflects an adequate understanding of Existentialism about to the same degree that Astrology reflects an
adequate understanding of Astronomy.

The apparent similarities between Existentialism and the Encounter movement proceed roughly from three factors. First, Encounter has simply adopted the Existential vocabulary. But a
shared vocabulary in divergent contexts does not produce same-
ness. Thus, for example, the term "Encounter" in Existential
thought refers to a dyadic relationship of dialogue between two
self-disclosing persons on what Martin Buber calls "the sharp edge
of existence" (1). In Encounter, encounter is the public confrontation of an individual by an individual or by the group. Confrontation differs from encounter in that it lacks mutuality. Only
the intentionality of the confronter needs to be present for it to
occur.

Second, Encounter has adopted the Existential conception of

the crucial importance for human life of the Mitwelt or "With-World."

In Existentialism, Mit-Welt refers to the world of interpersonal relatedness where persons meet as persons and not as objects. In other words where encounter takes place. Existentialism, however, distinguishes two additional modes of world. The Umwelt, literally meaning "the world around" and the Eigenwelt or "own world." A person is said to live simultaneously in all three modes of world and pathological disturbance in one affects the other two. Thus in Existential analysis functioning in all three modes is investigated. The Encounterists restrict their attention to the specific transactions that occur in the group and focus exclusively on the psychological significance of the Mitwelt as it is revealed through group interaction. With this focus, they uproot the conception of man from the natural biological world of his instincts, at the same time that they deprive him of his uniquely human achievement of self-conscious relatedness to himself.

Third, Encounter has adopted the Existential technique of Phenomenological observation, that is, observation without premises, for the investigation of behavior. I find this the only genuinely corresponding feature of the movement and incidentally it came to Encounter through the absorption of Gestalt techniques.

As for the rest, Encounter and Existentialism do not even appear to be similar. Existentialism is concerned with Ontology as it is manifested in the Single Being and not with group process; it is concerned with the authenticity of individual existence and not with "as-if" transactions engendered by inventive group leaders. Existentialism has traditionally entailed a tragic view of life, a recognition of the "thrown" quality of existence, a knowledge of solitude, an intimacy with the guilt of bad faith, a closeness to the anxiety of death. And traditionally it was in the face of this awareness that it affirmed again and again man's potential freedom and dignity. How could such a philosophy be conceivably reflected in a hedonistic carnival referred to as "Schutz's Flying Circus"?

The second image of Encounter is its Humanism. Now Humanism was an intellectual and cultural movement which occurred during the Renaissance and followed the rediscovery of ancient

Greek and Roman civilizations, their literature and art, and which stimulated a renewed interest in man and his capabilities.

Bertrand Russell says of it as follows (8):

> Most of the Humanists retained such superstitious beliefs as had found support in antiquity. Magic and witchcraft might be wicked, but were not thought impossible. . . . Astrology was prized especially by free thinkers; it acquired a vogue which it had not had since ancient times. The first effect of emancipation from the Church was not to make men think rationally, but to open their minds to every sort of antique nonsense. . . . Morally, the first effect of emancipation was equally disastrous. The old moral rules ceased to be respected. . . . I cannot think of any crime, except the destruction of ancient manuscripts, of which the men of the Renaissance were not frequently guilty. . . . Outside the sphere of morals, the Renaissance had great merits. In architecture, painting, and poetry, it has remained renowned. It produced very great men, such as Leonardo, Michelangelo, and Machiavelli.

And John Herman Randall writes of it thus (6):

> The Platonism of the Renaissance, if it lacked the full-bodied life of the Greek poet and wandered off into the vagaries of Neo-Platonic mysticism, of astrology and magic and strange secret lore, compounded of Arabian and Jewish dreams, had at least regained its joy in beauty.

And again (7):

> Humanism had an intensely practical interest in the forces within human nature, and bothered little with man's belief about the larger setting of his life; it was far more anthropocentric than the 13th Century, whose chief concern was God, or the 18th whose problems lay in nature.

Although the history of Renaissance Humanism differed quite a bit in the Northern and Southern parts of Europe, in general it was an intensely individualistic movement in the context of unstable political conditions. The spirit of the times was Pagan, pleasure seeking, orgiastic, superstitious, immoral, antirational, elitist, and for a number of specific individuals, staggeringly creative.

One can perhaps best sum up the Zeitgeist with Dr. Faustus' words (5):

Philosophy is odious and obscure; Both law and physic are for petty wits; Divinity is basest of the three. . . . 'Tis magic, magic that hath ravished me.

Dr. Faustus sold his soul to the devil for a chance to know everything, feel everything, do everything. He typified the Renaissance Being filled with eternal dissatisfaction and a restless, constant yearning for some great vague thing that when properly examined turned out to be personal power.

History reveals that the Renaissance and the Reformation could not and did not last. They ushered in Protestantism, fierce European nationalism and ultimately the worship of the Superman.

One can readily see that Encounter and Renaissance Humanism do share common qualities.

The anti-rational charismatic leader with his mystical aura and endless inventiveness in the search for new experience, is, even if rather threadbare and confined, the modern version of Renaissance man. His historical context however, is drastically different, as is much of the content of his psyche.

Twentieth Century Humanism is no longer bound up with an anthropocentric world view, and it does not take place in the context of Man's assured cosmic significance or even permanence. The Industrial Revolution ended all that. In the Twentieth Century man is a beleagured, helpless, irrelevant, anonymous being, unequal to the demands of his productions, dehumanized by his corporate complexity, mortally endangered by himself. He is entrapped, especially in America, in a Technocracy that is unresponsive to him, whose direction he is unable to influence, and whose ethic contaminates all his endeavors; so far including his attempts to re-establish his individualism. For on closer reflection, one discovers that Encounter after all is a group enterprise, with strict limits on individual freedom and with enormous pressures toward group conformity.

As to its spiritual orientation, I would like to quote to you some brief passages from Arthur Burton, who is an avid Encounter enthusiast (2).

Many clients tell me that they go to Encounter Group Centers not only for the encounter itself, but for the vast opportunities for sexual experience which are to be found there. One famous encounter center offers baths in which mixed nude bathing is the rule after the sessions themselves. One invariably gets a chance there to live sexuality rather than learning how to displace or sublimate it.

Here then is the new esthetic: sexual congress pre-packaged, TV Dinner Style, in the communal bath. This, in the name of freedom. Encounter Man no longer needs to wrestle with his soul to produce anything. Not a work of art, not even a personally chosen partner. They come compliments of the management, or the leader provides.

Again, elsewhere Burton writes (3):

> Encounter is experientially introjective rather than interpretative and it places little premium on intelligence with its function of rapidly manipulating symbols and placing and displacing them.

And he states (4):

> Encounter has a wider universality because it is not founded upon insight but upon experiencing.

Note this quote carefully because the tragedy it augers is not new in history. At the decline of every civilization the invading barbarian hordes destroyed that civilization's symbols and myths and insights and intellect. What is new is to get advanced notice of the coming event. I think we ought to pay serious attention.

Scrutiny then reveals that the Humanism of Encounter embodies all the worst features of Renaissance Humanism, such as for example its love of Pagan rites, its hedonism, its anti-rationalism, its irresponsibility, and its immorality, without manifesting any of its artistic and literary grandeur.

That this should be so is tragic but not surprising since these new "Humanists" are laboring in the shadow of the Megamachine that has contaminated their self image and corrupted most of their alternatives. It is to engineering that art is married today. Music is electronic and language is untrustworthy because it so frequently lacks referents.

I see Encounter then as chiefly a socio-political force symptomatic of the failure of the society to have met the psychic challenges that its technology imposed.

It is a political force because in its essence it is revolutionary toward the established order; because it is dissident to prevailing morality and because it responds to a felt need in the population.

Although poverty is by far not absent from contemporary America, the chief concern of the majority nevertheless appears to be not economic but psychological. The problem of the age is people's depression, isolation, alienation, anonymity. The problem is the decline of personal significance and individual autonomy. Encounter, I think, caters to these needs albeit in an illusory and detrimental fashion. I have made this point, however, in greater detail in another paper so I shall not go into it now.

A last word about the ideology of the politics of the Encounter Movement. I believe that in the United States they represent a crypto-fascist faction with real potentials for an overt fascistic stance. Fascism as a philosophy is anti-rational, anti-scientific, pseudo-individualistic, in that its individualism is verbally exalted but in effect depends on group support and group norms. It is ritualistic, ceremonial, it idealizes personal power based on Will and it is extremely dangerous for those who are not Humanistic but Humanitarian. I think it hardly necessary to prove to anyone who has ever attended an Encounter session the fact that the Encounter Culture menacingly fulfills all these criteria.

Let me now turn to Gestalt Group Therapy as sense in Sensitivity and encounter in Encounter.

To begin, allow me to say that Gestalt Therapy I do regard as the most complete and efficacious technical translation available today of Existential therapeutic theory into practice. Let me also say with considerable regret, that I do not think all Gestalt therapists practice with this awareness or this intent.

Existential Analytic work is characterized by two distinguishing features. First, the particular relatedness between the analyst and the patient which occurs in the context of a dialogue, and which involves on the part of the analyst a commitment of openness, selective and relevant self-revelation, and unwavering respect. The participation is that of equals in terms of responsibility, satisfactions or economics. In less fancy words, it is the patient hopefully who gets treated and not the analyst. (The analyst gets paid.)

I believe that Gestalt techniques facilitate this relatedness, especially when one regards the fact that even in group Gestalt therapy the primary work occurs on a one to one basis between the therapist and each of the members. Member to member interaction may occur but it is entirely subordinate to the therapist-patient dyad.

The second distinguishing feature of Existential analytic work is the nature of the analytic task, namely the phenomenological analysis of the patient's Being-in-the-World, his participation in the design of his world and his responsibility for the choices he makes within it.

In Gestalt Therapy, Perls has applied the term "Awareness Continuum" to the technique that translates into working reality the Existential aim of phenomenological analysis.

The awareness continuum consists of asking the patient to simply list all the exteroceptive and proprioceptive events of which he is aware at any given limited period of time. The specific instruction is something as simple as saying, "Please make up some sentences all beginning with 'Here and Now I Am Aware That.' " It is the therapist's task to call attention to the discrepancies that occur between verbal report and organismic expression, such as for example the patient saying, "Here and now I am aware that I am angry" while his tone is seductive and he is sporting a big grin. Also to call attention to the discrepancies between the verbal report and consensually demonstrable reality. Confrontation in the first instance gives rise to issues of psychic integration, denial, repression, authenticity, responsibility, the battle of the introjects and so on. Confrontation in the second instance gives rise to issues of projection, stereotypy in function, reality testing, etc. In either case, and whatever the specific problem that arises, the patient is in first hand organismic contact with his discrepant functioning and his difficulties appear to him with dramatic immediacy. A closely allied or perhaps even an integral part of the awareness continuum technique is what is referred to in a somewhat inelegant manner as "Could you stay with this feeling?" The purpose here is to confront resistance in the face of the discovery of a discrepant state. The patient is asked to familiarize himself with his discomfort in staying with the feeling in order that he may contact its ramifications and overcome his phobic avoidance of the feared state.

A third technique, really an abbreviated form of the awareness continuum is what I have come to call, also inelegantly as "Take a reading." "Take a reading" is an invitation to pinpoint, at a given instant, one's internal experiential state in order to orient one's self in relation to one's momentary Being-in-the-World. The instructions run something like this: "Please take a reading, by which I mean pay careful attention to where you are at this moment in your fantasy, here or perhaps someplace else. What is your most outstanding feeling at the moment? How is the comfort level of your body? Name what is the most important thing of which you are intellectually aware." The aim is to sharpen awareness of the figure of the Gestalt of one's momentary Being-in-the-World so that some relevant stance may be adopted in relation to it. I say stance and not action because often action is suppressed by other considerations even though one's stance is clarified. Thus, for example, if you were to take a reading right here and find yourselves bored, hot, hungry and tired, the relevant action would be to walk out. You may choose not to do this out of politeness but your organismic state and your stance in relation to it would be clarified and your inaction would be a matter of active choice and not a matter of passive martyrdom. The advantage is that it is very much easier to continue to sit in a state of responsible and noble courtesy than in an unidentified state of generalized discomfort.

I believe that it is possible to take almost any of the Gestalt techniques and demonstrate their correspondence to Existential theory. That project, however, exceeds the scope of this paper. I would like, therefore, instead, in the remaining time to briefly enumerate some points of difference between Encounter and Gestalt Therapy.

First, the techniques of Gestalt Therapy do not generate experience but rather allow individuals to become aware of the experience they spontaneously generate.

Second, Gestalt Therapy is not oriented toward catharsis in the pregnant instant, but is rather firmly committed to the need of disciplined working through of malfunction, in the context of a therapeutic dialogue of I and Thou.

Third, Gestalt group work is not primarily oriented toward the improvement of specific interpersonal relations in the group setting. In other words, its emphasis is not on "making it" in terms of approval, love, etc. with the other group members, but rather the group is utilized to sharpen self awareness in the context of the group, with emphasis on improved reality perceptions in relation to the group, and on the freedom of choice to relate or not to individual group members. The primary therapeutic interaction is invariably with the therapist on a one to one basis.*

Fourth, in Gestalt Therapy, dreams are still considered "the royal road to the unconscious" although of course, the vehicles of travel are not Freudian. This is in sharp contrast to Encounter which with its exclusive emphasis on interpersonal transactions, regards dream interpretation as useless.

But man is a symbolizing animal and his dreams are age-old repositories of his psychic evolution. They are the core of his creativity, the center of his being. Dreams are the heart of being human. To extirpate the dreams of men is to make them into robots. This is the greatest threat that Encounter presents–the reduction of Being under the banner of love!

Fifth, Gestalt Therapy is a therapy, not a culture. Its aims are curative and in a broader sense educative. But its aims are not political.

Gestalt Therapy, as I see it, is a disciplined attempt to help men change into what, at their best, they can become. It does not, however, partake of the delusion that possibilities are limitless. Elephants do not become birds through treatment, they become better and more able elephants. Encounter fails to recognize this truth. It suffers from a kind of hysteria† of exalting humanness.

In the Encounter ethos Paradise is no longer in the heavens, but it exists dormant in every human breast to be revealed in a matter

---

* I have originally made the preceding three points in another paper entitled: "Existential Gestalt Therapy: The Marriage of True Minds."

† I am using hysteria here in its popular meaning. The correct clinical term to describe the condition to which I refer is, I think: the manic phase of depression.

of two hours to two weeks, through Encountering. God is dead, long live the new Gods. The best quality of the Godhead is charisma. What charisma is nobody defines and if you need to ask you don't deserve to know.

I shall, nevertheless, attempt to say a word about it. I think it is personal power based on will. I think it is a composite of Evangelic zeal and television conditioned cool, sprinkled with a little flim-flam. I also think that only a society on the edge of despair at its powerlessness and disorganization would make it into a cult.

Balanced men are humble in their humanity, they know it as a task to be fulfilled with honor.

REFERENCES

1. Buber, M.: *I and Thou*. Edinburgh, T & T Clark, 1950.
2. Burton, A. (Ed.): *Encounter*. San Francisco, Jossey-Bass, 1969, p. 12.
3. *Ibid.*, p. 14.
4. *Ibid.*, p. 17.
5. Marlowe, C.: The tragical history of Dr. Faustus. In Woods, G. B., Watt, H. A., and Anderson, G. K. (Eds.): *The Literature of England*. Vol. 1, 3rd Ed. Chicago, Scott, Foresman, 1947, p. 457.
6. Randall, J. H.: *The Making of the Modern Mind*. Rev. Ed. Boston, Houghton Mifflin, 1940, p. 121.
7. *Ibid.*, p. 129.
8. Russell, B.: *A History of Western Philosophy*. New York, Simon & Schuster, 1945, pp. 502-503.

CHAPTER IX

MARATHON GROUPS AS INTENSIVE PSYCHOTHERAPY

Elizabeth E. Mintz

Dr. Elizabeth E. Mintz is a psychologist and group psychotherapist perhaps best known in group therapy circles for her work with marathons. A marathon as she uses the term is simply a time extended group. (Most usually these groups last for twenty-four hours with short breaks for eating and sleeping.) A group meeting such as this can utilize any theoretical orientation on the part of the leader and Doctor Mintz's orientation is varied using Gestalt, encounter, psychodrama and even psychoanalytic principles.

In her very thorough exposition of her own therapeutic orientation to marathons Dr. Mintz first carefully gives us the structure of marathons and her rationale for the various techniques she uses. She gives illustrative examples that clarify the actual process and its values—positive as well as negative. There is a large segment of the paper devoted to sexual implications with clinical examples.

What seems most apparent at this time, as with other techniques, in the hands of skilled professionals, is that it is a useful addition to other therapeutic tools. In this particular paper we are fortunate in having Dr. Elizabeth Mintz, one of the founders of the marathon technique, as our guide in outlining her perception of this technique. Her skills in describing the characteristics she views as essential to an understanding and use of this method are indeed reflective of her broad training in psychotherapy. The paper is also a testimony to her flexibility, spontaneity, and intellectual synthesis of the principles she knows and presents so clearly. It is this considered judgment of Betsy Mintz' that makes us secure that such new techniques will develop and can be used with skill and responsibility by mature professionals with the willingness to experiment and the judgment to define the effectiveness and limitations of a new instrument.

D.S.M.
G.D.G.

SINCE INFORMATION about marathon groups is becoming increasingly available in the literature, I will try to summarize briefly the material which can be found elsewhere; will then attempt to conceptualize what happens in a marathon and why this format is so powerful; and will finally discuss a topic which has received inadequate professional attention, namely, the value of physical contact among participants in these groups and its potential risks.

The term marathon in itself means simply a time-extended group, and does not imply any special theoretical orientation on the part of the leader. My own speciality is the unstructured marathon encounter group, usually meeting for two days with an eight-hour break for sleep, and including about a dozen participants. Some of the participants are clinically normal people, who wish to become more capable of intimacy and spontaneity. Some seek to alleviate a specific problem, such as sexual anxiety or a phobia or an irrational fear of authority. Many participants are referred to me by another psychotherapist who wishes his patient to try out newly-learned social skills in a protected environment, or hopes that fresh material for therapeutic exploration will be provided by the marathon experience. Other participants are drawn from my own part-time practice of individual psychotherapy. An equal number of men and women is desirable. My techniques include the Gestalt approach, psychodrama with its many variations, non-verbal encounters, the invention of scenarios and theater games, and sometimes fairly orthodox psychoanalytic interpretation. In general, an effort is made to follow each emotional experience by cognitive integration, rather than depending solely upon the impact of the experience in itself for therapeutic gain. However, in general it seems to me that the therapeutic value of marathons consists less in the acquisition of insight than in reparative emotional experiences; that is, the participant has an opportunity to re-live a traumatic experience in fantasy or through a group scenario with a happier outcome in which he feels less isolated and helpless than in the original trauma.

In using the word "unstructured" to describe my approach, I mean that it is not my practice to set up a series of prescribed, ritualistic games in which all group members engage simultaneously. Such games, usually involving physical contact, have some value in diminishing the sense of alienation and culturally-fostered inhibitions which afflict most of us. However, it is my belief that genuine intimacy cannot be achieved by means of physical-contact games arbitrarily introduced and supervised by the leader, and that there are grave dangers of inducing a pseudo-intimacy in which a meaningless physical embrace is merely substituted for equally meaningless social chit-chat. Similarly, pounding the couch does not release anger unless undertaken at a time when the individual participant is already angry or at least is interested in trying to reach his own angry feelings. The exercise of asking the group to lift and rock one of the participants can be extremely meaningful and touching, but must be properly timed according to individual needs. These techniques can be spectacularly effective. They can provide catharsis. They can elicit strong feelings which can then be explored. They can help provide a symbolically-reparative emotional experience. But they are not likely to be really effective unless they are selected to meet the needs of the group, or of its individual participants, as these needs become evident. And the exercises are far more meaningful if they are used only after the participants have begun to feel sufficiently at home with one another to be willing to reveal their deeper feelings.

Over the past six years, I have conducted about 150 marathons, including about a thousand participants, many of whom have returned for several marathons. Feedback consists of letters and evaluations from participants and from colleagues who have referred participants. With no exception, these colleagues have reported to me that ongoing psychotherapy has been stimulated by the marathon experience. Direct reports from participants immediately after the marathon are usually highly enthusiastic; however, various clinicians have pointed out that the marathon experience may create a kind of "high" which is not genuinely therapeutic but which indeed may lead to a let-down feeling or even a depression a few days later. This, in my opinion, can indeed occur, but only if the marathon leader aims toward achieving a kind of hysterical generalized excitement without serious regard for the dynamics of the individuals in the group, without attention to cognitive integration, and without recognition of the need to deal with the re-entry of the participants into their ordinary daily lives. Many reports from participants in my marathons have come into my hands several weeks after the group, or even many months later, and here are some quotations:

At first I felt terrible after the marathon. I seemed unable to achieve the kind of warmth and closeness of the rest of the group and I felt so left out. Then slowly I began to see how I keep other people away, which is what Dr. B. (his therapist) has been trying to point out to me for months, but I never saw it before. I'm working on it and I am really understanding myself better.

After the marathon I felt reborn. (This term is very often used by participants immediately afterward.) Some of the glow faded and some stayed. I'm still relating to my wife and children better than before. . . .

The marathon was almost a year ago and I'm still dating my life from Before and After Marathon. I just never knew people could be so decent and so nice and real. Of course they're not that way all of the time, not all of them, but I'm so much more willing to meet them half-way and take a chance. . . .

Such examples could be multiplied indefinitely; indeed, I am in possession of literally hundreds of such letters. Approximately half the marathon participants express a high degree of enthusiasm, and approximately one-quarter express a more moderate degree of appreciation. The remaining one-quarter either do not respond to a request for written feedback, or in about one case in twenty express disappointment or a critical attitude toward the marathon technique.

Why is the marathon time format so effective? Simple physical fatigue is sometimes adduced as an explanation. Exhaustion dissolves defenses, the participants become too tired to be polite, and they attack one another's insincere or defensive behavior, thus literally forcing one another to relinquish their poses. It is a battering-ram theory of therapy.

My own concept of the marathon is diametrically opposite. I do not think that fatigue dissolves defenses any more usefully than alcohol or drugs, and I do not think that people give up defenses which originally, in most cases, developed out of catastrophic childhood fears, simply because they are ridiculed or attacked. Rather, I believe that as the group remains together for a long period of time, its members develop a sense of safety in being with one another, which gives them courage to react to one another honestly and to reveal their feelings. As each participant experiments with revealing himself more and more deeply, the other participants in turn develop courage to explore themselves yet further. Cumulatively, an atmosphere of intimacy and warmth builds up as time goes on, to an extent which in my experience rarely develops in an ongoing therapy group.

Certain other specific features of the marathon time-format make it uniquely valuable. Strikingly enough, despite obvious differences, the marathon situation in some respects is analogous to the traditional psychoanalytic situation. Just as the analytic hour is conducted with no outside stimuli, and focuses solely on the patient's feelings and on his interaction with the analyst, so the marathon involves a set period of time during which, without distractions from outside, the participants have a maximally-favorable opportunity for self-expression and self-exploration.

The time-continuity of the marathon has other special values. It is more difficult for people to sustain false, stereotyped roles over a long period, not necessarily because of pressure from other people, but because few people enjoy posing and would far rather be spontaneous and open, once they can feel that it is safe. The marathon provides an opportunity for people to relinquish their social poses or stereotyped roles and behave in a more genuine way, whereas in more traditional forms of therapy, patients are likely to reconstitute their defenses, at least partially, in the interim between sessions.

Still another reason for the extreme potency of this time format is that it offers ample opportunity for an individual participant, often for several participants, to regress, to gratify his regressed needs on a symbolic level, and finally to re-integrate the adult personality, nearly always at a more mature level. For instance a participant may be permitted to go into an infantile temper tantrum, kicking and screaming, and then be held and comforted by the group. My experience is that after such an episode, the regressed participant *invariably* not only regains adult poise and control, but shows an increased alertness and sympathy for other members of the group. Such episodes, of course, would not be encouraged in the concluding hours of the marathon, when there might not be time to work them through. Indeed, it seems to me that regression is rather less risky in a marathon situation than in a 45-minute therapy hour, where the patient may depart in anxiety or conflict which may last until the next appointment. Of course, no capable marathon therapist would encourage regression if there was clinical doubt about the ability of the patient to handle it, just as would be the case in any other form of therapy.

Now let me try to convey the actual process of a typical marathon group, though every combination of people is unique. The setting is informal, with cushions strewn on the floor, since it is necessary for people to shift positions frequently over so long a time. Coffee and snacks are continually available. Group members are asked to remain together at all times and not to engage in one-to-one conversations, and they are reminded that everything revealed in the group must be confidential. Liquor is not served, except that sometimes wine is offered at night just before the group breaks up.

Sometimes, for the first few hours, the marathon resembles a rather dull party. People remain wary, and talk may be superficial. If the group is very slow, I may ask each participant in turn to tell the group the most personal and intimate thing he can reveal without embarrassment. Otherwise, I remain passive. The movement toward deeper and more authentic self-revelation is best facilitated if group interaction is spontaneous instead of being artificially stimulated by structured activity.

In many marathons, an outburst of anger is the first strong feeling expressed. This may be because the beginning of a marathon naturally produces anxiety in most participants, which is converted into anger, or it may be simply because an encounter group is one of the few situations in which hostility is socially permissible. Hostility may take the form of criticism of the leader, antagonism between two participants, or resentment toward a parent or some other outside person. Often this is the point at which I may become more active. For instance, if anger toward a parent is being expressed, I may ask the participant to speak to the parent as if he were present in the room, following the Gestalt principle of trying to translate every past event into the here and now. If there is antagonism between two participants, I encourage its full ventilation unless it seems that one of them is in danger of being too deeply wounded. Sometimes the antagonism dissolves after full verbal expression; sometimes the insight occurs that it is actually transferential hostility (you remind me of my mother); and sometimes it is best resolved by a non-verbal encounter, such as arm-wrestling, a procedure which allows the two combatants to put forth their full strength without any danger of injury.

As with any physical encounter which is appropriately chosen, arm-wrestling may lead to worthwhile, spontaneous insights. Here are comments from letters of marathon participants on their experiences with arm-wrestling.

> I didn't realize until we wrestled that Saul (his opponent) got on my nerves mainly because he sounded like my brother, who always bossed me around. I spent half my life trying to catch up with my brother, and even now I've been preoccupied with his being more successful than myself, even though I wouldn't like the kind of work he does. After we wrestled, I suddenly liked Saul and didn't care who won. For some reason, ever since then I haven't so much minded that I drive a Ford and my brother has a Buick.

Here is another comment, from a woman who had arm-wrestled with a man, a situation in which I recommend a modification of the procedure by which the woman uses both hands and the man but one, to equalize their strength. In this case, after a dramatic struggle, the woman was the victor. She wrote:

> I think I was brainwashed to believe no man could like me unless I was kind of girlish and dopey. After I beat Paul he laughed and hugged me and it was great. I'm a strong woman, and I'm gradually getting used to the idea that it's all right.

Like any other physical encounter game, arm-wrestling is followed by a brief discussion of its meaning to the participants and the group. This particular game, which has been described at some length to give a feeling of a marathon's atmosphere, is of course only one of dozens of encounter procedures which can be useful both to foster intimacy and to elicit emotions. If these experiences are cognitively integrated, they are usually more meaningful in terms of personal growth.

After a few such episodes, it rapidly becomes easier for the participants to begin sharing their feelings more and more completely, and a sense of intimacy and warmth emerges. This, in my belief, is because the participants have been permitted and encouraged to express feelings which can seldom be expressed in groups, not only anger and competitiveness but also anxiety and insecurity and grief. Each individual discovers, more and more deeply, that it is not only safe for him to share his feelings, but that this is actually acknowledged with understanding and even with affection by the group. Each individual also empathizes with others who speak of their own inner lives. As empathy and trust develop, many participants tell the group of feelings they have never told to anyone before. A capable businessman confessed that he had never fully recovered from a boyhood fear of the dark, and was relieved and delighted when the group heard his confession with concern and without ridicule. A young mother spoke in great pain of her occasional impulse to strangle her baby; the group did not reproach her or intensify her guilt, but understood her anguish and successfully persuaded her to enter individual psychotherapy. The group itself is an immensely powerful therapeutic instrument, and once they are at home with one another, marathon participants often develop fantastic insight and great creativity in being helpful.

My groups usually work until one or two hours after midnight, then break for eight hours of rest. In the morning, when they return and greet each other, there is usually an atmosphere of friendship and exhilaration. Dreams of the night before are often reported, and are treated much as in any other therapy group, sometimes by interpretation, sometimes by the Gestalt method of asking the dreamer to impersonate every person and object in his dream. The resulting insights are often similar to what might occur in a psychoanalytic situation, and typically several participants identify with the dreamer and share his insight.

In the second day, the atmosphere of trust and warmth usually reaches a peak. It is not infrequent for several participants to weep, often over childhood traumas which were never completely overcome. Grief or fear or anger which may have been repressed or denied for half a lifetime are expressed. In our culture there are surprisingly many men who have not been able to cry since boyhood, and often such men are able to weep for the first time in marathons, thereafter feeling great relief.

As the marathon moves toward its ending, some form of separation anxiety appears. Sometimes the group asks to convene again or to continue for a longer time. Sometimes there is a rush of meaningless social chatter, as if the participants were already preparing to re-enter a world in which it is not always wise to be spontaneous or intimate. The group can then be asked to face their feelings about separation, and perhaps to discuss how they will feel when they return to job and family. If this is done adequately by the leader, few marathon participants experience a sense of let-down after the group terminates. This does occur occasionally, but participants who report it usually indicate that it is of short duration and is balanced by the general value of the marathon experience.

In many marathons, the group itself spontaneously devises some type of separation ritual, often very beautiful. Some groups simply link their arms and stand together in a circle, swaying and singing. One group improvised a circle folk dance, taking turns doing solos in the middle. And one group invented a special form of communion which was acceptable to Christians, Jews and agnostics in the group, and which involved passing around a ceremonial glass of wine and bowl of crackers. There is something very touching about these moments, which are difficult to describe, because in many groups and for many participants they constitute a true peak experience of feeling, a deep closeness to humanity.

Concern has been expressed by many responsible clinicians that the physical contact games used by most encounter leaders, along with the frank interaction sought in these groups, may diminish the precarious controls of impulse-ridden personalities or precipitate a degree of anxiety which could be dangerous to latent schizophrenics. Marathon groups, naturally, are especially suspect. These dangers exist as in any type of therapy, but are minimal if participants are screened, if the marathon leader is a skillful therapist, and if the group is small enough so that the leader can be alert to every participant. To my knowledge, every report of a psychosis being precipitated in a marathon arose in a group which did not meet these conditions.

However, I believe that it is time for us to face openly the whole question of sexuality in encounter groups, which is closely related to the above considerations. Until recently, most group therapists regarded it as part of their responsibility to discourage sexual contacts among group members, and some even forbade any form of physical contact within the group. Today there is considerable divergence of opinion, which ought to be recognized and discussed. Many responsible therapists are concerned lest the prolonged intimacy and permissive atmosphere of a marathon group should lead to inappropriate acting out, as for example with a married participant whose religious or social values would be violated by sexual infidelity. Other therapists, some of whom are professionally qualified, openly encourage sexual intimacy in the belief that such encouragement may help release participants from crippling sexual inhibitions. Leaders without professional qualifications are known to offer groups in which the terms "marathon" or "encounter" merely denote an orgiastic experience; for instance, a Manhattan movie house recently offered a film called "Encounter Group" which was openly pornographic and included considerable sado-masochistic material. Commercially-advertised marathons often scarcely disguise their promise of providing sexual adventure. Professional therapists must consider carefully the whole question of what attitude to take toward sexuality in groups, and must familiarize the public with their standards. Let me offer for your consideration the approach which I have developed in my own practice, with full recognition that some of my colleagues will find my views over-conservative and repressive, while others will view them as negating personal ethics and professional responsibility.

Without any encouragement from the leader, physical intimacy does develop spontaneously in encounter groups. A participant who has just gone through an episode in which he has expressed feelings of loneliness or grief will always be comforted by an embrace. Affection usually is expressed freely on a physical level before the first day ends. There is undoubtedly some element of sexuality in these physical contacts at times, but my groups rarely engage in any physical contact which would be regarded as inappropriate at an ordinary social gathering. It seems to me that in our society people are actually more hungry for affection than for sexual experience, and literally hundreds of marathon participants have written to me that the physical affection of the marathon was a joyous and liberating experience which made it easier for them to show affection physically in their own families with spouse and children. Men, particularly, often have a hunger for contact with other men which is more-or-less taboo in most settings because it implies effeminacy or perhaps homosexuality, and in almost every marathon some man will for the first time experience the joy of sharing comradely physical affection with another man. An especially charming episode of this kind occurred with a rather naive young man whose background had given him a very exaggerated fear of homosexuality although in reality he had no difficulty in controlling any homosexual impulses. His feelings were expressed and the group discussed them freely, offering him support. Toward the end of the marathon, he went around and joyously embraced every man in the group, exclaiming with real delight, "I'm not homosexual! I'm not homosexual!" These physical encounters occur spontaneously; I would never request two participants to show physical affection toward one another as a routine exercise. Also, I would discourage overt sexual activity occurring in the group, but this is scarcely ever necessary.

In other respects, however, my approach has changed during the six years that I have been conducting marathons. At first, I rather actively discouraged group members from making any sexual contacts on the Saturday night of the group or even after the group ended. My rationale, which I shared openly with the group, was that the intimacy of the marathon might lead participants into romantic adventures which they might later find inappropriate and regrettable. My specific suggestion was that if any of the group members wished to meet again, they should exchange phone numbers and get in touch a week or so later, after the glamor of the marathon wore off. I still think such a suggestion would be therapeutically appropriate with groups in which self-control and judgment might not always be dependable, such as younger adolescents and certain psychiatric populations. However, my groups in general are composed of intelligent adults who function well, and today it seems to me that an attempt to control their private behavior on the Saturday night of the marathon would infantilize them and would show inadequate respect for their ability to make appropriate decisions. Since our society is in a considerable state of flux over sexual standards, it seems to me that the values of the individual participant rather than the values of the group leader should determine his sexual behavior, hence today I neither encourage nor forbid sexual experiences between the participants when the group breaks up for rest on Saturday.

Results so far have been gratifying. To my awareness, no participant has ever been carried away into behavior which he himself, according to his own personal or religious values, would experience as guilt-provoking or inappropriate. Participants whose personal values include the acceptance of free sexual behavior sometimes become involved with one another, sometimes transiently and sometimes for a period of commitment. The incidence of these episodes is approximately as high as what might occur at a pleasant cocktail party. The emotional atmosphere of a marathon is so intense and its interaction is so honest that it is actually not conducive to meaningless, superficial sexuality.

It can happen also that a sexual episode can have enormous therapeutic value. A homosexual man in his mid-thirties, who had undergone two years of individual psychoanalysis, had remained very unhappy about his homosexuality but had never been able to achieve a heterosexual experience, and in fact had never dared even try. He discussed this openly in the group, which like most of my groups did not view the homosexuality as reprehensible but did sympathize with his anxiety. As the day went on, he became more and more attracted to a young divorced woman in the group who told him she returned his feelings. In this instance, I offered them open support, by rather lightly, saying, "Bless you, my children." This remark was based on my knowledge that to this man I was a mother-figure, and that his homosexuality involved a deeply-lying anxiety at being rejected by the archaic mother if he were unfaithful to her with another woman. The couple left the marathon together, and a few days later, for the first time in his life, he successfully achieved heterosexual intercourse. His eventual choice of a way of life is still in doubt, but certainly–according to his psychoanalyst, to whom he returned to work out the experience–it brought him an enormous increase in self-esteem and in his masculine self-image.

Another sexual episode, highly theraputic in my judgment, occurred with a man in his early thirties, whom we may call Clem. When he was in his teens, Clem had been hospitalized, and when I first saw him, he would have been clinically diagnosed as extremely schizoid or perhaps even as an ambulatory schizophrenic. He could hold a job, but had no personal friendships whatsoever, had *never* had a date with a woman, and although he had been seeing a fine psychiatrist for some years of individual treatment, little progress was made. He was referred by his psychiatrist for a marathon, and thereafter attended nine marathons over a four-year period, concomitantly with some individual treatment. Nine marathons may sound an excessive number, but with Clem they had a spectacular effect.

In Clem's first marathon, he sat hunched up, pale and anxious, hardly speaking. Later I found that he had sat close to the door and drunk as little fluid as possible, because he was embarrassed to use the bathroom. On the second day, even more withdrawn, Clem told us that the preceding night several participants had gone out for coffee without inviting him, and that he was very hurt. Though I was alarmed by his withdrawal, it did not seem to me that a discussion of his feelings would be helpful, and I waited for an opportunity to involve him in the group through play.

Play, especially with a very frightened patient, offers a way to drain off some of the terrifying feelings, so that they can be dealt with more easily later. Play provides a symbolic outlet for agonizing feelings; it can diminish guilt; for many people, it provides an experience which they missed in childhood. My chance to play with Clem came when Clem broke his silence, as the group was discussing their relationships with parents, to remark that he had never expressed any resentment toward either parent and could not even imagine doing so. As lightly as I could, I said to Clem, "Well, let's pretend that I'm your mother. How would it feel to execute me?" I handed him a rolled-up newspaper and knelt before him, bowing my head.

Clem struck me like a feather, then retreated to his corner. I had made an error, by trying to help him release hostility before he was ready. Moving back, I sat down some feet away from him and turned the murder weapon of the paper cylinder into a toy, rolling it gently toward him. To my relief he rolled it back, and for several minutes we played with the cylinder while I moved cautiously closer. When he seemed no longer anxious, I again attempted to get him to release some of his hostility on a symbolic level, placing my hand plam-down on the heavy carpet and inviting him to strike it. When it is done with the aggressor's palm open, this game is painless; if the aggressor clenches his fist, it can hurt. Clem was clenching up his fist, and I warned him to use only his open palm. He complied, slapping with his palm several times, and then it seemed to me that once more he was clenching his fist, so I stopped him. He drew back abruptly, resumed his hunched-up posture, and began to cry bitterly, saying over and over "I didn't use my fist; I wasn't going to!"

Repeatedly I told Clem that I had been mistaken and owed him an apology. Meanwhile the group, moved by his misery, drew closely around him. Clem needed physical comfort, like a hurt child, and so I signalled to a girl who was already reaching hesitantly toward him. She clasped his hand, Clem put his head on her shoulder, and gradually stopped sobbing. At last he looked at me and said, "This is the first time in my life anyone ever admitted that I was right and they were wrong." Then he put his arm around the girl's shoulder, not like a little boy but like a man. It was the first time in the course of the marathon that he had touched anyone, and the first time in his life he had related to a woman as a man.

Thereafter Clem changed, became responsive and alert, and made several helpful and relevant comments to others. This is among the basic processes in marathons–a movement away from miserable self-absorption to interest in others. My two errors, trying to get him to release hostility prematurely and mis-perceiving his half-open hand as a clenched fist had been effectively rectified and turned to good account, thanks to the long time-span of the marathon.

Clem's psychiatrist reported that Clem regarded this marathon as his life's greatest experience. What remained most vivid to him was the moment when he looked up from his withdrawn sobbing to see the ring of friendly, worried faces. Over and over again, Clem's psychiatrist told me, he kept saying, "I looked up, and there they all were, all around me!"

The successive stages through which Clem passed in the marathon are worth conceptualizing, because they give a picture of what can happen in a time-extended group. First, he attempted fearfully to remain withdrawn. Next, he refused a chance to express anger, because the harmless "murder weapon" may have been too strong a symbol. Third, in our paper-rolling, he accepted a playful relationship with a mother-figure. Fourth, he expressed anger physically through the hand-slapping. Fifth, his self-respect and sense of contact with reality were strengthened by my apology. Finally, supported by the warmth of the group, he could express affection to a woman, a totally new experience in the life of this self-depriving man.

By Clem's fourth marathon, he was more relaxed, more talkative and more interested in others. He was also beginning to be somewhat more active socially, but still had no relationships with girls. Then there occurred another major breakthrough. One of the other group members was speaking of how he resented his mother's unconscious seductiveness, and Clem told us that lately he had recalled a boyhood fantasy of actually being intimate with his mother sexually. Because in an anxiety-laden situation psychodrama is often best conducted on an imaginary telephone, I asked Clem if I could represent his mother on the phone, and Clem agreed, and he established our conditions.

"You're at home and I'm calling you. Dad isn't there. I've just arrived at the airport. Hello, Mom."

"Hello darling! How are you?"

"I'm fine, Mom. I'd like to sleep with you."

Astonished by his directness and apparent lack of anxiety, I responded with fantasy-frankness. "You mean have sexual intercourse?"

"That's right."

"Why, darling, I'd love to! I always hoped you'd ask me."

"Well, Im asking you now. Will you be in bed when I get there?"

"Why, yes, of course."

"That's good. I'll hurry home then?"

"Oh, do, please hurry!" There was a long pause, then in the same level tone he had used all along, Clem put an end to the conversation.

"DIRTY OLD WOMAN!" he said firmly and hung up the imaginary phone. The group exploded into laughter, and there was actually a smattering of applause at Clem's wit and perfect timing. Thereafter, Clem became much less anxious about incestuous feelings toward his mother. He wrote, "The discussion about mother-love and seduction was the first guilt-free discussion I ever had on this topic. I found my emotions were not so intense and uncontrollable as I had feared."

In his next three or four marathons, Clem showed that he had lost most of his fear of physical contact. He wrestled vigorously with a male co-therapist, who represented a father-figure to him. He often pressed my hand or put his arm around my shoulders, with no anxiety or dependency. Most important, he was able to embrace and be embraced by the young women in the marathons. Remembering the Clem who had been embarrassed to use the bathroom, the description of therapy as a corrective emotional experience seemed highly relevant.

Three years from entering his first marathon, Clem was able to speak openly about his shyness and fear of rejection in approaching women sexually, although he was now able to date them. The groups were reassuring and supportive, helping to alleviate the guilt which Clem himself regarded as irrational. After his ninth marathon, a sympathetic and sophisticated young woman invited Clem home for coffee, and gently and tactfully conveyed her availability. Thus Clem had his first sexual experience, which was successful to his great delight, under almost ideal conditions. If "acting-out" after this marathon had been forbidden, it seemed to me, and also to Clem's psychiatrist, that perhaps several years of additional treatment would have been required before he could have approached a girl under the circumstances of his usual life. On the other hand, if a more radical marathon therapist had attempted to push Clem prematurely into a sexual experience before he was ready to cope with it, I am equally certain that there would have been a possibility of a psychotic break.

Attitudes toward sexuality today range from those who regard it a simple biological need which should be gratified easily and directly to those who view it as involving deep personal values and emotional communication. Most therapists, I believe, still consider that extensive sexual activity which does not include mutual respect or emotional involvement is likely to be clinically associated with disturbances of gender identity, low self-esteem, and difficulty in forming satisfactory relationships. Yet most of us are also particularly concerned about the impotent, frigid or emotionally withdrawn person who may lead an asexual life or may have an unsatisfactory pseudo-adjustment. For the sexually over-active personality, an encounter leader who openly encourages overt sexual contacts merely offers a social rationale for the behavior which helps him deny his inner dissatisfaction and may prevent him from undertaking self-exploration in a bona-fide therapeutic situation. For the inhibited and cold and withdrawn personality, intolerable or even dangerous anxiety could well be aroused in a group where acting-out was encouraged. Such considerations, in my opinion, make it unwise for a group leader to encourage sexual activity in the group as a whole, even though in some highly-specific individual cases an exception can be made, as with the homosexual patient whom I described earlier. Another exception, perhaps, would be a group attended by couples for the specific, recognized purpose of improving their sexual adjustment, in which the skills of the leader and the screening of applicants would be at the professional level of, for example, the Masters and Johnson Clinic. My personal opinion is that if a group leader encourages nudity or fosters overtly-sexual behavior *without having made it clear in advance that this is to occur in the group,* he is not only unwise clinically but is professionally irresponsible. It would be tragic indeed if the powerful therapeutic marathon approach should be misunderstood or debased.

CHAPTER X

THE PSYCHODRAMATIC APPROACH

JAMES SACKS

Psychodrama, as developed by Moreno, is one of the earliest techniques in the arena of psychotherapy. It also varies in its conception and implementation somewhere between an individual and group technique. Since it involves in number, because of the audience, more than the participant and the director, it falls more classically in the group process sphere. As such, it again historically leads the way. Because of its coeval existence at the beginnings of the psychotherapy movement, it has an extensive literature covering many important details of technique and theory. It is difficult to determine why it had for so long a period of time been kept on the periphery of the psychotherapeutic mainstream. However, its technical and theoretical notions have been, directly or indirectly, adopted and adapted by many therapeutic schools. It is fascinating to conjecture about the source of many of the ideas presently in vogue or practice, but it is not too difficult to discern in many of them at least a modicum of the spirit and influence of Moreno.

This concise and consistent presentation by Dr. James Sacks has that same imprint. Although in this presentation he does not attempt to cover all of psychodrama but merely highlight some of its most salient features, the encompassing feeling is present. Again and again, as he proceeds to detail some psychodramatic ideas and techniques, one is impressed with their relevance to other issues that have been debated and innovated in recent years. We begin to learn that there are not only the roots of many group techniques that sprang from the fertile soil of psychodrama, but many of the branches of all forms of therapy seem to have evolved from the trunk of this formidable tree.

D.S.M.
G.D.G.

PSYCHODRAMA, a contribution of J. L. Moreno, was begun in Vienna as early as 1911 and has been under development by its practitioners since. In initiating psychotherapy for groups, Moreno considered how groups in the past have been reached emotionally. Since classical times the theater has been the major

means to accomplish this purpose. When Moreno combined selected elements from classical drama with modern psychotherapy,
psychodrama emerged as a new form. In this method a protagonist
is chosen from the group and under the direction of the therapist
(called the director) and with the help of therapist-actors (called
auxiliary egos) dramatic scenes are improvised which bear on the
protagonist's problems.

If the reader will indulge a facetious reference to Jewish ritual,
I will pose four questions:* Wherefore is this method of group
psychotherapy different from all other methods? 1) In all other
methods patients work either sitting or reclining but in this method
they move freely. 2) In all other methods events remain in their
proper time but in this method time shifts. 3) In all other methods
we work within the patients' reality but in this method we also
work with the patients' surplus reality. 4) In all other methods patients speak as themselves but in this method they may be anyone.

These "four questions" appear grammatically as one question
and four statements. As in the liturgical reference the implied
preface to each statement is, "Why is it that? . . ." Mere descriptions of group techniques are of some value but much recent literature leaves the reader waiting for a theoretical explanation.

Our first question refers to the use of acting out, a method
unique to the psychodrama approach. The negatively loaded term
"acting out" is used in analytic literature to refer both to pathological modal behavior or to almost any behavior on the part of
the patient during the session other than a report of thoughts and
feelings (4, 7, 8, 13). The usual rationale for the prohibition on
acting out in the session is that if the patient gratifies his impulses
by acting he no longer needs to deal with his frustration by insight.
How then can we justify the use of acting out within the therapeutic hour? Again, in the analytic model, the therapist tries to weak-
en the counter-cathexis by the analysis of transference and resistance. If, despite these efforts, the repressed material is still not
available to consciousness, the analyst provides the further help

---

* In the Passover ceremony the Jewish child asks four questions about the
meaning of the rituals. "Wherefore is this night different from all other nights?
. . . On all other nights we eat and drink either sitting or reclining but on this
night we all recline." etc. The father then gives the rationale behind them.

of interpretation of content. He informs the patient what certain of his repressed ideas might be. He thus introduces into the patient's awareness the cognitive content of unconscious material. Assuming that the counter-cathexis has been sufficiently reduced, the similarity between the new conscious idea introduced by the analyst and the unconscious material serves as a further facilitation to enable the repressed material to enter consciousness (with all its attendant memories and affects). The greater the similarity between the new material introduced by the analyst and the repressed material the more likely it is that the two entities will merge. A limitation of the analytic style lies in the fact that the material introduced by the analyst includes only the cognitive content whereas the repressed material itself includes the potential participation of all ego functions. In this respect the interpretation and the repressed material are dissimilar. Therefore in psychodramatic technique the patient is encouraged to experience the therapist's suggestions with as much of himself involved as possible. He thinks, sees, feels, acts, and experiences his own actions. This raises the level of effectiveness of interpretation by increasing the degree of similarity between the repressed and the suggested material. In a scene chosen by the director to correspond to his repressed wishes, the patient cannot easily resist the temptation to allow himself to feel. An analytic interpretation such as, "I think you are angry with your boss," is less likely to help the patient get in contact with this anger than suggesting a scene in which he waves his arms and yells at his boss. Assuming that in both cases the unconscious anger with the boss does exit and that the resistance has been equally worked through, going through the motions of this anger seems more frequently to call forth the genuine affect.

Other uses of acting out do not depend on the director's suggestions and hypotheses about the patient's unconscious. Frequently the patient becomes aware of his feelings by spontaneous acting out in the controlled environment of the therapeutic session. Many psychodramatic scenes are nearly self-directed and the director simply follows the protagonist's lead. Acting out in life is famously ineffective in producing insight. Acting out in psychodrama, because of the "as if" nature of the situation involves a stronger observing ego on the part of the protagonist. The protagonist allows himself to act more freely than he dares in life. By looking at his own actions he becomes aware of how he feels. It is a frequent experience of psychodramatists to hear the protagonist sigh after a particularly passionate scene, "My God, I had no idea I felt that way."

The psychodramatist is free to use the acting out procedure when indicated or on the other hand, to suggest the suppression of action according to the analytic formula in situations when the analytic tactic seems more applicable.

"In all other methods events remain in their proper time but in this method time shifts." This second "question" refers to the flexibility of the temporal dimension in psychodrama. In Moreno's writing emphasis is placed on the *hic et nunc,* the here and now. This emphasis on the present has frequently been misunderstood. It has led some therapists to exclusive attention to the interpersonal relations within a group or to an exclusive emphasis on the transference in analytic therapy. The point of the psychodrama is not that only the present counts but that for the neurotic patient the past or future is experienced unconsciously as present. Past traumatic events are experienced in the unconscious as if they were still present. Indeed only what is experienced as present is emotionally significant while what is experienced as having past is emotionally neutralized. When a patient narrates traumatic events of the past he tends to deal with them only in so far as he experiences them as past events. This is not too helpful since this is just the aspect of those events with which he can already cope. In psychodrama such traumatic events are brought into the present by re-enactment. Those parts of the patient's psyche which still experience the traumatic event as being in the present and which therefore cause symptoms, thus become accessible to the realization that the event is indeed past.

A 30-year-old woman with a pattern of masochistic sexuality described a horrible experience from her adolescence. An intruder had locked her in an apartment, raped her, and spent a full hour ransacking the apartment for valuables and making occasional threats to kill her. At the end of the hour the rapist suddenly left the apartment and was immediately apprehended by the police.

The patient had described the incident frequently to her former therapist with mild affect in the re-telling but without apparent influence on her masochistic symptom.

Throughout the one hour ordeal the patient did not know from moment to moment whether she would live or die. Every resource down to the deepest and most primitive parts of the psyche were drawn upon to cope with the crisis. She considered grabbing the telephone, jumping out of the window, attacking the intruder, remaining passive, etc. All parts of her being were aware that her survival hung in the balance. When suddenly the intruder left and was arrested, the cessation of the danger was almost anti-climatic. The information of her safety did not penetrate to the same depths as had the awareness of her jeopardy. A great part of the unconscious continued to believe that she was still in that room in immediate danger of death. Recounting of the events in her previous therapy had not penetrated to this emotional level. The deeper parts of her mind had not been open to receive the reassuring fact that the danger was past. It was necessary to gain access to these emotional levels. Since the psyche reluctantly opens itself to such depths, intense emotional situations alone can penetrate. In the re-enactment of the scene in psychodrama the patient was able to re-experience these horrible past events as if they were occurring in the present. She again became frightened but achieved a powerful catharsis on several occasions. Each time the scene included the happy ending–the arrest of the rapist. It seemed reasonable to attribute her reduced masochism to these sessions.

In a sense, the psyche is more concerned with the future than with the past. The reason for this patient's masochism was to master the unconscious fear that she would be killed in the very near future. A nagging unconscious question persisted. "What are you going to do about the fact that you are about to be killed?" The psyche is well aware that nothing can be done about the past once it is experienced as past. The fear is that it will happen again. For this reason many psychodrama scenes deal with hopes and fears and are largely future oriented.

This takes us to the third question. "In all other methods we work within the patients' reality but in this method we work also with the patients' surplus reality." Moreno uses this term to refer to events which did not actually occur but which are real as fantasies, wishes, or fears. Both negative and positive futures can be experienced as present by psychodramatic means.

An engineer with a cardiac phobia once suggested the engineers' term "worst case analysis" for the acting out of his feared future. Although he had no history of cardiac illness he avoided even mild exercise for fear of a heart attack. In the enactment of this part of his surplus reality the patient became aware of the details of his fantasy. This fantasy had never been consciously thought through and was experienced only in the psychodrama. In the scene he fell to the ground and had himself carried to the hospital and catered to by nurses and relatives. During the period of recuperation he lay completely helpless. The helplessness was emphasized each time he enacted his fear and it became apparent that what he feared most was not death but dependency. He then became able to look into previous events which caused him to long for and yet fear the dependent role.

Using the future projection technique the patient may also explore the positive side of his fantasies. Making the assumption that all has gone well in the interim, he acts out some future life situations. The compelling nature of the drama enabled one confused young man to experiment with several possible life adjustments. Such scenes often help to confirm some possibilities or eliminate others. Sometimes the very failure of these scenes helps to make patients aware of the extent of their aimlessness.

The final question: "In all other methods patients speak as themselves but in this method they may be anyone." This refers to the flexibility of role in psychodrama. The protagonist may act and feel like another person. The capacity to change roles has its roots in the development of identity. The six-month-old baby begins imitating and identifying with people in his environment (1). He is already taking the role of the other. Throughout the developmental years and to a lesser extent throughout adulthood identity is expanded by means of identification. Ultimately an integrity of the self is established which is greater than the sum total of the internalized roles. Still the self is never totally integrated and retains remnants of its having been acquired through identification. Early identification requires both observation and rehearsal in active role taking. The spontaneous dramatic play of children is the practice they give themselves for developing their identity. While natural role playing is more evident during childhood, we can use this regressive behavior as a tool in psychotherapy with adults. The encouragement of regression in a controlled setting is familiar from other forms of therapy as well (9, 10).

Role playing has numerous strategic applications depending on the pathology. One of the most important uses is the release of repressed identifications and roles so as to place them within the sphere of conscious control. Once freed, these unconscious roles not only lose their destructive effect but actually serve the interests of the ego. A further scene with the patient with the cardiac phobia serves to illustrate this point. The patient asked to reverse roles with the auxiliary ego (therapist-actor) who took the part of the nurse. He then was in the position of catering to himself as the passive invalid. In adopting this role he showed great involvement, obviously enjoying the controlling, stifling love he was pressing on the victim. It emerged that the patient identified with both sides of the symbiotic relationship which had existed with his mother. He feared the control by the pseudo-loving mother figure but also feared his own wish to control others. He had warded off awareness of his unconscious identification with the mother as aggressive lover. It had disturbed him sufficiently so that the phobia was elaborated partly to maintain this repression. The psychodramatic device of role change had released this inner identification. Awareness of the aggressive side of himself proved not to be so dangerous after all. The patient later, in fact, remembered this scene and mentally adopted the role of the aggressive nurse in certain life situations in which he had previously been submissive. Just as Fairbairn (3) sees all the characters in a dream as a part of the self, the psychodramatist sees every role that the individual conceives in the drama as representing a conscious or unconscious segment of his identity.

Role change may at times be helpful with people who fear the very process of role change itself (6). These patients cannot allow themselves to benefit by imitating others. Some have lost this capacity so early that a great part of personality development has been blocked. Having suffered a lack of respect from significant figures, their sense of identity is insecure. Should they become involved in a role there is anxiety that they will dissolve into it rather than be expanded by it. This danger may indeed be realistic for some schizophrenics. One psychotic may, in fact, lose his identity and believe that he is Napoleon even outside the psychodrama while another may cling tightly to his "true" identity and cannot even pretend to be Napoleon. With such patients caution should be exercised in the use of role changing techniques. They may be treated by working with them in their own role at earlier ages when their sense of personal integrity was more intact. If this phase of treatment is successful they may then slowly learn to take other roles, beginning with relatively neutral ones. Non-psychotic, rigid adults with this problem may also benefit from the practice effect of role playing in graduated degrees.

Those patients who role play constantly in life represent a special problem for psychodramatists (2, 5, 12). These people are so quick to take on the roles and values of those around them that they lack all stability. They may appear grossly opportunistic. They may enjoy psychodrama as a way to exercise their chameleon-like versatility but benefit little from the experience. The director must set scenes which enable the protagonist to act as his most integrated self. This may require re-enacting scenes from a time when he was still aware of losing something when he compromised his integrity. If the patient is able to return to this period of his growth he may be able to reunify his roles.

Moreno describes role reversal as a special form of role change (11). This technique helps us to see ourselves as others see us. Confrontation groups whose members rub each other's noses in their faults not only produce traumatic effects but such hardening of the defenses that self-perception may become all but impossible. Role reversal by contrast brings the protagonists face to face with themselves in the heat of the dramatic situation. When roles are reversed between conflicting individuals both parties warm up to their new roles and their very tendency to cast blame works in the interest of self-understanding.

Still another use of role shifting is role rehearsal or role training (14). This refers to the use of psychodrama for the acquisition of new roles which were not previously available. This phase of treatment is sometimes considered a kind of emotional education, either omitted or deferred until after "therapy." As such, it is usually placed outside the rubric of insight oriented treatment. Actually most psychodramatists prefer to integrate role rehearsal into the analytic sessions as the protagonist's needs indicate. Frequently the confidence gained in acquiring a new role raises the self esteem needed to face some inner pain.

The complexity of psychodrama makes any attempt to extract its distinguishing characteristics in a short essay necessarily incomplete. The distinctions in this paper are therefore best taken as facets of psychodrama rather than as an exhaustive list of its essential qualities.

REFERENCES

1. Brenner, C.: *An Elementary Textbook of Psychoanalysis.* New York, International Universities, 1955, p. 44.
2. Deutsch, H.: *Neuroses and Character Types.* New York, International Universities, 1965.
3. Fairbairn, W. R. D.: *Psychoanalytic Studies of the Personality.* London, Tavistock, 1952.
4. Fenichel, O.: *The Psychoanalytic Theory of Neurosis.* New York, Norton, 1945, p. 375ff.
5. Freud, A.: Problems of infantile neurosis. *Psychoanalytic Study of the Child,* Vol. IX. New York, International Universities, 1954.
6. Greenson, R. R.: The struggle against identification. *J Amer Psychoanal Assn, 2:*200-217, 1954.
7. Greenson, R. R.: *The Technique and Practice of Psychoanalysis,* Vol. 1. New York, International Universities, 1967, p. 23.
8. *Ibid.,* pp. 263-268.
9. *Ibid.,* p. 85.
10. *Ibid.,* p. 288.
11. Moreno, J. L.: *Psychodrama,* Vol. 1. Beacon, N.Y., Beacon House, 1945.
12. Riesman, D.: *The Lonely Crowd.* New Haven, Yale University, 1950.
13. Schuman, E. P.: Acting out and the analytic atmosphere. *J Clin Issues Psychol, 2:*26, 1971.
14. Seabourne, B.: Role-training. In Blatner, H.: *Psychodrama, Role-Playing and Action Methods.* Norfolk, England, mimeo, 1970.

CHAPTER XI

MULTIMODAL PSYCHOTHERAPY: MULTIPLE MARITAL COUPLE GROUP THERAPY, AUGMENTED BY PHASE-SPECIFIC INDIVIDUAL, COUPLE AND CONJOINT FAMILY THERAPY

LEONARD I. SIEGEL AND CELIA DULFANO

As reflected in the approach in this book, most of us do not see therapies as being considerably different or with little overlap in functioning. For example it is fairly usual to combine individual therapy with group therapy for patients. However, in this model there is the danger that the application could become fairly routinized and ritualized. This is certainly not true of the approach of Doctor Siegel and Mrs. Dulfano who have experimented with a variety of approaches to the treatment of persons seeking assistance. For them each mode of treatment has a specific utility for dealing with a more general social problem and is very specific to a phase in the development of that individual.

The family and the couple are examples of two different social structures. Each member of the couple has a different relationship to each other depending on the structure that exists within them and within which they are functioning. For Siegel and Dulfano, the utility of the treatment process and its effect on the individuals varies at different times. Although they are not able to define this in the most specific fashion, what they suggest is at different times different approaches may be more effective and appropriate. At times a couple may be in individual treatment, at other times in family treatment, or in a couples group at another point in their growth. Additionally, even a change in that therapeutic structure may be necessary and desirable. Thus, a marathon is introduced into the couples group at specific times depending on the development and evolution within that particular treatment modality.

If this flexibility, and its consequent demand for skillful introduction of different formats did not provide enough complications the additional fact that the majority of their therapeutic interventions is also as co-therapists introduces even more therapeutic problems. However, the desirability of this co-therapist approach is clearly indicated in the different modes of therapeutic intervention that they utilize. It is also quite apparent from their thorough presentation that their approaches make more than the usual demands upon the therapeutic skills and maturity of the therapists. Their skillful utilization of a variety of approaches more specifically geared to the time specific needs of the patient also seems to offer an opportunity for greater therapeutic gains by the patient. The variety of perspectives on personality and therapeutic dynamics presented in this paper will yield the interested reader a rewarding and refreshing experience.

D.S.M.
G.D.G.

OUR WORK WITH FAMILIES is based on the theoretical premise that there must be change in the internal structure of the family to effect permanent personality change in family members.

For example, a family comes into treatment with a typical structural skew. There has been prolonged alienation between the parents, with alternations between unresolved, rageful arguments and mutual silent withdrawals. There is continuous feedback of hurt and revenge. To compensate for what is lacking in his marital relationship, each parent tends to form a symbiotic or pseudo-marital relationship with one of the children. The mother is too closely connected with her son in a pseudomarital or symbiotic relationship; the father is overly involved in a pseudomarital quasi-incestuous relationship with his daughter. The mother is on top of the family power system. She alternates between agitation and depression. The father, at the bottom of the family power hierarchy, is depressed and obsessively walled off from his feelings. In such a family, the son might be school-phobic and the daughter schizoid.

Their symptoms are related to the skewed family structure. The goal of our therapy would be to change the skewed structure. Father should move up in the family space to a position equal to and closer to mother. Healthy distance between mother and son and father and daughter should be created. Each child should move towards his peers outside the family.

If such a change in structure is achieved, it will be accompanied by behavioral changes in the patterns of interpersonal relatedness between all the members of this family system. These behavioral changes lead to repetitive emotional gratification, and are built into each person as permanent personality changes. Each member is liberated to change and grow in facets of his personality that are locked into family structure and in other facets as well.

We use various combinations of couple group therapy, conjoint family therapy, marital couple therapy, and individual therapy to achieve our central therapeutic goal of permanent personality change concomitant with family structural change. This paper will present our work with a couples group.

THE COUPLES GROUP

The couples were selected from the part-time private practice of the male co-therapist. They were all well educated and middle class or upper class. Three of the couples were Jewish, one was Protestant, and one was Catholic. Each had at least two children, ranging in age from five to fifteen. The group members ranged in age from the middle thirties to the middle forties.

All the couples had been in combined unit couples and individual therapy with the male co-therapist alone, and all had been seen with all of their children for at least two sessions. All the couples had first made contact with the therapist with presenting complaints of disturbance in a child, though all of them had been aware of a marital problem.

Group Functioning

The group met for weekly ninety-minute sessions for ten months. A two-day marathon was held, followed by the resumption of weekly sessions.

A typical group session follows a characteristic progression. There is an initial five or ten minutes of social chitchat. The couple suffering the highest level of tension and conflict on this particular evening moves from this verbal groping for a theme to talk about their current conflict. Usually the group allows this couple to elaborate its own argument with minimum intervention. A marital couple systems theme usually emerges from their dialog.

After the group has helped the couple resolve its conflict, each couple reveals how similar conflict is played out within its own sphere.

Usually by this point the central theme of the session is clear to all the couples. If it is not, the co-therapists will spell it out. The couples reach a peak of insight into their own version of this common dyadic systems difficulty, and achieve some idea of how to begin to resolve this conflict. There is a final short period of working through toward the end of the session.

Co-therapist Collaboration

We have found the male-female co-therapist relationship especially useful in couple group therapy. The co-therapists of this group had worked together in a multiple family therapy group, and had found the co-therapist relationship useful for modeling open communication and conflict resolution, collaborative cooperation, change in a couple over a period of time, and ways of supporting each other under stress. We felt that the synthetic marital system of the co-therapists' long-standing professional interpersonal relationship was a promising tool for the modificaion of marital systems in the couples group as well.

The couples in the group had all been in therapy with the male co-therapist. The female co-therapist was entirely new to the group, and she became somewhat underactive because she was afraid of driving her co-therapist's patients away.

The male co-therapist was anxious about dealing with a group because of his experience of being scapegoated in his family of origin. Although he had worked out some of his counter-transferential problems in the multiple family therapy group, there was a certain amount of regression in his response to the new couples group. In addition, he was relatively inexperienced in doing group therapy. As a result, he became rather inactive and intellectualized during the initial phase of the couples group, though he had been quite active and upfront with his patients before starting the group.

Most of the couples in the group suffered from a similar skew in their relationship. The men were silent and repressed; and the women, in the superordinate position, were overly emotional and overly talkative. The therapists wanted to avoid reproducing this relational skew and model the kind of couple in which the male was at least as active as the female. However, they modeled a couple who were controlled and emotionally unexpressive.

They worked on their own relationship in conferences before and after each session as well as in dialog during the sessions. They were able to move up and become more active and more expressive. The male encouraged the female to give up her anxieties about driving his patients away, and the female encouraged the male to be more active. It took the co-therapists the better part of a year to develop what they considered an optimum degree of activity in the group.

During this period the couples were dealing with their own anxieties about starting in a new group. They reacted to the female co-therapist as to a stepmother, and were fearful of being displaced in therapy by their surrogate siblings.

During the first six to nine months of the group, the emotional climate was mild and intellectualized. As the months wore on and the therapists became more assertive and more expressive of their own feelings, the group paralleled this deepening and this expression of feelings and socially unacceptable thoughts.

The co-therapist model was also useful when a therapist engaged in confrontation with a patient. The therapists encouraged the confrontation of angry and tender feelings between the couples and between cross-couple dyads more than they did between themselves or between themselves and the patients. But occasionally there was a therapist-patient confrontation.

Such confrontations are not simply confrontations between two people in a group; they are extremely complex. The therapist shifts from revealing personal feelings about the patient to validating therapeutically accurate perceptions of the patient to interpreting certain parataxic distortions of the patient. The co-therapist model enabled one of the co-therapists to split off for this purpose. When one co-therapist moved into the role of group member to make such an intervention, the other could move into the more objective and less emotional therapeutic role. The co-therapists could also complement each other in confrontation and interpretation. If one adopted an ego-threatening stance, the other could move in with an ego-supporting stance; both would be designed to help the patient accept and integrate the insight.

The Marathon

The marathon was instituted after ten months of therapy because the couples in the group had frequently expressed the feeling that a one and a half hour session was insufficient to achieve closure in conflict resolution. The therapists also felt that the marathon might serve to increase group cohesion, especially since the group at that time was struggling with the introduction of a new couple.

We met for eight hours during an afternoon and evening and for four hours the next morning. We designed the marathon to straddle a night's sleep in order to utilize the self-reorganizational process of sleep, giving the members a fresh start and another chance to express themselves. The group shared two meals together, and the sharing of visceral gratification seemed to facilitate the sharing of emotional gratification. The therapists introduced the use of family role-playing and physical contact between group members.

Prior to the marathon, the emphasis of the group had been on working through marital problems. The therapists had encouraged an emphasis on the here-and-now interactions of the conjugal family rather than on historical material. There had been little focus on sexual problems, and the tone was largely cognitive and unemotional.

During the marathon, however, there was a shift to the spouses as individuals. Historical material from the families of origin was brought in, and the shift to the emotional and private areas was accompanied by a shift to the area of sexual functioning. This change continued after the marathon.

In retrospect, it seems to us that the couples had to resolve certain malevolent processes in the marital systems before they could be relaxed enough to concentrate on themselves as individuals.

These couples were characteristically overly enmeshed with each other. Consequently, a spouse misperceived marginal differences in his spouse as an implicit putdown of his own characteristics. It was vital for the spouses to decrease such symbiotic relationships, individuate themselves, and give each other the freedom to separate and be different.

The marathon marked the possibility of such individuation, accompanied by a shift to emotional immediacy. The favorable changes in the spouses as individuals were fed back in a favorable way into the marital systems.

For example, Betty Kaufman mothered her husband, but resented this. She had been locked into a pseudomaternal role in her family of origin and had reproduced this in her relationship with her husband. She tended to become involved with her friends in a similar role. The group had confronted Betty with this, but becoming aware of this characteristic of her marital relationship was not sufficient. During the marathon, she was made to see how she had the same tendency to overextend herself in all relationships. She was able to modify these, and to re-enter the marital system without continuing to mother her husband. She learned how to give as a wife without resenting it.

The post marathon phase has been characterized by an optimum mixture of the cognitive and emotional levels, and of the present and the past. Sexual problems have been made available to the therapeutic process. Consequently, we plan to build marathons into our couples group therapy as a regular feature, two or three times yearly.

THE COUPLES GROUP IN MULTIMODAL THERAPY

The couples group is useful as a single therapeutic mode. It helps each spouse become more in touch with his feelings, more courageous in revealing them to his spouse, and more skillful in resolving conflicts. Whereas there might be a severe systems impediment within the marriage which hampers openness and directness, there is no such impediment in the relationship between group members. The cross-couple relationships are useful in breaking the impasses of the marriages and revealing and consolidating areas of health which have been driven underground by malevolent processes within the marriage.

The goal of permanent personality change concomitant with change in the structure of the family can be achieved by multiple couple group therapy, as changes in the structure of client families are affected by changes in the relationship of husbands and wives to each other. For example, if the couples group helps a mother get what she needs from her husband, she can give up a pseudomarital relationship with her son.

In the Schwartz family, for example, one of the goals of conjoint family therapy was to create space between the mother and her son. When other forms of therapy reached an impasse, the couple entered the couples group and for six months this was the only form of therapy they received. The therapist, however, kept tabs on what was going on in the structure of the whole family during this period. When the husband and wife underwent periods of alienation, the mother and son regressed toward a pseudomarital relationship. When the group helped the parents move closer together, the mother-son relationship automatically normalized.

But multiple couple group therapy can also be used in combination with other forms of therapy. As a phase-specific form of therapy used within a multimodal approach, it has great effectiveness.

Sometimes the couples group can stimulate changes which can be utilized in another form of therapy. For example, the central goal of the individual therapy Edward Kaufman was undergoing was to come up front with his feelings. He had a strong tendency to assault people under the banner of revealing his true feelings. But if the individual therapist had pointed this out and pressed the point home, he would have lost ground. When Edward entered the couples group, the group did this job for the therapist.

Furthermore, though the couples group deals only with marital issues, the themes that are posed have total family systems implications. A wife may pose a dyadic theme: "When we are putting each other down, I feel hateful and ugly, and then I am afraid you will leave me and go off with another woman." This theme, however, is one part of a total family systems theme when seen in the context of the whole conjugal family system: "When you put me down, I feel ugly. I'm afraid that you will either go off with another woman or go off and be seductive to our daughter. I feel ugly and hateful with you, so I console myself by babying our son."

The themes in the couples group are pieces of the marital couple skew common to the families of the couples in the group. Desirable changes in the structure of the families are advanced in regard to the relationships of the spouses, but they automatically feed into changes in the total family structure. If the total family needs more active therapeutic intervention during the course of couples group therapy, the therapists can see the whole family in sessions separate from the couples group.

In other words, skews in intrapsychic structure overlap with skews in conjugal family and marital couple structure, which overlap with skews in the therapy group structure. We will try to reveal these overlaps by paraphrasing themes as they appear in the course of group sessions with themes as they appeared in the course of marital couple and individual sessions.

> If I reveal my inner fears and shameful secrets to the group, overcoming my fear of being hurt by other group members, I would be able to reveal my inner fears to my spouse. I would have to transcend my experience of being scapegoated when I revealed similar fears in my family of origin.

> I could commit myself to the group if I set aside my narcissistic wound long enough to give of myself generously to other members of the group. If I discovered that they would in turn give of themselves, I would be able to do this in my marriage. At the same time, I would have to change my experience in my family of origin, in which revenge was more important than tenderness.

> If I trust the co-therapists as benign parental surrogates and stop trying to kill them off, I can work on getting closer to other group members. If I succeeded in this, I could get closer to my spouse. To do this, I would have to give up my lifelong battle with my parents.

> If I gave up trying to kill off the new group members I could give up my murderous rivalry with my siblings in my family of origin. Then I could comfortably share my spouse with my children without resentment.

> If I can accept the therapists as human beings and stop hating them for their faults, I can accept what was good about my parents. Then I could accept what is good in myself and my spouse. I could stop hating myself for my faults and stop hating my spouse for his.

The synergistic working of multimodal therapy is enhanced by different factors.

First, different facets of personality emerge in different social contexts. This accelerates individual and intrapsychic change.

Second, the multiple couples group is like a family. The male and female co-therapists become "parents," and other group members become surrogate siblings. Group members re-enact their roles in the skewed structures of their own families of origin, just as they have re-enacted them and do re-enact them in their conjugal families. The couples group provides an excellent substrate for the members to make changes in their family of origin patterns, their conjugal family patterns, and their peer-group and social network systems.

The analogy of group interactions and family interactions was shown vividly at certain transitional points. We have already mentioned the effect of the professional marriage of the therapists. The female co-therapist was new to the patients, and the group initially attempted to exclude this "stepmother." When this attempt was frustrated by the "father's" consistent support of his professional wife, the group accepted her as completely as they did him. Group members occasionally refer to the co-therapists as a "couple," or as "the father and the mother."

Group reaction to changing composition was also analogous to a family's. Two couples became permanent members of the group. Three, including two of the charter couples, stayed only a short time. The group did its best to keep these two couples involved by motivating them toward changes in their marriages and in themselves and toward commitment to the group. But the transitory couples' lack of commitment and motivation to change galvanized the permanent couples' resolve to change; and the increased commitment of the permanent couples toward change provoked the transitory couples into leaving.

The permanent members seemed to provoke personal and marital crises in the transitory couples. Both of them underwent periods of trial separation following their departure from the group.

Bernard and Helen Goldstein had entered the group after a

crisis around adopting a child. Helen had originally entered individual treatment because of a severe psychosomatic disorder. This
responded to individual therapy, and she made satisfactory improvement in developing insight. It was clear from the outset that
a serious marital difficulty existed, but she was unable to change
the nature of her marital relationship by herself or to talk her husband into coming for treatment. The Goldsteins discovered that
they had a fertility problem, the exact responsibility for which was
never clarified. Bernard was evidently very ashamed of this. Under
the stress of repeated gynecological examinations and marital
crisis, Helen decompensated into a state of extreme agitation.
During this period her husband consented to see the therapist in
the role of an interested family member, and some preliminary
marital therapy was done in this context. On the eve of adopting
a child, Bernard went into an acute state of indecision about
whether he wanted to adopt the child or break up the marriage.

The group served a major purpose for this couple, revealing
their lack of commitment, their fear of change, and their con-
spiracy of secrecy. It was particularly valuable in revealing to
Bernard his lack of commitment to life. Bernard was afraid of exposure, and withdrew himself and his wife from the group, entering individual therapy.

In individual therapy he discovered that he was using his wife
to give him an ersatz feeling of power in order to cover over his
feelings of impotence as a man as well as his actual sexual impotence. In order to clarify his feelings toward Helen, he effected a
trial separation lasting several weeks. During this separation, he
discovered how isolated and empty he was as a person. He moved
back home, and brought Helen in for marital couple therapy. This
moved quickly and in depth to their sexual difficulties, which they
had never mentioned to the group. Bernard became more giving
to Helen, who began to learn to respond warmly after years of
hurt and resentment. At the time of writing, their sexual relationship was showing some improvement, and Bernard was beginning
to be more active as a father to his adopted son.

The couples group also provoked valuable personal and marital
crises for the Smiths. The Smiths were an upper class Protestant
family with three sons ranging from four to ten. Two years before

entering the group, June had gone into a severe agitated depression and made a serious suicidal attempt. After she was discharged from a four-month hospitalization, she developed an extramarital affair which she soon confessed to her husband. He brought her for marital couple therapy, feeling that individual therapy had been unsuccessful for her.

The Smiths were an interesting family. When the entire family was seen, it was obvious that though the spouses had severe marital difficulties, they functioned well as parents; the three boys were remarkably healthy. In contrast to the other mothers in our group, June had not sought substitute emotional gratification in her children, but rather in an extramarital relationship. Charles had not developed unhealthy relationships with his children because he had felt basically satisfied in his marriage.

When the Smiths entered the group after two months of individual and marital couple therapy, two factors emerged vividly. June expected her husband and the group members to applaud her relationship with her lover, as having implications for growth. The group confronted her with the quasi-psychotic inappropriateness of this expectation. It probably would have taken months in combined individual and marital couple therapy for the therapist to deliver the insight that June was essentially uncommitted to either her lover or her husband. If this insight had been pressed too quickly by the individual therapist, June would have withdrawn prematurely from therapy in a paranoid huff.

Second, Charles was passive, unable to confront his wife with a firm ultimatum either to give up her lover or separate. The group was helpful synergistically with individual therapy by making an ego transfusion to Charles, helping him develop the image of himself as an attractive male who could make it with his wife or integrate a more satisfactory marriage in the future. Charles confronted June with the ultimatum; June was unable to make up her mind; and Charles made a trial separation. The couple withdrew from the group and re-entered couple and individual therapy. June decided to give up her lover and commit herself to her marriage, and Charles moved back.

June replaced her lost lover with a total preoccupation with an evangelical religious movement, in a manner characteristic of the essentially psychotic personality. She withdrew from therapy. Charles continued in individual therapy for six months and then withdrew. It is clear that our ultimate goal of permanent personality change was not achieved in this instance. However, the wife was helped through a major suicidal psychosis with a rebalancing on a level comparable to the precrisis level. The couple was helped through a major marital crisis, making an adjustment apparently satisfactory to both of them.

Frank and Hilda Jones entered therapy in a marital crisis. Frank had fallen in love with an old college girlfriend and was on the verge of leaving Hilda. They had evolved a marriage in which Frank was the selfish, withdrawn tyrant and Hilda the long-suffering doormat.

When they entered the group, the group reacted as children react to the birth of a sibling. Intense hostility to the new couple flared up, and the group challenged them to become deeply committed to the group immediately. A major crisis to the life of the group itself was posed; many of the old members threatened to leave the group if the Joneses stayed.

The male co-therapist initially reacted with a high degree of self-neutralization because of his own ambivalence as to the appropriateness of the new couple's entrance and his countertransferential guilt about bringing in new members. The female co-therapist was neutralized by the new members' paranoid reaction to her attempts to make a tender connection with them and protect them from the others. As a result, both therapists procrastinated in making interpretations to the old members as to the transferential nature of this reaction. The interpretation was finally made early in the marathon, and the new couple was temporarily accepted as part of the group.

The group confronted Frank with his essential inability to feel and to relate; they confronted Hilda with her fear of closeness and her tendency to live life purely on the basis of the rule book and surface behavior. But even after they were accepted by the group, this couple was not ready for the group at this particular stage of development. Frank and Hilda decided for themselves to withdraw from group therapy and re-enter marital couple therapy. The group helped them develop a clear picture of their individual and joint problems, and motivated them for marital couple therapy in depth.

We had thought of the couples group as a post-graduate course of therapy following prolonged family, couple and individual therapy. The Smith and Jones cases, however, demonstrated that the group could be useful for couples with very little previous therapy.

THE MULTIMODAL APPROACH

We have mentioned the impact of the multiple couples group used as a phase-specific form of therapy within a multimodal approach. The Schwartz case may help illustrate this.

The Schwartzes were an upper middle class family which entered therapy because of problems around the integration of a new stepfather. Conjoint family therapy succeeded in helping Frances make space for her husband to function as a father to her son and daughter. A pseudo-marital relationship between her and her son diminished. But a year of combined conjoint, marital couple, and individual therapy yielded only slight improvement in the problems of the marital relationship, which was characterized by prolonged arguments about peripheral issues with mutual putdowns, alternating with prolonged periods of silent, angry withdrawal. Frances was furious with Milton for his obsessive, convoluted way of ruminating over a problem and for his limited capacity for tenderness. Milton was chronically angry at Frances for her sharp-tongued expressions of anger. He had an idealized model of a woman similar to his mother—sweet-tempered, compliant, and sunny. Whenever Frances departed from this ideal model, he would try to intimidate her into being nice by withdrawing or angrily putting her down for her style of expressing anger.

During the first six months of couples group therapy, the only therapy the Schwartzes were then engaged in, little progress on couple interaction was made. Repeated arguments in front of the group only served to reveal the ritualized feed-back pattern of hurt and revenge. No significant change was accomplished.

But within the group context, striking individual insights emerged. Frances reported a dream to the group, which revealed her inner sense of aloneness. She felt unconnected to her friends, her husband, and her family of origin. She could be direct and emotionally expressive with her friends, but this gave her no sustained feeling of comfort and self-esteem. When there were difficulties with her husband, she felt alienated from him and everyone, and she would go into a severe state of fear and loneliness.

During the course of the group, Frances also developed insight into the fact that she was still perpetuating the pseudo-maternal role she had played with her mother and sisters in her family of origin. When these insights struck her with full clarity during a group session, she re-entered individual therapy with a new high level of motivation. In the course of individual sessions which paralleled the group sessions she integrated these insights and made true intrapsychic change. She changed in the context of her marriage concomitantly, lowering her overinflated expectations of her husband and becoming more tolerant of his failures.

The group confronted Milton with his essential passivity and his use of passive aggression. His refusal to assert himself either in improving his marital relationship or moving out of it was also delivered with great emotional impact. Milton also re-entered individual therapy with a high degree of motivation. During individual sessions, he saw that his parents had in truth been alienated from each other. Their superficially placid relationship, which he was re-enacting in his conjugal family, was far from an ideal model. He began to be more assertive, replacing his typical pattern of ruminative, obsessive thinking with decisive action. He was able to be more active and generous toward his wife.

In summary, we use various combinations of group, family, couple and individual therapy sessions to make use of the fact that different facets of personality emerge in different social contexts. During pre-group therapy phases of treatment, the marital couple session is the central process, with individual sessions used as a subsidiary supportive modality. During the group therapy phase, the group becomes the central process, with couple, individual, and occasional full-family sessions as the subsidiary supportive modalities.

The use of a phase-specific multimodal approach reflects the synergistic interrelationship of themes: the conjugal family, which is a replay of the family of origin, which is replayed in the couples group. The couples group seems to bring out individual and marital couple difficulties which adjunctive sessions can work through. Changes in the positioning lead to permanent personality change. Therefore, we feel that this multimodal utilization of several therapeutic models accelerates both intrafamilial and intrapsychic change.

CHAPTER XII

GROUP PSYCHOTHERAPY WITH SCHIZOPHRENICS

HYMAN SPOTNITZ

Dr. Hyman Spotnitz, a psychiatrist, psychoanalyst, and group psychotherapist, is well known for his expertise with schizophrenic patients as reflected by his articles and book in this area. In this clear, direct and well organized chapter he has outlined the major issues that are relevant to understanding the problems of practice and technique in the treatment of the schizophrenic patient by group methods.

In this very illuminating article, Doctor Spotnitz first reviews the literature describing group treatment of schizophrenia. He concludes that in the early years group therapy was accomplished primarily with hospitalized patients where the goals were minimal and primarily of a supportive nature. However, he notes and delineates a trend toward the development of a more optimistic and individualized treatment philosophy. In the first major section of his paper, Doctor Spotnitz traces the evolution of the mutually interactive threads intertwining the theory of schizophrenia and group methods for treatment of this problem. He indicates as central in this transition the change of focus in treatment from anxiety to aggression. He continues with an exploration of the importance of the more recent attention to the patient's need to inhibit action and of the therapist's inhibition of countertransference reactions. Treatment goals were expanded along more realistic lines and practitioners began to determine group composition on the basis of severity of ego pathology and type of defenses rather than diagnostic label. Doctor Spotnitz describes the treatment of the schizophrenic patient in a heterogeneous group, pointing out the advantages and disadvantages of this group structure. In addition, he alerts us to several warning signs that may occur when such treatment is not appropriate at a particular time for a particular patient.

In the next section he shares with us his fully developed and original theory of the treatment of the patient with a schizophrenic illness. In this model, group treatment is seen as an adjunct to intensive individual psychotherapy. It is directed toward the resolution of obstacles to the appropriate release of aggression through defense-freeing exercises and the development of patterns of checking or releasing it constructively. Communication through language is stressed rather than motoric discharge. His discussion of handling resistance is particularly well delineated and described. In the final section of his paper, he offers a clinical il-

162

lustration from his practice. The discussion of this clinical material combines and makes explicit the general and specific theoretical issues he has raised earlier. In an article that is both practical and theoretical, Dr. Hyman Spotnitz details for us his formulations regarding group psychotherapy with ambulatory schizophrenic patients. He has brought light, clarity and optimism to an area all too frequently both unclear and pessimistic in outlook and, therefore, frought with anxiety for the practitioner.

D.S.M.
G.D.G.

A SERIES of lectures conducted by Lazell for World War I veterans confined to the schizophrenic wards of St. Elizabeths Hospital in Washington, D.C. initiated the literature on the group treatment of schizophrenic patients in 1921. This venture, which served to attenuate feelings of isolation among the young physician's audience, was later characterized by him as "mental reeducation." In the half-century that has elapsed since them, the literature has focused primarily on improving the lot of hospitalized schizophrenics, alleviating their psychotic symptoms, and restoring them to community life at their premorbid level of functioning.

Notably absent from a review of 404 reports published from 1956 to 1966 (4) are claims of curing the condition or suggestions that anyone works, let along knows how, to produce such an outcome. When Stotsky and Zolik (8) scanned the literature from 1921 through 1963, they found no "clear endorsement" of group psychotherapy as an independent modality for psychotic patients. The common theme running through the reports was that a group therapeutic experience can help these patients achieve a "more successful treatment outcome" when combined with other therapies and an "aggressive interest" in helping them.

The copious literature on inpatient group treatment highlights the paucity of reports on group psychotherapy with ambulatory schizophrenics. A large majority of practitioners are reluctant to accept patients with a firm diagnosis of schizophrenia for groups conducted in private practice; others place one or two such individuals in a heterogeneous group and do not report the specific results achieved in these cases.

Most therapists conducting such treatment adhere to the basically supportive goals that are typically pursued in the inpatient group treatment of psychotic patients. Hence, descriptions of group psychotherapy with schizophrenics that is addressed to more ambitious goals, usually as one aspect of a total treatment program, sound an exceptional note in the literature. The authors of these reports, rejecting the notion of helping the patient "learn to live with" his illness because "once a schizophrenic, always a schizophrenic," strive to provide a group experience that will convert him into a nonschizophrenic (1).

Against the backdrop of many years of psychotherapeutic activity oriented to socialization, the emergence of this more optimistic treatment philosophy parallels two other historical developments: (1) a change in views about the nature of the core problem in schizophrenia that significantly influences the clinician's approach to the patient; (2) the ongoing transformation of group procedures from a miscellany of relatively crude and more or less similar instruments for "doing psychotherapy" in a general sense into an armamentarium of different instruments, each refined to achieve highly specific objectives (7).

Consonant with these broader developments in the field, new ideas about how schizophrenic patients should be treated, and a definitive technique that exploits the potentials of group process more fully for that purpose, have been evolving.

EVOLUTIONARY TRENDS

Some of these changes can be retrospectively traced in two books on group psychotherapy published a decade apart—one by Powdermaker and Frank in 1953 (3) and the other by Johnson in 1963 (2).

Shift from Anxiety to Aggression

The observations and clinical experiences reported in the books just mentioned reflect a gradual shift in interest from anxiety to aggression as the fundamental factor to be dealt with in the group treatment of schizophrenic patients. The psychotherapists who conducted groups of chronic schizophrenics under the Veterans Administration research project discussed by Powdermaker-Frank addressed themselves primarily to allaying anxiety and its manifestations. Hostility was viewed at that time as one of the prominent defenses against anxiety. Nevertheless, the material reported suggests that progress in the group was a function of securing the appropriate discharge of aggressive energy in language. Much evidence is advanced that the patients did well in the group when the therapist could accept their hostility. When, for some reason, they had to inhibit its expression, they manifested catatonic or withdrawal reactions. The counter-hostility of unconsciously antagonistic therapists was repeatedly observed to make these patients more upset and eventually unmanageable.

Three of the first four groups had to be reshuffled at the end of the first year. The group that remained intact was the one that had reached the stage of expressing intense hostility to a "hostility-inviting" therapist. What was therapeutic was not the expression of the hostility but the therapist's ability to accept it undefensively and help the members of the group verbalize and eventually understand it.

Ten years later, Johnson also stressed the focal role of anxiety. However, his approach reflects definite movement toward dealing with the defenses against massive rage, awareness of guilt over the rage, fears of retaliation from others, and fears of close relationships. He recognized that such feelings were the source of much of the anxiety demonstrated by schizophrenic patients in group relationships.

It is evident that Johnson worked on the problem of hostility. He viewed the symbolic and metaphorical communications of the schizophrenic as a "necessary and safe means of expressing hostility to the group therapist." Early in treatment, displacements of hostility from the therapist protect the patient from examining feelings that might evoke fantasies of rejection, retaliatory hostility, or loss of dependency. Indefinite delay in confronting the patient with these feelings was recommended because of his acute need for love, dependency, security, and help from the group.

Foreshadowing another element of the modern theoretical approach—the need to inhibit action—Johnson commented on the tendency of schizophrenics to control homosexual impulses triggered in group relationships. He also called attention to their "highly developed radar" for detecting the unconscious feelings of others. He recognized the importance of the therapist having the proper feelings for them.

The initial concentration on anxiety as the crux of the illness has been abandoned because it proved to be therapeutically unrewarding. The unconscious ego-sacrificing attitudes that bind aggression—the primitively patterned defenses of the schizophrenic against the acting out of destructive impulses—are now regarded as primary and his anxiety as a sign that the defenses are threatened. In the contemporary literature, one finds far fewer references to the patient's anxiety than to that he arouses in the therapist. Projection of the therapist's anxiety onto the patient apparently helped to confuse the issue. Countertransference reactions that make it difficult to provide the type of emotional experiences that facilitate the reversal of the schizophrenic reaction are now viewed as the main obstacle to effective treatment.*

Expansion of Goals

Specific goals were not formulated for the groups of hospitalized schizophrenics treated under the Veterans Administration project. Each therapist was permitted to set his own. Powdermaker-Frank state that the leaders of these groups tended to err "in the direction of overambitiousness," because of their research orientation. Johnson, pointing out that group therapy does not produce a high percentage of recoveries, advocated limited goals in the treatment of schizophrenic patients, as follows: increasing repression, bringing about new, positive identifications, sociability, expiation of guilt, strengthening of old defenses and establishment of new defenses, and the lessening of inner tensions.

The current tendency, as already mentioned, is not only to resolve the fundamental problem but also to help the patient continue on the road to personality maturation. Outpatient treatment is recommended to a postpsychotic patient leaving the hospital.

---

* Powdermaker-Frank and Johnson describe many appropriate and inappropriate responses of the therapist to the schizophrenic patient, but rarely discuss them in terms of countertransference. The index to the first book (3) contains no reference to countertransference, and that to Johnson's book of more than 400 pages (2) lists only half a dozen brief references.

The prognosis has brightened over the years. The specific nature and severity of the condition become less significant when the patient is helped to manage his aggression. Techniques are available to help him achieve a mature personality and his potential for creative accomplishment and happiness in life.

Composition of Groups

Retrospective study of the Powdermaker-Frank and Johnson books elucidates other evolutionary trends that are of interest in the present context.

The first inpatient groups in the V.A. research project were formed on the basis of diagnosis, each group being composed of patients with the same subtype of the illness. Inter-member relationships developed in these groups but they remained at a primitive level. One patient tended to monopolize the sessions of the group of paranoids, silences that could not be broken developed in the catatonic group; the hebephrenic group, after barraging the therapist with intense hostility, subsided into hostile silence. None of the so-called pure or homogeneous groups fared as well as those subsequently formed on the basis of blending patients with different diagnoses and behavior patterns, and giving consideration to the personal characteristics, tolerance of aggressive reactions, and techniques of the therapists. One of them said, for example, that he felt more comfortable when the members of his group were openly hostile in the sessions.

The principle of disregarding diagnostic labels and composing groups on the basis of the severity of ego pathology came to the fore during the next ten years. As stated by Johnson, "Regardless of the clinical picture put forward [by patients with overt psychotic conditions], there is severe ego psychopathology present which poses certain problems in their management in group therapy." On the other hand, ambulatory schizophrenics can be treated together with neurotic patients and function well with them in outpatient groups.

In composing heterogenous groups to be treated in private practice, some therapists regard diagnosis as an inadequate source of information on how patients will function together (7). These practitioners therefore try to ascertain the types of defenses that each candidate for a group activates in interpersonal situations. An assessment of current impulses and defenses is one aspect of achieving a balancing of personality types; this facilitates the functioning of the group as a unit.

Therapists who conduct group treatment as a primarily emotional experience, seek to blend placid and volatile persons with some who tend to arouse excitement and others who check it. There are no generally accepted criteria for excluding a candidate, but reciprocal tolerance of each member for the psychopathology of his co-members is an important consideration.

The schizophrenic patient who undergoes treatment in a mixed group performs valuable functions for his co-members, and they for him. Even though he tries to inhibit his own tendency to engage in discharge-directed behavior, his strong impulsivity and imperious attitudes create tension in the group. Their attitudes, on the other hand, have a dampening effect on him, thus helping him develop methods of controlling and regulating the release of aggressive energy.

In a mixed group, too, the schizophrenic patient is usually the first member to express the deepest resistances of the group as a whole. Successfully dealing with his resistant attitudes often has the effect of alleviating problems of the other members of the group.

The schizophrenic patient who undergoes treatment in a mixed group requires more attention than its other members. Because of his tendency to mobilize their aggression, the therapist may have to intervene more frequently and rapidly. Guidance of the group may be necessary to protect the schizophrenic from acting on his impulses, to help him deal with his defenses against the verbalization of his resentments, and to provide him with special psychological nourishment.

During the initial period of treatment, the therapist needs to be on the watch for a rapid exacerbation of symptoms in the schizophrenic patient–a clue to defensive regression. Does he demonstrate a need to withdraw from the group when under verbal attack? Does he need to discharge his tensions in immediate action? Does he engage in ego-damaging explosions? What is the anxiety content of his silences? Does he come in and talk "scared"? Can he be protected from attack without inhibiting the emotional inter-changes of the other members? These are questions that it is de-sirable to investigate during the trial period. If the patient regress-es rapidly and severely in situations of stress, he may not qualify at that time for treatment in an outpatient group.

GENERAL THEORY OF TREATMENT

*Working Hypothesis**

Schizophrenia is an organized mental situation, an intricately structured but psychologically unsuccessful defense against de-structive behavior. Both aggressive and libidinal impulses figure in this organized situation; aggressive urges provide the explosive force while libidinal urges play an inhibiting role. The operation of the defense protects the object from the release of volcanic ag-gression but entails the disruption of the psychic apparatus. Ob-literation of the object field of the mind† and fragmentation of the ego are among the secondary consequences of the defense.

Hereditary, constitutional, and environmental factors appear to be implicated in the illness. In some cases, only one of these factors seems to produce the schizophrenic reaction; in other cases, highly specific combinations of two or all three factors ap-pear to be involved. Regardless of etiology, the schizophrenic re-action is psychologically reversible, most readily so when the pre-dominant factor is life experience.

No cases have been reported in which the schizophrenic reac-tion has been reversed through group psychotherapy alone, but it is a valuable adjunctive procedure to long-term individual psycho-therapy.

The major thrust in group treatment is the resolution of the ob-stacles to the appropriate release of aggressive energy through defense-freeing exercises and the development of understanding of the patterns of checking or releasing it constructively. In the course of working through these patterns, psychological growth

---

* This hypothesis is quoted from a detailed conceptualization of the illness in a book on individual treatment (5).

† Encompassing the earliest representations of the self as well as object repre-sentations. These overlap in the undifferentiated phase of development during which the situation appears to be organized (5).

is facilitated through verbal and emotional communications and enhancement of the capacity for emotional differentiation. The ultimate goal of treatment is personality maturation.

Operating on the assumption that the patient enters the group in a state of psychic regression, the group therapist accepts responsibility for safeguarding him against further regression and psychotic breakdown. For the schizophrenic (and other group members with preoedipal problems) the treatment is structured as a process of self-regulated progress alternating with brief periods of retrograde movement.

From the opening session, the group members are inculcated with the idea that verbalizing feelings and thoughts is cooperative functioning and that acting on them in any way is out of order. In other words, the group is a forum for open discussion, *not* an arena for action. The distinction between communication in language and motor activity is maintained by appropriate reminders when the latter is engaged in. This approach dampens tendencies to act in, and its influence extends into the interpersonal situations of daily life.

The therapist sees to it that the treatment climate is salubrious,* and that the patient is provided with ego-syntonic communication. However, he experiences sufficient frustration to activate his psychopathological defenses against the release of aggression. These unconscious maneuvers, evoked by and studied in the transference situation, are dealt with when they interfere with progressive verbal communication and cooperative behavior in the group sessions (8). The patient is not exposed to pressure to give up these resistances; but, as he is made aware of them and gets to understand how they are activated in the group interchanges, he tends to give them up voluntarily.

Since explanations of the emotional logic of his behavior tend to make the schizophrenic more self-absorbed, it is desirable to withhold interpretations until he is able to freely verbalize the resentment they engender and is capable of utilizing insight in his

---

* A too sudden or too intense mobilization of feelings that cannot be freely and adequately released in language signifies that the schizophrenic is being exposed to an undue degree of excitation.

own interests. However, resistive behavior that, if permitted to continue, would make the continuance of treatment impossible, is discussed with him as a matter of urgency. Such behavior early in treatment characteristically includes repeated absences from the sessions without advance notification to the group, chronic tardiness, and failure to adhere to the payment schedule.

The schizophrenic patient is drawn gradually into spontaneous verbalization; some degree of noninvolvement is permitted. By and large, resistances to verbal communication are sanctioned, and may even be reinforced. Such resistances are regarded as primitive modes of communication that will be outgrown as the treatment proceeds (6). When the group interchanges fail to resolve these resistances, the therapist may psychologically reflect (join) them —with or without feelings—ask questions that will draw the patient's attention away from his ego preoccupations and toward external objects (object-oriented questions) or intervene in other ways to minimize the counterforce to talking.

Schizophrenic symptomatology, such as delusions and hallucinations, are studied but not interpreted. They are responded to only when they interfere with meaningful communication. The patient is neither encouraged nor discouraged from revealing psychotic material in the group, but no attempt is made by the therapist in the initial phase of treatment to modify the patient's thoughts and feelings. When misperceptions and distortions of reality are accepted and objectively investigated, the patient experiences feelings of being cared for. More than that, he tends to move away from his original attitude; he may respond with feelings of appreciation for the group's help.

The schizophrenic patient mightily defends himself against experiencing and verbalizing hostility to his co-members, conveying the impression that he was inordinately sensitive in early childhood to hostile feelings—his own as well as those of his parents. He may need considerable help from others in the group to develop the ability to talk out his negative feelings. Especially difficult to verbalize are feelings of worthlessness, depression, nothingness, hopelessness, incurability.

Cathartic release is not worked for deliberately since it is of minor significance for long-term personality change. However, much of it occurs in the framework of defense-freeing exercises that help to liberate the schizophrenic group member from the compulsive grip of his maladaptive patterns. Another important aspect of this unlearning process, mediated through identification with the other group members, is the creation of new action patterns that will facilitate the discharge of aggressive energy in personally and socially desirable ways whenever it builds up in the future.

Emotional Induction

The propulsive charge (in the form of feelings) that is needed to move a schizophrenic patient into emotional maturity may have to be provided by his co-members and the therapist—a much greater commitment than the group makes to a member who responds more therapeutically to insight into his problems. In effect, the schizophrenic is told: Feel and talk out all the bad feelings you experienced as a child with your parents and siblings. In turn, you will be helped to express these bad feelings, and we will help you deal with them. We will also help you acquire all the good feelings you needed and failed to experience in childhood.

The feelings of the schizophrenic patient arouse similar and complementary feelings in the other group members and the therapist (5). The induced feelings are a great aid in reconstructing the patient's primary relationships in life and in guiding him toward experiences that will help him achieve emotional maturity.

If the group commits itself to this process of emotional induction, all kinds of feelings will be experienced in relation to the patient—some disagreeable or strange, others pleasurable. The expression of these feelings immediately is not helpful. However, if they can be tolerated and sustained, the realistically induced feelings are an important source of therapeutic leverage when communicated to the patient at the proper time.

CLINICAL ILLUSTRATION OF MODERN APPROACH

The following material, drawn from the case of an arrogant and severely troubled schizophrenic patient, illustrates the types of interventions used to reduce tendencies toward destructive action and facilitate the resolution of defenses against the verbalization of hostile feelings.

Dick was a good-looking young man, twenty-six years old, when he entered a group on the recommendation of several practitioners who had treated him individually over a period of eight years. The patient, a dental technician who worked in a laboratory operated by his father, was placed in an open group composed of men and women who were expected to have considerable tolerance for his psychopathology.

Within a few sessions, Dick initiated a battle for control. He tried to dominate the group's communications, making repeated efforts to limit their content and impose restrictions on the language to be used in the sessions. No member had the right to raise problems that were not, in his judgment, strictly psychological. He did not talk about other matters, and he expected the others to behave as he did.

When these attempts at group control and group censorship were hooted down by the other members, Dick threatened to leave the room or to beat up anyone who referred to him as "vicious" or called him a "lousy bastard." Winning his respect for the principle that each member had the right to speak freely without being put under the threat of physical violence required numerous explanations; these were advanced by the other patients. Dick's threats were also met with threats (joined). The therapist informed him that, if he wanted to remain in the group, he would have to accept what was said about him.

Moreover, special attention was paid to his objections. For example, he was invited to draw up a list of the epithets that provoked him. After receiving this attention, Dick changed his mind. He informed the other group members that they could express whatever they felt about him.

Dick's efforts to suppress rage led to increasing emotional tension. The suppressed rage and tension were recognized, and he was told that he had the right to express whatever he felt in language. He came to see that, although certain group members aroused intolerable feelings in him, he was able to verbalize these reactions, no matter how childish or degraded he felt when doing

so. Hence, he did not have to strike anyone. When the verbal release of rage was blocked, he was told that he wouldn't be executed for having hostile thoughts or feelings or for using violent language. Dick's richest curses did not meet with damaging retaliation. In a climate of acceptance, his tolerance for his own feelings
of being childish or degraded gradually increased. It was explained to him that these feelings inhibited verbal release. Eventually, he was able to verbalize comfortably his urges to strike others, and he mastered his tendencies to act on these urges.

Other destructive behavior, such as running out of the room,
setting himself up as the final arbiter of group behavior, and refusing to attend sessions, slowly yielded to the same approaches.
Dick was helped to perceive his own feelings. Interchanges among
the other patients and the therapist bearing on the significance of
their feelings about Dick served to sharpen his perceptions of his
group associates. His own ego boundaries were more clearly delimited.

The technique of joining resistances figured in the process of
dealing with Dick's controlling attitudes. When, for example, he
announced that he wouldn't attend the next session, he was told
that he wasn't required to come. On one occasion when he said
that he wanted to leave the group, the therapist did not oppose the
idea, and when Dick decided to return two weeks later, the therapist again joined him. At that time, Dick wrote the therapist that
he would like to return but would do so only if he was invited to
come back. The joining of these resistance patterns enabled Dick
to talk more freely and to act more consistently in harmony with
feelings that were not potentially destructive to others.

Dick's disclosure of his willingness to pay girls for dates that involved only dancing together evoked critical remarks from the
men, and the women in the group speculated that his penis must
be an awfully unappealing one. The group interchanges at this
juncture aroused intensely hostile feelings in Dick. When he was
able to describe these feelings without action, he observed–to his
surprise–that the women in the group found him much more attractive. They displayed growing interest in helping him with his

everyday concerns. The men expressed warm approval of his new courtship activity. The positive feelings communicated helped him acquire a sense of identification.

During the second year of group treatment, Dick's communications were marked by spontaneity. He reported that he was deriving more satisfaction in his social life, enjoying the company of attractive young women, and working more productively. He behaved appropriately in the group situation, and participated helpfully in discussions of the problems of the other members.

The group experience just reviewed indicates that a domineering, hostile, and potentially psychotic individual, when placed in a suitable group, can be effectively educated to give up asocial attitudes dominated by feelings of intense hatred, infantilism, and degradation—feelings that urged him toward violent action. He responded favorably to the attention and interest of the group, to joining techniques, to the meeting of his threats with threats, to reminders of the rules he had accepted on entering the group, and to the praise and admiration that rewarded him for more mature functioning in the treatment situation and in his own social environment.

In a follow-up report several years later, Dick said that his two years of group treatment had been the most effective of all the psychiatric procedures to which he had been exposed in moving him along the road to emotional maturity.

REFERENCES

1. Berne, E.: *Principles of Group Treatment*. New York, Oxford University Press, 1966.
2. Johnson, J. A.: *Group Therapy: A Practical Approach*. New York, McGraw-Hill, 1963.
3. Powdermaker, F. B., and Frank, J. D.: *Group Psychotherapy: Studies in Methodology of Research and Therapy*. Cambridge, Harvard University Press, 1953.
4. Schniewind, H. E. Jr., Day, M., and Semrad, E. V.: Group psychotherapy of schizophrenics. In Bellak, L., and Loeb, L. (Eds.): *The Schizophrenic Syndrome*. New York, Grune & Stratton, 1969.
5. Spotnitz, H.: *Modern Psychoanalysis of the Schizophrenic Patient: Theory of the Technique*. New York, Grune & Stratton, 1969.

6. Spotnitz, H.: Resistance phenomena in group psychotherapy (over-view). In Ruitenbeek, H. M. (Ed.): *Group Therapy Today.* New York, Atherton Press, 1969.
7. Spotnitz, H.: Comparison of different types of group psychotherapy. In Kaplan, H. I., and Sadock, B. (Eds.): *Comprehensive Group Psychotherapy.* Baltimore, Williams & Wilkins, 1971.
8. Stotsky, B., and Zolik, E. F.: Group psychotherapy with psychotics: a review—1921-1963. *Int J Group Psychother 15:*321, 1965.

CHAPTER XIII

BLACK AND WHITE GROUPS AND THERAPISTS

THOMAS L. BRAYBOY

Thomas L. Brayboy, a psychiatrist and group psychotherapist, received his psychoanalytic training at the White Institute. He is black and has considered the interrelated issues of blacks, society, psychotherapy, and group psychotherapy. In a provocative paper, Dr. Brayboy shares some of his feelings and reactions with us on these topics. His paper is a commentary on our times and more than solely a paper on group methods with blacks. In this form of reference its message of pessimism should not be taken lightly.

In a brief historical and sociologically oriented survey, Doctor Brayboy recounts the forces he sees as leading to the black revolution. He feels that the racial tensions generated by social developments impose a profound influence on the therapy scene. He evolves a thesis that the role of the therapist has been altered and he has had to become a more real person. This occurrence particularly when there are racial differences between patient and therapist, leads to heated confrontations which he feels are social reality and cannot be explained as solely transference phenomenon. Forcefully, feeling fully, and at times almost angrily Doctor Brayboy traces the discrimination against black patients both in individual and group treatment. He deals with ramifications of blacks entering racially mixed groups as patients. The social climate of the group is immediately altered with white liberals seeing themselves all too frequently in a new perspective. Rational racial discussion he feels is difficult, if not impossible. He laments the scarcity of black group therapists and highlights the need for them particularly with recently arrived southern Negroes. The group he feels mirrors society's patterns even to the point of blacks moving in and whites moving out of both groups and neighborhoods—a sad commentary on both group and therapy and Society.

Doctor Brayboy has in this paper given his commentary on blacks, whites, groups and therapists. It is provocative in its content both for his anger and his pessimism—but it should also hopefully inspire us to greater effort at implementing more effective dialogues not only within groups but within society.

D.S.M.
G.D.G.

AFTER THE MASSIVE GENOCIDE of the Nazis and the horror of nuclear holocaust over Japan as World War II ended, mankind was forced to reexamine itself in preparation for a future destined to be very different from the past. Nationalistic feelings had to be subordinated in a world that had become so small that what one country did affected all others. The non-nuclear powers were strong in their demands for control and limitation of radioactive material. Chauvinistic doctrines became irrelevant for how could one person claim superiority to another when both were so vulnerable to instant non-being by that great leveler, the bomb. The United States government was showing guilt as charged by a world indignant at the brutal annihilation of so many non-combatants. Later efforts at medical reparation admitted and emphasized this guilt. A type of social revolution swept through all countries in a demand for freedom and justice. It was quite natural that black people in this country were influenced by this mood and movement. Thus began the so-called Negro revolt. As one critic said, "All of Africa will be free before we can get a cup of coffee in a corner drugstore." Riots swept the country as the black revolution proceeded against a society which seemed determined to make no attempt to accommodate any of the aspirations of black American citizens. Not only the poor participated in the riots but also some middle-class blacks made token contributions for they felt equally frustrated. Although having fulfilled all of the tenets of the Protestant ethic they found themselves no more accepted within the society than their lower achieving brothers. The concept of power through coalescence brought together many divergent black groups and all began to assume a more militant attitude as it became clearer to everyone that this was the quickest way to achieve social change. Black groups advocating violence caused hysterical fear in white society and this brought on violent repression. Thus the black-white confrontation led to increased polarization with immediate effects felt in all areas of social life. The change in attitude of blacks who began to try to accept themselves as they are rather than trying to become lamp shade white imitations was a narcissistic wound to the collective white ego and the pretentions of superiority.

The racial tension generated by these social developments had a profound effect upon the psychotherapy scene which was already undergoing serious changes after World War II. Living under the threat of nuclear war made everything more immediate, more existential. Orthodox Freudian doctrine and technique were felt by some to be outdated and newer ideas and methods were sought. Zen Buddhism, Existentialism and Behaviorism have all had their day in the sun. Efforts to shorten the process of therapy by briefer more direct techniques have produced many new approaches, some retaining the concept of unconscious motivation and others rejecting it entirely. Traditional group therapy has been extended to include family therapy of many varieties and encounter groups of every description. In all of these changes the role of the therapist has been altered. No longer can he be a reflecting screen but must become more of a real person. Where there has been a difference in race between therapist and patient this new emergence of the therapist as a person and the more militant stance of a patient becoming a person has led to some interesting new developments in psychotherapy. Except for the monumental work of Kardiner and Ovesy (3) the psychiatric literature has not placed much focus on interracial interactions in the past. Now with patients and therapists involved in marathons, confrontations and encounters within and outside of the therapy situation we can never return to the ivory tower where the therapist reigns supreme, transference distorts all and social reality is considered to be irrelevant.

In the beginning there were only white psychotherapists. If any black patient was treated psychotherapeutically it could be done only by one of them. Treatment ranged from very good to very bad. Some therapists refused to treat black patients and some still do. Of the early ones to treat blacks some had separate and unequal waiting rooms and some required their patients to ride on the freight elevator. Since the vast majority of therapists have had no form of analysis or other process of self evaluation of any kind it is not unexpected that their prejudices would be similar to those of the general population. In fact some psychiatrists along with colleagues in psychology have helped to support discrimination and segregation by offering so-called "scientific" proof for the theory of black inferiority. Social workers have recognized for a long time and have written about the problems inherent in working across the racial line. A few analysts who have worked with famous or well-to-do blacks have also done so. Only recently, however, has there been much concern about racial factors as they are involved in treatment of poor blacks or those seen primarily in groups.

As black patients have entered groups their presence has altered the content of discussion as well as the social climate of the therapy setting. Some have been accusatory and have caused some white members to become defensive. The therapist cannot remain immune and his true colors are often revealed in such a situation. Some so-called white liberals find themselves to be surprised when they become aware that their liberal rhetoric does not match their underlying feelings. Others get into difficulty by trying to defend a society and its entire record of racial fanaticism rather than accepting it as historical fact and defending only their own personal history including whatever they may have done to change the overall situation. However, rapping on race is a highly emotional experience and requires personal stability and maturity on both sides in order to be really productive. Since these are not characteristics usually associated with group therapy patients and frequently not with group therapists either, the sessions may degenerate into polarized debates that block constructive therapy and in some cases can destroy groups. Various kinds of encounter situations often have been set up specifically in order to decrease racial tensions but have broken up with greater bitterness than before due to lack of leadership, or the temporary nature of the project, but the basic rock has been the immovable determination of the "haves" not to give up anything to the "have-nots." This has never happened in the history of the world and has therefore forced the various revolutions of the past.

Black group therapists are few and far between and most have come upon the therapy scene relatively recently. Except in institutions few have conducted groups that are predominantly white. The reason is simple. White patients do not seek black therapists unless they come highly recommended by other white patients or else they are patients who are very young and this is part of their rebellion against the establishment and its highly discriminatory social order. Referrals from white colleagues do come in occasionally but they come like a left handed compliment with apologies. (He's a good man even though he is black.) Therefore the white group members are more likely to be tolerant of a black therapist and not pose the type problem presented to white therapists by black group members. In fact there are a few of that rare type of patient who come voluntarily to black therapists because they believe them to be superior due to the fact that they had to overcome special obstacles to work out their own problems and to achieve the role of therapist. However, given the present racial polarization any discussion concerning race may be difficult for a black therapist whose orientation is militant. He may be unable to remain objective and prevent his feelings from interfering in work which should be done in the best interest of the patient. When this occurs, of course, he is likely to loose a patient just as a black patient will flee an obviously bigoted white therapist. Recently black patients are leaving white therapists claiming that they lack "soul" or cannot understand the black experience. These patients usually are using race as a screen defense covering many other things with which they fear to deal. They do not tend to work well with any therapist of any color. Black therapists are practically essential in one situation. This involves black patients usually raised in the South whose experience with white people has been so negative that he cannot speak truthfully with any of them. If a black therapist is not available for such a patient he will not enter any group. His counterpart is the white bigot who could not possibly accept a black therapist. Both types were seen and described by Brayboy and Marks in a paper concerning transference variations evoked by racial differences in co-therapists which was presented at the AGPA conference of 1967 and later published in the *American Journal of Psychotherapy* (2).

Since then the polarization of racial attitudes has increased generally and has affected all areas of psychotherapy. It seems to be more important in group than in individual therapy. In a one to one situation almost any combination of colors, religions or sexes can be accommodated if both parties are willing and color becomes no more significant than any other variable if the relationship lasts long enough. However in group the social and cultural influences from the outside exert pressures in the group which mirror those of the society. Field theory postulates the manner in which each member is affected and like magnetic forces bring about the polarization we are now seeing in group and in society. Several black therapists report that as blacks enter groups whites flee much as the pattern seen in residential communities. The transformation of such a group from all white to all black was described by me in a recent article (1).

This inability to discuss race is typical of our society which has made skin color the most important single factor in determining the nature of interaction between any two people of different colors while at the same time denying that our country is racist oriented, second only to South Africa. Some day our descendants will look back on us with the same awe with which we now regard the Salem witch burners. If racial differences cannot be discussed in a therapy group, what other forum could contain such a dialogue or what other vehicle could accomplish such a task? Because racism in this country has become institutionalized it has become very complicated. Sometimes it exists without appearing to be present and then extends through a range to the other extreme wherein it does not exist but appears to do so. Some racists declare themselves openly as George Wallace did when he said that of course all white folks hate all niggers and likewise all niggers hate all white folks. The same rigidity is seen when blacks proclaim that all whites are devils and imply that all blacks are angels. Others are more deceitful when they practice racism openly but give lip service to goals of integration and freedom. The state department in its cultural exchange program is one good example. However, the larger percentage of our national population who make the issue so complex are those who are unconsciously racist or who make up their own definitions of racism to suit themselves. Of course there are also those who practice racism out of pure ignorance. Perhaps they are a faction that might best be able to use mixed group psychotherapy. Anyway to paraphrase Myrdal (4) of many years ago, the present blacks are much more of a burden to America than a promise and group therapy seems to offer little in the way of a method to improve the situation.

REFERENCES

1. Brayboy, T.: The black patient in group therapy. *Int J of Grp Psycho, 21:*288, 1971.
2. Brayboy, T. L., and Marks, M. J.: Transference variations evoked by racial differences in co-therapists. *Am J of Psycho 22:*474, 1968.
3. Kardiner, A., and Ovesy, L.: *The Mark of Oppression.* New York, Norton, 1951.
4. Myrdal, G.: *An American Dilemma.* New York, Harper, 1944.

CHAPTER XIV

DRUG ABUSE, COMMUNITY GROUP PROCESS, AND THE TRAINING OF NATURAL TALENT

Robert U. Akeret

Dr. Robert Akaret, a William Alanson White Institute trained analyst and group psychotherapist, shares with us in this paper two of his experiences with community group consultation. In a personal, anecdotal style he recounts his struggles as a consultant group psychotherapist to establish drug rehabilitation programs within a new store front treatment center and a wealthy middle class private school. Both attempts ended in what could be termed a failure, but each, because of his frank, open style of communicating, provides us with lessons on the problems to be faced.

In his work with the store front community, Doctor Akaret did not know if he would be a staff group therapist, a supervisor, or a resource person. In the initial phase, he decided to train the workers in group dynamics and self awareness. He did this by using his rather intense encounter like "movement oriented method" where they acted out in a structured way their feeling toward him, each other, and the young addicts. The group, mostly Puerto Ricans and Blacks, rejected him almost totally because he was white and they felt he couldn't really understand them and their experience. They wouldn't tolerate his turning the sessions into a personal growth experience for themselves, but instead wanted him to provide ideas, supervision and support. It was only on this level that he could help the staff improve their working relationships with one another. The lesson to be learned from this experience appears to be that in the area of black-white interaction basic distrust permits only the more cognitive of interactions.

In his work within a private school he introduced a one-year self-exploration training group for teachers before they themselves could become group leaders for the students. The teachers too were defensive, questioning and fearful, though more amenable to learning group process dynamics than the store front leaders. Unfortunately this project also ran into a great deal of resistance and ended in failure.

184

This innovative and rather flexible use of group process techniques somewhat illustrates how a well trained group psychotherapist improvised in his attempts to control drug abuse in young adolescents. He reaffirms his belief that people with natural talent can be trained to do useful and effective group work and that the best approach to drug abuse is to not focus directly on the drug problem but to help people to be more self aware. In this paper Doctor Akaret has given us what he did and the problems in doing it—further explanation and amplification are eagerly looked for in future papers.

D.S.M.
G.D.G.

ABOUT FIFTEEN MONTHS AGO two community organizations approached me for help with their difficulties in coping with the growing drug abuse by young adolescents. The first group had recently been funded by state and city grants to establish a new street-front treatment center for young heroin addicts; the second group was a large, well established and wealthy private school. Both community groups had no preconceived ideas about how to approach the problem of drug abuse or how I would be used as the consultant.

This paper describes my experiences as the consultant. Special attention is focused on what was helpful and what was disruptive in my participation.

For a number of years I had become increasingly restless as a psychoanalyst in private practice. I wanted to become more actively involved in community group work. Thus the offer to work as a consultant was both refreshing and challenging, and also provided me with the opportunity to pursue two deep personal interests: (a) my interest in training people with natural talent for therapeutic work with others in need of help with their problems in living, and (b) my interest in group therapy.

For a number of years I had been experimenting with different forms of group therapy, and I had evolved an approach to group work that I call "movement" oriented group therapy. In this approach the problems, feelings, dreams, fantasies presented by the group members are placed into movement in order to create an intensity of experiencing that could help facilitate personality change. I welcomed the opportunity to use this approach in my community work.

The two community groups could not have been more divergent. The first group operated out of a run-down, street-front building located in a slum area; the second group was housed in a magnificent new building located in a well-to-do neighborhood. The staff group workers in the first setting were primarily young, black and Puerto Rican ex-addicts; the teachers in the second group were white, middle-class with little personal drug experience. The young adolescents coming for help in the first group were primarily court referred black and Puerto Rican heroin addicts, and the adolescents in the second group were white, upper middle-class students who were just beginning to experiment with drugs. Paradoxically, the first group had adequate funds for their drug program, and the second group had practically no funds available. Both the ex-addict leaders in the first group and the teachers in the second group had little previous individual therapy.

STREET-FRONT COMMUNITY GROUP

My expectation was that I would be welcomed with open arms as the consultant even though I had considerable doubt about how to be useful and resourceful. Although the director of the drug program had asked for assistance, I soon discovered that many staff workers did not want my help. They even boycotted the group meetings I attended. There was also some confusion about my role as the consultant. Would I be a staff group therapist, a supervisor, or simply a resource person? What authority did I have? I was convinced from the beginning that some form of training for the workers was essential if they were to be effective, resourceful leaders. It was not, however, my ideas, my personal style of participation or even my insistence on worker training that was disruptive; it was simply that I had the wrong color and background. I would be confronted with, "How can you know the black experience?" I said, "I knew something about the human experience," but everywhere in the program decisions were based on—That's not black enough. I felt frustrated and angry even though I realized I was getting a heavy dose of what the staff had often experienced in their own lives—rejection based on color rather than talent.

After two months of partially attended meetings, we finally had the first staff meeting with all the staff workers present. I assumed that since most staff workers had group encounter experiences when they were overcoming their drug addiction problems, they would be open to intense emotional experiencing. I was ready to apply my group movement approach. Some of the workers focused on the usual black-white-Puerto Rican conflict. The talk appeared circular. Everyone seemed entrenched. They were not really listening to each other. They were simply making pronouncements. I asked one of the more resistant black workers to make up a group fantasy while lying on the rug with his eyes closed. He created the following fantasy:

"I see two lines of people–one white and the other black. They're facing each other. A large ferocious cat appears . . . like stalking its prey. The whites are scared–they show it . . . the blacks remain cool. The cat keeps coming closer . . . closer. Everyone in the white line starts to panic . . . and the blacks panic . . . and I begin to run. Everyone runs . . . all in different directions."

After a long silence, the black worker sat up, opened his eyes and reflected, "When the shit hits the fan, man you run . . . when the shit hits this agency . . . everyone runs alone . . . no one sticks together."

This theme of scattering and "each into his own thing" roused individual feelings of loneliness and isolation. We had progressed beyond the familiar color war. One of the white workers became overwhelmed with his personal sense of isolation and coldness. He started to weep, at first within himself and then openly. His weeping created enormous group tension. No one made a move, and the white worker felt even more isolated. Then another worker responded with comforting thoughts and physical touch. Soon we were all talking about our own emotional reactions to what was happening. After the meeting I felt almost elated–now the group was finally beginning to work together.

The next meeting, however, was cancelled! I realized that an almost panic reaction existed because the meeting was cancelled a few minutes before starting time. Some of the workers were upset about the strong, open display of feelings. "Too painful to cope with." "We don't want to know each other that intimately." "That's not what we want to learn." I had the distinct impression that two of the black workers were elated with the cancellation.

They were for disruption and against supervision and learning. After some additional meetings which were partially attended by the workers, I decided to resign. I felt that prejudice against me based on color–by some of the workers was too great an obstacle to overcome. I encouraged the group to find a black consultant. After weeks of searching and lack of agreement about the new consultant, I was asked to return as the consultant. I accepted after learning that the two most disruptive and resistant black workers had been fired after using drugs personally while working with their groups.

Since then I have met regularly with the staff workers, and the number of workers attending is directly related to the needs of the individual workers. I find myself constantly changing roles from therapist to supervisor to resource-idea person to friend. My primary effort has been to create an effective working relationship within the staff. Coping with problems of resistance, hiring and firing staff workers, developing program objectives, evolving methods of group work with young drug addicts are some of the themes that keep emerging. I did not find that intense encounter experience through my movement oriented group therapy was helpful as the primary method of working. The staff members were more interested in ideas, in supervision, and in support; they did not want personal growth experience in such a peer-work group setting.

THE PRIVATE SCHOOL

The private school's psychologist had initially asked me to meet with the upper school faculty in order to explore with them what actions could be taken by the school to cope with their growing drug abuse problem. I reviewed for the faculty some of the traditional approaches to the problem of drug abuse, and then I expressed by personal conviction that lectures and films by experts would probably have little lasting impact on the students. I then suggested that a program be established in which teachers with natural talent in relating with students be trained in a workshop to eventually lead student self-exploration and self-confrontation workshops. The faculty group would train for a year in a similar self-exploration workshop, and then such groups would be open to the students the following year. If the student workshops focused primarily on drugs, I felt certain that they would fail. I suggested that the workshops should emphasize awareness of self and others and that attention be given to the process of how significant life choices are made. With some apprehension, the faculty decided to follow my suggestions.

Fifteen teachers including the head of the high school signed up for the training workshop which met after school hours. Soon I realized that I was facing a very similar problem to the street-front community group. The teachers varied sharply in their readiness to participate with feelings and personal openness. Only a few had previous therapy and only about a fourth were open to emotional experiencing. Most teachers were defensive, questioning, and fearful. The issue of privacy was always present. How much do you tell? Feel? As faculty members they had to face each other each day outside the workshop experience. As with the previous group, I discovered that intense, personal emotional experiencing was upsetting and painful for most of the teachers.

The teacher workshop turned out to be an experiencing and teaching of group process skills. The typical format would be that I would initiate an activity based on some current group problem. For example, I would ask a group member who was having difficulty expressing his feelings about other group members to simply "sculpt" the group. Then we would discuss the form of his sculpture, and each person would express his thoughts about how he was placed. Many of the outside ongoing conflicts between faculty members surfaced–efforts were made to resolve the conflicts. Gradually I encouraged other faculty members to initiate a group experience.

The self-exploration teacher workshop turned out to be quite meaningful for most of the participating members. As teachers they became freer and more open with each other. A few teachers dropped out of the workshop; one teacher was too upset by his emotional experiencing and another felt he had no talent for group leadership work. While the workshop did open the communication between faculty members in the workshop, the very existence of the program created a communication gap between those teachers in the workshop and the other teachers in the school.

We worked together as a group for one year, and in the final meeting each teacher talked about his readiness to lead a group of students. The teachers were frank about themselves and each other. We decided to have two leaders in each group–a "man and woman" team. They could act as a control as well as a resource for each other. From the group we had four "teams" ready to start leading student groups.

Then I spoke to the upper school students and presented my thoughts about the self-awareness workshops to be offered. There were many questions and much enthusiasm. Who would lead the groups? How would the groups be selected? One faculty member present at the meeting asked, "At the risk that even one student would become emotionally disturbed by the group experience, could I seriously start such a program?" I answered, "I certainly would take the risk. I would always support a program that could potentially benefit many students even if a student responded negatively." This particular faculty member was obviously against the program, and I was informed at a later date that he actively started to lobby against the student program. "They're tampering with emotions of children–they're not professionals." Unfortunately, the *New York Times* magazine section carried an article that weekend on group encounter work–focusing on the dangers of group work by non-professionals. A special "fatal" faculty meeting was called after the weekend. Some teachers brought pressure on the headmaster to postpone the beginning date of the workshops. More than forty students had already signed up for the experience. The headmaster decided to "wait" for additional studies about such group student workshops in other schools. Unfortunately, I did not attend this last faculty meeting, I had assumed from the start that the faculty had approved the program. Some of the faculty members voting for postponment did not realize that I would continue to supervise the teacher "teams." The faculty decision to postpone the groups was a real disappointment for the entire teacher group. I realized too late that I should have kept more in contact with faculty members who did not participate in the workshop. The experience reinforced my observations that so many educators who believe in the education of the "whole" person become frightened when the "whole" person begins to include personal awareness, feelings, self knowledge. They shy away from the self and focus on the "outside" world of academic subjects; evidently feelings and the personal self are not a part of the whole person!

SUMMARY

The paper described my experiences as the consultant for two community organizations that were attempting to cope with growing drug abuse by young adolescents. I always had the sense in the two community experiences that I was "on my way" but never quite sure where I was going. My participation and my particular role as consultant often became defined as I experienced the situation and the individuals involved. I was constantly shifting roles from therapist to supervisor to educator to friend.

In both community experiences I was repeatedly confronted with the problem of resistance. The street-front group resisted my help because I was white and therefore could not comprehend the black experience; the private school administrative faculty resisted my help because I was encouraging the "tampering with emotions by non-professionals."

I discovered that both community groups resisted the strong emotional experiencing in the group meetings. Training individuals with different levels of openness, competence, and talent–in the same group–was also difficult.

My experience in both community groups re-affirmed my belief that people with natural talent can be trained to do useful, effective group work. My experience confirmed my previous belief that the best approach to drug abuse is not to focus specifically on the drug problem, but rather to help individuals to become self-aware so that their life choices are meaningful and appropriate–whatever they may be.

CHAPTER XV

CHARACTERISTIC PHASES OF DEVELOPMENT IN ORGANIZATIONS

Seymour R. Kaplan

The application of material gathered in the psychological sphere to other areas has been attempted numerous times, with some success and some failure. In the area of organizational development it would seem almost patently obvious that there would be some direct relevance to psychological theory and particularly the knowledge of group process. The utility of such an approach also seems fairly obvious. When one further considers the interrelationship of organizational structure and group process dynamics and their common expression in a mental health program, the implications for improving the manner of delivery of mental health services seems to be another extension of theory into the realm of community psychology. It seems highly desirable to use the skills we as professionals have developed to assist patient populations now translated into principles that may enable us to put our houses in order.

Dr. Seymour Kaplan has approached this topic with originality and creativity. Beginning with a model derived from group development, he outlines the substantive phases he sees as characteristic of the usual mental health group. He then defines those specific attributes he feels are characteristic of organizational development. With these two seemingly divergent developmental schema as a back drop, he begins to interrelate the aspects of each that are similar to each other. The dynamic structure that he formulates is both interesting and informative. It provides an excellent frame of reference for understanding and dealing with organizational problems and particularly their application in developing mental health programs.

Although the task he has set for himself and accomplished is a difficult one, and by itself would be a significant contribution, he has contributed something else as well. In his effort to analyze and synthesize the complicated structure he approaches, he draws on material from a variety of sources. The power that comes from having at one's disposal material from various disciplines is an example that might be used in dealing with other complicated issues as well. Thus, he provides us with a model of how the social sciences working together might be able to understand and solve major problems that a single discipline working in a more isolated fashion might find insoluble.

D.S.M.

G.D.G.

F OR A NUMBER OF YEARS I have been interested in the behavior of members of small groups with a special interest in the study of group processes to which characteristic phases of developments have been ascribed. My observations primarily have been derived from my work with therapeutic and human relations sensitivity groups in a hospital or medical school setting. These groups, composed of patients, staff or students, numbered about eight to ten members in the instance of group therapy, about twelve to fifteen members in the human relations groups and thirty to fifty members in therapeutic community meetings on a psychiatric ward or in a day hospital and about a similar number in the staff development meetings.

Although the major part of my research and clinical studies were with the smaller group constellations, I have been impressed over the years that a similarity of structure and process existed in all these group formations. Other investigators have reported observations which correspond to this point of view (4, 5, 8, 16, 21-25).

In the recent past I had the opportunity to participate in the initiation and development of a large mental health organization in a municipal general hospital. The program was sponsored by a university department of psychiatry and included a community mental health center. This organization, whose membership came to number over 250 individuals, underwent a developmental process to which I would ascribe similarities in its organizational structure and process that I had observed in small groups. As a result of my experiences with this and other programs and the formulations about organizational dynamics by social scientists with which I have become familiar, I began to explore the hypothesis of characteristic phases of development in organizations, particularly mental health organizations in hospital and community settings, which are directly or indirectly supported by public funds. I would like to focus my discussion about group process in the hospital setting upon these explorations.

I urge your attention to the application of group process to organizational dynamics as among the most important areas to which we can address ourselves. We hear a great deal about the crisis in health and mental health care in the country today and much of the onus for the crisis is blamed upon the problems in the health delivery systems. It is an oversimplification to seek out one cause for the complicated state in which we find our health and mental health care services, but there is little doubt that the organization and delivery of the services leaves much to be desired.

One of the reasons for this is the curious disinclination of the mental health professional to occupy himself with the problems of administrative management and organization. This disinclination is all the more difficult to explain among those mental health professionals interested in group process theories and practices since they have access to a body of knowledge which can be expected to help to contribute solutions to the many vexing organizational problems with which we are confronted in the mental health care field. The discussion which I am going to present about phases of development in organizations is an aspect of organizational dynamics to which group process theory can be expected to contribute in the future.

CHARACTERISTIC PHASES OF DEVELOPMENT
IN SMALL GROUPS

Before turning to the dynamics of organizations, I would like to first review my thinking about the developmental process in small groups. The following quote is from an article I wrote with Roman about phases of development in adult therapy groups. "In the foregoing we have presented a phenomenology of group behavior in order to demonstrate how a collection of strangers organized themselves into a psychological group. We have attempted to draw attention to the two frames of reference currently utilized in the study of small group psychology. On the one hand, we have focused upon the subjective reactions of the individual member, with special reference to the role relationship to the therapist or a substitute for him. On the other hand, we have focused upon the group as a dynamic system and observed its development from a relatively loosely organized state in which role differentiation was nonspecific to one in which a greater degree of differentiation became tolerable. It is our hypothesis that the therapy group, as any small group, goes through specific phases as it develops from the undifferentiated to the differentiated condition. Each phase brings with it a specific theme or conflict, a specific interaction pattern, a specific perceptual framework. All the members to some degree participate in this development. Each phase is dependent on the resolution of the previous phases, which is experienced as a developmental crisis by the group. This has been outlined in Chart I (13). The chart is reproduced here.

Since I am going to compare the concept of phases of small group development that are outlined in this chart to the development of organizations, I should like to amplify some implicit aspects of the chart. Although the outline of the behavior of the members of the group includes the consideration of their interaction as a social system, the group themes, the social and family models to which we compared the members' group behavior, as well as the group symbolic constructs, emphasizes the individual or dyadic psychological viewpoint of the shared behavior. This, of course, was consistent with the purpose of providing psychological treatment for which reason the members had been convened. More specifically our attention always included an attempt to understand the members' behavior in terms of their expressed or inferred feelings and thoughts about the therapist-leader, even when the peer group interaction was predominant.

The categories and content of the chart, therefore, are theoretically based upon a leader-oriented concept, following Freud's constructs of the nature of the basic emotional bond of social groups as well as his emphasis upon the technical use of the transference relationship for therapeutic purposes. However, the group behavior referred to under Phase II, subphase A, which occurs usually within the first ten meetings, is group or patient-centered and the actual technical use of the transference relationship is quite modified compared to the classical psychoanalytic approach. Nevertheless, although there are therapeutic benefits in group therapy to be derived from the group relationships between the members, it is my impression that a significant, and perhaps the basic, motivation for the group therapy members' behavior will be reflected

CHART I

PHASES OF DEVELOPMENT IN AN ADULT THERAPY GROUP

PHASE I: THE LOOSELY ORGANIZED PSYCHOLOGICAL GROUP (Medical Model)
↓ Regression
PHASE II: THE COALESCENCE OF THE PSYCHOLOGICAL GROUP (Interaction Models)

Structure	Theme	Family	Social	Mythological
A: *Patients interact as part of the group as a unit.* (Common bond on the basis of a shared mythology)	Dependency	Child-Parent	Student-Teacher	Disciple-Demigod
B: *Patients interact as part of a subgroup of men or women as a unit.* (Common bond on the basis of shared sexual identity)	Power	Younger Sibling-Older Sibling	Teenager-Young Adult	Follower-Heroic Leader
C: *Patients may interact as part of a pair as a unit.* (Common bond on the basis of complementary character traits)	Intimacy	Husband-Wife	Friends	Individual-Society

↓↑

PHASE III: THE PARTIAL DISSOLUTION OF THE PSYCHOLOGICAL GROUP
(Minimal Interaction. Individual Transference)

by their relationship to the therapist and by their perception of, and fantasy about, their direct or indirect impact upon him. Also important, are the patients' real and fantasied perception of the therapist's leadership method, the motivations they ascribe to the reasons he employs the method and their capacity to utilize it.

Other aspects of Chart I require some explanation to clarify its use in the comparison to an organizational setting. The column at the far left of the chart, under the heading of structure, outlines the sequential phases of the structural differentiation of the group as a social system. It presents the hypothesis that the structure of a given phase or subphase can be determined by the observer's understanding of the basis upon which the emotional bond between the members are formed and the configuration of the membership groupings that evolve from this bond. Initially, in my experience, the emotional bond is characteristically an identification relationship based upon the members' shared mythological construct of the nature of the events that are occurring in the group (i.e., that they are all being magically cured of their symptoms by virtue of their group membership). The mythological construct includes a representation of the members' perceptions of their relationship to the therapist-leader which, corresponding to their magical expectation of cure during this initial phase, is deistic in nature.

In the quotation from the article from which this chart is taken, it was hypothesized that the differentiation of the group phases is a progressive one.* This is represented in Chart I in all the categories. The emotional bond and the resulting configurations among the members become more "object-oriented" although still based upon an identification relationship; the family and social interaction models reflect more mature phases of psychosocial development, and the collective themes more socially-valued interpersonal needs.

The members' perception of the meaning of the events and the symbolic constructs of their relationship to the therapist becomes less bedded in magical thinking. The thoughts and attitudes of the

---

* "Progressive" is used here as the converse of the "regressive" influence of group emotions that characterize the early formative phase in groups. The progressive changes refer to the maturation or developmental growth of groups in the subsequent phases.

members and the method by which they use the treatment process becomes more "scientific." The idealization of the therapist-leader or of a group member is more clearly influenced by the members identity and purpose for attending the meetings. The category, "individual-society," probably should be characterized by a "patient-doctor" relationship, using "doctor" here in the sense of a culture hero* of the likes of Marcus Welby or Ben Casey, that is, as a romantic personification of a self-less, socially dedicated individual willing to sacrifice personal needs for others. "Individual-society" was used to represent the human conflict between self-interest and social consciousness.

This latter point emphasizes another implicit and fundamental aspect of the theoretical point of view outlined in the chart, namely, that the theory is based upon a conflict-resolution concept of human behavior, from both the psychological and social system framework, although the source of conflict is viewed differently in each. The psychological framework emphasizes individually internalized anxiety or guilt over conflicts arising from unconscious wishes for a unique and special relationship with the therapist or other group members, and the social system framework emphasizes the individual member's more overt, perhaps preconscious, distress about the disequilibrium-producing aspect of his behavior or attitudes.

According to this hypothesis, the members' conflict is mitigated or controlled by the preconscious shared participation in, or compliance with, the prevailing norm of the group, specific to the particular phase that has generated the conflict. The member is able to experience dependency needs, act "as if" he wishes to be a child or to have a special student-teacher relationship with the therapist or another group member, provided his behavior or attitude *in concert with the other group members* enacts the groups' prevailing consensus that they are in the presence of a diety, who dispenses or will soon dispense magical cures to all the membership. The member who will be extruded from the group, either by leaving or emotional withdrawal, is not the member who expresses the phase specific theme, or interaction models, but rather the mem-

---

* I use this term as described in an article by Myerhoff & Larson, The doctor as a culture hero: the routinization of charisma. *Human Organization, 24:3,* 1965.

ber who refutes by behavior or attitude the collective group-evolved hypothesis about the nature of the common bond that underlies the relationship of the members to one another and the therapist.

In terms of the therapeutic use of group therapy, the theoretical views that I have noted above imply specific limitations upon the extent to which transference phenomena can be analyzed. In my opinion, group therapy is best adapted to treat the emotional derivatives of these phenomena as they are expressed in the interpersonal context or by other manifestations of ego functioning. However, it is not my purpose in this paper to discuss the use of the small group setting for psychotherapy but, rather, to use the observations of the therapy group for data about phases of development in small groups and to see what comparisons if any there are to observations about organizational development. Assuming for purposes of exposition that the material presented has some basis in fact, I would like to explore the parameters of the issues discussed in relationship to a "work" group of employees.*

A HYPOTHETICAL MODEL OF PHASES OF ORGANIZATIONAL GROWTH

I was encouraged by the hypothetical model of organizational growth (Chart II) to explore the concept of developmental phases in organizations. I am indebted to Sherwood for this model and the following descriptive characteristics of three phases in the growth of organizations.† The comparison of these observations

---

* The phrase "work" group will bring to mind the classic work of W. R. Bion and his concepts of group behavior. Although the "work" group referred to in this context is not being used in the same sense as Bion's "work group," his thinking nevertheless has influenced the concepts the author is presenting in this chapter. Bion's views will be referred to and discussed below.

† The chart and the discussion of the phases of organizational growth were presented by Sherwood at the American Psychiatric Association Institute on Theory and Practice of Administration, April, 1971. The Institute was jointly sponsored by the Committee on Certification in Administrative Psychiatry of the A.P.A. and the Division of Social and Community Psychiatry, Columbia University. The curriculum was the result of the joint efforts of Archie Foley, M.D., Director of the Division of Social and Community Psychiatry and Sidney Mailick, Ph.D., Professor of Public Administration and Director of Doctoral Studies, Graduate School of Public Administration, New York University. Arthur R. Sherwood, Ph.D., is Associate Professor of Public Administration, New York University.

to the social psychological schema of phases of development in small groups that I have postulated will be presented in the following section.

A HYPOTHETICAL MODEL OF PHASES
OF ORGANIZATIONAL GROWTH AND DEVELOPMENT

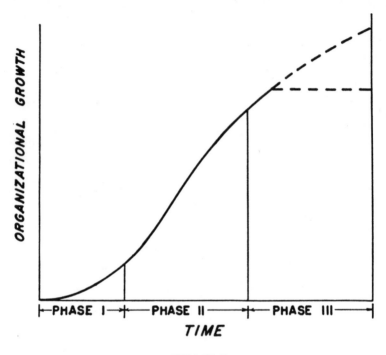

PHASE I

At the beginning of the organization, its goals and purposes and the functional relationship of the membership to one another is untested and exists primarily on paper as general ideas and concepts. There will be varying degrees of preorganizational relationship among the initial members who will, for the most part, be identified by their prior career experiences. The task at hand is the initiation of the programmatic objectives so that hard work, commitment and optimism are personality attributes valued among the members. The sanction and assistance of the sponsoring institution or institutions is usually necessary in the early stages of recruitment of staff and the arrangements for facilities. (This description applies, therefore, primarily to institutionally supported organizations, especially those funded directly or indirectly by public resources.)

In the early part of phase I, there will not be any complex intraorganizational issues with which to contend until such time as the characteristics unique to its structure and membership have emerged. This is not to say that there will not be any interpersonal difficulties among the members, or any organizational problems, but these will reflect upon the relationship to the sponsoring institution or upon the idiosyncratic nature of individual members.

PHASE II

This is reflected on Chart II by the accelerated growth rate and expansion of the organization. One of the most important issues with which the organization is faced in this phase is the competence of the staff and the availability of resources to provide the services and programs to which the organization has made commitments. The successful organization will be making adjustments and corrections of its original goals and plans and, as needed, will innovate new concepts and obtain the necessary resources to provide for the innovations.

Aside from these professional and management observations Sherwood suggests the following. The accelerated growth and increasing complexity of the organization during phase II will of necessity require a flexible organizational structure so that to various degrees and at various transitional points the administrative organization will be loosely structured and possibly, at times of rapid change, it may be chaotic. A staff characterized by the quality of its enthusiasm and commitment may be more adaptive during this accelerated growth phase than a staff characterized for its attention to detail or its "productivity."

Sherwood correlates this intraorganizational development with a characteristic interorganizational development. In order to be successful, the organization during phase II must compete with other similar organizations to demonstrate that it can achieve the goals and purposes better and more effectively. To a greater or lesser extent, the competition entails political considerations. The organization must therefore, concomitantly with its internal developments, occupy itself with developments in the "political arena." Sherwood uses the political context in the broadest sense of "the body politic," although its application would be more relevant for public health programs, or programs largely supported by public funds, than for privately sponsored and supported organizations.*

PHASE III

The bifurcation of the growth curve in phase III shown on Chart II is meant to illustrate two characteristics of this phase, which tend to conflict with one another. These refer to the simultaneous need to consolidate the developments of the organization, in order to improve efficiency and to shore-up the quality of the work, while at the same time maintaining a continued capacity for growth and change, although at a less accelerated pace than in phase II. Sherwood considers this the critical point in the organization's growth and development, upon which its continued success depends. In management terms, the need for consolidation at this point is due to increased costs as the result of a variety of organizational developments. To begin with Sherwood points out that during the initial phases many of the members of a successful organization will work quite hard and there is an inevitable slowing down after a period of time, at least among those who initially have been carried along by the enthusiasm and excitement of the formative phases. If one views the time dimension of phase II over a number of years, in the latter part of the phase the organization would include among its members a higher percentage of senior staff than at the beginning, including many on pensions or who have available other financial privileges that accrue with seniority.

In addition to these management characteristics Sherwood suggests that, with the development of more consolidated administrative structure, the qualities of enthusiasm and flexibility among the staff which were assets during the accelerated growth of phase II become translated into fiscal liabilities. The staff members who functioned best during the transitional phases of program de-

---

* Professor Harry Miller of Hunter College suggests that an organization's need to occupy itself with its "environment" allows for a broader theoretical applicability of these concepts.

velopment and innovation tend to be less productive and efficient when program consolidation is accomplished.

During phase III the role of middle management becomes crucial if there is to be an improvement in competence and maintenance of quality. This may in effect entail a significant recasting of the organizational structures and operations. The delegation of increased decision-making authority to middle level staff and the development of improved methods for program feedback at all levels, while always important, are critical at this point. The personality characteristics which were effective in the formative phases will be most sorely tested around issues of authority and power. The need for individual changes coupled with the need for organizational changes at this phase would contribute to its critical role in the development and growth of the organization. The normal human resistances to individual change and "bureaucratic sclerosis" could be expected to interdigitate at this point.

APPLICATION OF SMALL GROUP DYNAMICS TO THE DYNAMICS OF ORGANIZATIONS

One can recognize the influence of group dynamic theories among the general characteristics which Sherwood has suggested for the three phases of organizational growth. Notable among these are the interrelationship of personality theories and theories of behavior in task-oriented groups. Also, implicit in Sherwood's observations are the leadership styles that each phase would tend to promote, or respond to, about which there is considerable literature in the social psychological field. The inter-relationship of personality and a group's (or family's) "work" has been one of the major contributions to social psychology by Talcott Parsons (17, 18). His formulation of the coterminous need for expressive (or emotional) and instrumental (or task) functions in group behavior has in fact been extensively applied in modern management theory, for example by Blake in the "managerial grid" concept (7).

Kurt Lewin's studies of the influence of different leadership styles upon the productivity of groups (14, 15) is interwoven in management theories in the intervening years since his pioneering work. The influence of psychological theories of personality upon concepts of organizational dynamics is indirectly manifested through the work of Parsons and those who have followed his approach. Another indirect influence of personality theories upon organizational dynamics has come via the work of Bion, whose concept of the "basic assumptions" group mentality (6) is a derivative of Freud's theories of personality. Bion's concepts have been directly applied to organizational dynamics by Jaques (10) and Rice (16, 19-22).

However, to my knowledge there has been no concerted attempt to consider the applicability of the concept of phases of development in small groups to the larger aggregates of individuals in organizations. Although there has been some degree of cross-fertilization between personality, social psychological and sociological theories, as witness the work of Parsons, Bion, Lewin and many others, the concept of developmental processes has not been extrapolated to any major extent from the studies in human development.* For the most part, the concept of a predictable process of interrelated developmental phases remains the province of the biological sciences.

In a larger context, the lack of interest in developmental processes reflects the "cultural lag" that exists before theoretical concepts from the separate disciplines become mutually assimilated. Often this appears to be a philosophic issue, dependent upon whether one sees the human situation in terms of the psychological man, the biological man, the social man, the economic man, or the political man. We tend to orient ourselves this way although we are well aware that no one discipline is adequate in itself. However, we so far have lacked the capacity to form theoretical bridges across disciplines. As Rice has stated it, "The problem is to raise the level of conceptual abstraction: the danger that in so doing we shall not only lose the simplicity and richness of existing descriptive concepts, but lose ourselves in an arid complexity of irrelevant variables" (22). With this caution in mind, I am going to recapitulate the hypothetical model of phases of organizational development. The presentation is a mixture of clinical ob-

---

* There are references in the literature to organizational growth and development, particularly influenced by economists. Rostow's *The Stages of Economic Growth* combines an historical and economic approach.

servations and cross-discipline references which I believe reflect characteristics of phases of organizational development. However, I have not attempted to achieve conceptual clarity. Specifically in the following section, I will add to the hypothetical model that Sherwood has suggested for organizational development the type of observations and concepts that are summarized in Chart I about characteristic phases of development in small therapeutic groups as well as observations from my personal experiences in the development of mental health organizations.

PHASE I—THE MYTH OF THE OMNIPOTENT LEADER

Although during phase I, there are no unique organizational complexities generated by the structure itself, there are important developments which, I believe, are characteristic of the early formative stage of all organizations. I refer to the establishment of a leadership mystique unique to the members of the organization. This has been frequently identified with the individual charismatic qualities of a leader, who is viewed as attracting a following by the power of his appeal as though this is imposed upon a group who submit in a passive manner. Since the mystique of leadership is a central element in my thesis, I would like to review my thinking about this phenomena.

I should first point out that I am making a distinction between the personal, idiosyncratic, social and professional roles of the organization's membership before they become members and their behavior and roles which emerge as the result of the influence of their membership. The mystique of the charismatic leader, in my opinion, is a group-evolved phenomena to which all the members contribute emotionally. This is not to deny that certain proclivities and individual characteristics are required of a leader in order to fulfill the group-allocated charismatic role. However, considering the extraordinary diversity of individuals who have come to be seen in this light by their organizational membership, to which one can bear witness by a random review of a variety of different organizations, the nature of the predisposing individual characteristics are difficult to identify.

What appears to me to be much more significant than the individual differences among leaders is the differences among organizations for the need of a leadership mystique. Although in my opinion it can be observed to some extent in all organizations in the formative stage, the extent of the need and the duration to which the members of organizations are involved in maintaining the mystique appears to be the result of many intra- and extra-organizational factors. For one thing, the need for the mystique would appear to be proportionate to the lack of definition of the organizational goals and the lack of clarity about the competence of the members or the availability of resources to realistically achieve those goals that are defined or are capable of definition. Any new program which has innovative objectives, which by intent are not readily definable, or any established program undergoing a major change in personnel or goals, could be expected to manifest among its members the emotional characteristics of individuals being led by a leader to whom unusual and larger-than-life qualities are ascribed.

The ubiquitous development in early phases of groups, regardless of their size and goals, of a symbolic construct ascribing mythological or idealized qualities to a leader, attests to the importance of the emotional relationships between the members of an organization. This has been stated in another way by Rice about the modern-day enterprise organizations. "To perform a task, activities must be carried out. But however automated their processes, enterprises have to employ human resources for some activities. Such activities seldom use the total capacities of the individuals so employed and individuals can seldom, if ever, give to an enterprise only the capacities it requires. If an enterprise fails to provide outlets for the unused capacities, they are likely to interfere with task performance" (22). Rice goes on, in the article from which this quotation was taken, to suggest that the conjoint application of systems theory, psychoanalytic object relationship theory and Bion's theory of small group behavior may serve as a bridge upon which one may construct new conceptual abstractions. I share with Rice a similar interest in these theoretical approaches, although there are some differences in my understanding of the applicability.

Although Rice is well aware of the importance of organizational changes and discusses temporary and transitional task systems, in which he refers to the concept of "project organizations," he is not very sanguine about efforts to administer organizations undergoing significant change. "In conditions of social and technical change, the attitudes and behavior of members of a group to each other, and to the external environment may not only jeopardize the survival of the task systems but put such strain on internal group relaionships that group survival is also jeopardized" (21). Rice's pessimism is supported by the evidence of the extraordinary disruptive impact of recent social changes in this country upon many institutions. However, the fact that he did not expand his conceptualization of transitional task systems is in part due to the way he interprets the theoretical constructs from which he derives his concepts, or perhaps, more appropriately, the emphasis he places upon aspects of these constructs.

The aspect of the systems concepts he refers to, as well as the object relationship concepts, emphasizes their "boundary maintenance" functions. Rice does not explore their possible application to developmental processes or their application to conflict-resolution. "System conflict does not arise in conditions of stable equilibrium–in other words, where environmental forces are unchanging or do not impinge too differently on the three systems" (21). Similarly, in considering Bion's concepts of the "basic assumption" group formations and the "work group" formation, Rice emphasizes the dichotomy between irrational emotions and rational behavior in the achievement of a group's task. However, Bion was influenced by Freud's personality theories, which were based upon a conflict-resolution model, especially the constructive resolution of conflicting irrational and rational feelings and thoughts. Freud postulated this resolution as a synthetic process necessary for the development of mature ego functions.

I have attempted to demonstrate that the dichotomy between irrational group emotions and group members' rational task-oriented attitudes and behavior is an artificial one by illustrating how the group members' shared symbolic constructs of the role of a leader functions as a unifying and synthetic factor in group development. In a prior publication I presented the following thesis. "The leaders were cast in the image of deified or heroic figures as part of the shared mythology about the nature of the group situation. The implications for the small group of this group-evolved myth may be similar to the function of the cultural myths for society-at-large. Arlow comments about the function of cultural myths that, 'The shared daydream is a step toward group formation. . . . (Myths) are instruments of socialization' (2). Freud speculated that civilized man emerged from privimite (primal horde) group formations through the use of the epic myth. 'We have said that it would be possible to specify the point in the mental development of man at which the advance from group to individual psychology was also achieved by the individual members of the group. He who did this was the first epic poet. . . . He invented the heroic myth. . . . The myth, then, is the step by which the individual emerges from group psychology' (9). It is hypothesized that, apart from what the deified or heroic images projected upon the leaders represents in terms of individual psychology, the process reflects a method by which the members collectively attempt to define the reality of the situation and at the same time to organize and give structure to the group" (11).

In terms of object relationship theory, one may also explain Rice's tendency to dichotomize rational and irrational group emotions by his failure to give adequate attention to the role of "identification relationships." As a summary comment about phase I, I refer to the previously quoted article. "The members' emotional contributions to the shared group mythology and the related ritualistic behavior appear to serve the common task of the group both in the evolving of a social structure and in providing the data from which the members may achieve their work goal. These goals or task-oriented identifications are of a "functional" nature as the result of the interdependency of group members upon one another, and they refer to mechanisms within the ego that have not been extensively considered in this context in analytic theory" (11).

PHASE II—THE MYSTIQUE OF THE PLENIPOTENTIARY ADMINISTRATOR

I have attempted to make a case for the similarity of the symbolic role of the leader in small groups and in larger organizations in the early formative phase. I am now confronted with the critical question of whether a similarity exists in subsequent phases of development between small groups and larger organizations to which predictable characteristics can be ascribed. It is important to first take note of obvious differences that exist between organizations and the type of small groups from which I had derived my observations, that is, small therapy groups of patients, larger groups formations of patients in "therapeutic communities" and work with students in small human relations or sensitivity (T) groups.

One of the most obvious and important differences pertains to the reality of power and the exercise of authority in the relationship between organizational members. The "theme of power" was prominent in the development of all the small groups with which I have had experience in a phase which would correspond to hypothetical phase II in organizations. I believe there may be a useful correlation to make between the preoccupation with power by patients and students in small groups and the group emotions evoked by the competition and "the body politic" which Sherwood suggests characterizes organizational life in phase II. It would however be unfortunate to give the impression that, whatever similarities that might exist in phantasy among the membership in these various group configurations, that the exercise of authority over the livelihood and careers of staff members is to be equated with the role of authority of therapists and teachers in relationship to patients and students.

Other similarities between a hypothetical phase II in organizational development and the structural, thematic and symbolic constructs that I have listed in Chart I, under phase II, subphase B, are the emergence of the influence of psychological subgroup formations. It is my impression that subgroups among staff members have an increasing and significant influence upon the organizational development during this phase. The organizational subgroups will exist prior to this time, just as the subgroups have been observable from the outset in small groups with which I have worked. However, as in the instance of small groups, I refer here to their emergence into the consciousness of the membership and to the overt influence of the subgroups upon the attitudes and behavior of the membership.

During phase II there will be an increased structure emerging with the formation of service subdivisions and special programs, although the various subdivisions will develop unequally. The emergent role specificity and the differential in status will encourage the reemergence of normal competitive reactions. The members' identification with the organization-as-a-whole will have diminished as they become more closely identified with their own subdivision or team. The competitive spirit is also stimulated by the rivalry between subdivisions as they each tend to see the contributions of their particular program or service to be the most highly valued in the organization, as well as consisting of the most superior members. When all is going well this competition spurs the subdivisions to greater efforts and the competitive energies are more or less channeled into the competitive power struggles with outside organizations for recognition.

Nevertheless, the competitive atmosphere is contagious and also may be fostered by the inevitable unequal development of the subdivisions and the inevitable unequal rewards of the members within the subdivisions, especially during the accelerated period of growth when the organization's administrative capacities cannot keep pace with the developments. It is, therefore, during phase II that the emergence of internal competitive struggles can be anticipated with the usual rivalries and petty differences.* The members' reactions will tend to be magnified out of proportion to the issues over which the differences arise because of the overvaluation of the organizational goals that had taken on mythological qualities in the early phase, and because of the exaggerated powers and prestige ascribed to the organization and the idealized leaders during the second phase.

The subgroups which emerge during phase II may or may not correspond with the formal service subdivisions or program components. When the psychological subgroups diverge from the formal structures of the organization, they tend to increase the divisiveness among the membership and assume the characteristics

---

* Freud's observations about the "narcissism of petty differences," which he noted was most marked among individuals who have a close relationship to one another, suggests a theoretical basis for these events to which Roman and I have referred as "group narcissism" in an unpublished manuscript. I hope to be able to clarify these observations and concepts in the future.

of coalitions organized around their own informal leaders.* Since this corresponds with the accelerated growth of the organization when its administrative capacities are strained and membership competition is rife, there is also increased pressure upon the formal leadership. If realistic external power conflicts simultaneously converge upon the organization, either because of bureaucratic, political or other reasons, this is the time when changes in leadership are most likely to occur. Nevertheless, if one keeps in mind that the realistic internal and external events can and often do determine organizational developments, regardless of the influence of group emotions, the symbolic aspects of these emotions are a useful consideration. Besides providing some understanding of the extraordinary impact of group emotions upon individuals, which

---

* The word "coalition" is used to infer that the subgroup members share an emotional bond on the basis of their common identification of a perceived difference from the organizational membership-as-a-whole, which may be of a minor nature. Regardless of the real differences and the rational basis upon which the subgroup members identify with one another, the use of the hypothetical concept of the "psychological coalition" in this context is meant to infer that it is a "group evolved" emotional power alliance with its own subgroup leadership. The symbolic construct of the role of the subgroup leader, however, will be identical with the prevailing symbolic construct of this phase of the organization-as-a-whole, i.e., the idealization of heroic qualities based upon a mystique of leadership. In this sense, therefore, a considerable degree of group emotionality may emerge around critical realistic issues and reorganization may occur around divided opinions over these issues, but in terms of the phase of organizational development the changes may be of a regressive or status-quo nature. The eventual developmental outcome of these changes will depend upon the reality of the issues and the appropriateness of the changes made in terms of the many complex social, political and economic factors that also determine the viability of an organization. The contribution to organizational planning that would be entailed in the hypothetical phases of development is that there would be a greater likelihood of group-evolved influences playing a role in the pressure for change in the latter part of phase II than at other times in the organizational life. The anthropomorphic term "group narcissism," to which I previously referred, might be a way of characterizing a normal human need among organizational membership to preserve their prevailing group emotional bonds, which evolve from their shared experiences and which become ritualized around a shared symbolic construct of a leadership model. In the psychological sense, members may leave the organization and leaders may change, but the members' internalized percept of the configuration of the organization-as-a-whole and the symbolic construct of the role of the leader is preserved.

Bion has referred to as "psychotic anxiety," successful planning may require consideration of these influences.

As indicated in the heading of this discussion of phase II, I have referred to the symbolic role of the leader as an "administrator," whom I suggest the membership at this phase perceives as a plenipotentiary figure. The change from an "omnipotent leader" to a "plenipotentiary administrator" is meant to indicate that in a successful organization although the membership continues to have a need to weave a symbolic construct about the leadership role, with associated ritualistic behavior, that a progression in collective group emotions has taken place. (For a socioeconomic approach to this transition, see the reference to Myerhoff, who uses Weber's concept of the "routinization of charisma.") The emergence of "the plenipotentiary administrator" as the symbolic construct of the leadership role is seen to occur in organizations during phase II when, although successful in its endeavors as evidenced by its accelerated growth, administrative conflicts as a result of its rapid growth are very much in evidence.

The use of the term "administrator," rather than director for example, corresponds with my experience and apparently reflects the realistic recognition of the inevitable administrative problems that occur during rapid organizational change, as well as reflecting the ambivalence of the membership toward efforts to deal with these problems. The "administrator" is the traditional bete noire of the professional and has provided a ready-made symbol by which professionals can discharge their responsibility for facing and undertaking the organizational changes which modern-day social demands require. The irrationality is indicated not only by the plenipotentiary powers which are ascribed to the "administrator" but by an almost ubiquitous application to staff whether they have administrative responsibilities or not. My own failure to appreciate this phase in the development of the programs with which I have been associated was the result of many factors, not the least of which was my former concurrence with the professionals' traditional negative attitude toward administrative functions. The existence of realistic administrative problems and the conjoint development of formal structural changes tends to obscure the informal emotional subgroupings and the symbolic aspect of the leadership role.

However, it bears repeating that when there is a convergence of emotional subgroup coalitions with realistic power factions, the usefulness of explanations of human behavior from one frame of reference has a limited value, since it fails to include other considerations which may be of greater significance. The issue of power and the exercise of authority in organizations are among the notable areas of human behavior in which the application of social psychological explanations should be used with deference to the importance of sociocultural, economic and political factors. Nevertheless, with these reservations in mind, it is suggested that the subgroup formations and the idealization process adumbrated above may represent a characteristic property of the structural and perceptual reactions of the membership during phase II of an organization's development.

PHASE III—THE ILLUSION OF THE SELFLESS HEALER

During phase III an organization is seen as having to achieve a balance between the need for efficient administrative management and the need for individualized personal services. It represents an ideal which organizations hope to approximate but seldom, if ever, are able to achieve. The use of the symbolic construct of "the selfless healer" as the conjoint model for the roles of the leader *and* membership is meant to indicate that there are unattainable collective values which continue in any human organization, no matter how invested in their task and how efficient and "productive" the organizational membership. These collective values have a function similar to the myth and the idealization process in the earlier phases, although with less regressive implications. To state it another way, man always depends on illusions to define as well as to mold his reality.

"The selfless healer" as a role model is meant as a specific reference for the membership of a health or mental health care organization. It is being used as an overdetermined symbolic construct which simultaneously represents the realistic pride of the membership in their individual contributions to the work of the organization; the ideology of the organization toward which it must continuously strive in an everchanging environment; as well as the achievement of realistic goals based upon the competence of the membership and the soundness of the organizational structure, which the members have evolved through a difficult process of

CHART

CHARACTERISTIC PHASES OF DEVELOPMENT

Phase I	Organizational Structure	Organizational Relationship to Superordinate Bodies
The Beginning	The organization is loosely structured. The members identify with the organization-as-a-whole on the basis of a shared mythology about its goals and purposes.	Official sanction of the sponsoring bodies.
Phase II		
Accelerated Expansion	The subdivisions are unequally more or less well structured but loosely integrated. The members identify with their subdivisions on the basis of its superiority over the other subdivisions.	Competition with other organizations for recognition of its superiority by the superordinate bodies, including support by "the body politic."
Phase III		
Consolidation and Efficiency	The organization is integrated through a balance between centralized administrative and decentralized operational functions. The members identify with one another on the basis of their pride in their collective achievements.	The organization becomes established on the basis of consumer support and use of its services.
Phase I	Expressive (Emotional) Roles of the Organization	Instrumental (Task)Roles of the Organization
The Beginning	Dedication to the organizational goals. (Optimism)	Initiation of programs and hard work.
Phase II		
Accelerated Expansion	Dedication to the collective goals of the subdivisions and the organization-as-a-whole. (Cooperation)	Expansion of programs and extraorganizational promotion of the organization.
Phase III		
Consolidation and Efficiency	—Intraorganizational and interorganizational— cooperation and collaboration.	

growth. This hypothesis about psychosocial maturation of the membership of an organization is similar to the third phase in the developmental process in the small therapeutic groups, although it is focused upon the organization's "productivity" rather than the individual's personal development.

III

IN A MENTAL HEALTH ORGANIZATION

Membership Relationship to the Organization	Interorganizational Conflicts Over Power	Intraorganizational Conflicts Over Power and/or Status
Commitment to organizational goals and optimistic belief in its achievement. (Hope)	The power of the mandating authorities versus the autonomy of the organization.	Extraorganizational status versus emergent status in the organization.
Conviction of the organization's superior achievements and its imminent success. (Enthusiasm)	The power of the organization to obtain scarce resources in competition with similar organizations versus the need for interorganizational collaboration.	Competition with colleagues for personal power and/or status versus the developmental needs of the member's subdivision.
Confidence in one's contribution to the overall organizational goals and services. (Competence and productivity)	—Personal and organizational needs and goals versus societal needs and goals.	

Symbolic Role of Formal (or Informal) Organizational Leader(s)	Individualized Expression of Organizational Conflict	
	Psychological	Role Identity/Diffusion
Omnipotent leader(s). (Mythology)	Dependence versus independence.	Preorganizational role versus emergent organizational role.
Plenipotentiary administrator(s) and/or member(s) (Idealization)	Personal gain versus friendship and loyalty.	Specialized role versus "team" role.
Selfless healer(s). (Ideology)	Personal interest versus social consciouness.	Established organizational role versus reorganizational role.

I have summarized in Chart III a number of the organizational and membership characteristics that I have been discussing which correspond to each of the three hypothetical phases. This chart bears some similarity in its format to Chart I but it is less cohesive and does not reflect the extent of clinical observation upon which the therapy group chart was based. Chart III is rather a summary statement of the points of view discussed, although some attempt has been made to correlate them systematically.

In Chart III I have listed various organizational situations that potentially are conflict-generating for the membership. Under the category of organizational structure I have attempted to combine the hypotheses about the structural characteristics of the phase with the nature of the emotional bond upon which the members identify with one another during that phase. The differences between the small therapy groups and organizations become more apparent during the second and third phase as the structural changes increasingly reflect realistic administrative and management requirements for role specificity and organizational efficiency. There are corresponding differences in the nature of the emotional bond.

The constructive resolution of conflict among members will depend upon such factors as the clarity of their task objectives, their competence to perform these objectives and the soundness of the organizational structure. Unfortunately, at this point in time, the existing health and mental health organizations are confronted with inherent dilemmas that complicate these factors. Among these dilemmas are the contradiction between the need for organizational control over staff and the staff's need for sufficient autonomy of function so that, as providers of services, they can invest their efforts with the degree of personal pride and concern for the individual patient that are so necessary for adequate health and mental health treatment. It is not realistic to expect that a staff member will maintain this personal concern for patients in his work after a period of time, no matter how well motivated, if the organization in which he works relates to him to an impersonal way, while at the same time imposing significant restraints on his freedom to exercise independent judgment.

We have suggested that in phase III an organization can achieve effective integration through a balance between centralized administrative and decentralized operational functions and that this will result in the members identifying with one another on the basis of their shared pride in their collective achievements. Unfortunately what we cannot suggest are the detailed means by which this balance between centralization and decentralization can be implemented. The usual guidelines of modern day management by which this would be attempted do not apply to the health and mental health care organizations. The distinction between "line" and "staff" functions upon which a table of organization is based, from which one draws the schema for centralized and decentralized structures, are not so readily distinguished in health care organizations. This is just one aspect of the problems of administrative organization that have to be resolved before sophisticated management plans can be formulated.

In addition to the speculations about the organizational structure, I have listed on Chart III hypotheses concerning specific conflicts in each phase that originate from the organization's relationship to superordinate bodies; external and internal organizational conflicts over power and/or status; as well as individualized expressions of organizational conflicts in terms of interpersonal and role identity reactions. The chart also contains categories based upon Parson's concepts of expressive and instrumental roles as they may relate to each of the hypothetical phases. In future work, I hope to present a more sophisticated assessment of these categories and their comparison to prior studies of developmental processes and the nature of object relationships in small groups.

SOME CONCLUDING OBSERVATIONS

Although I have not attempted in this presentation of hypothetical phases of organizational development to reach any conclusions about its applicability for the planning and administration of mental health organizations, it is my hope that future studies of these concepts will lead to practical contributions. This has proved to be the case in the study of phases of development of small groups, at least to the extent that it has added to the attention of the importance of group emotions as seen from the vantage point of the group-as-a-whole. The importance of group processes is particularly evident in groups conducted in hospital or institutional settings which in part accounts for my interest in this area. Such critical therapeutic reactions as that which we refer to as an "institutional transference" cannot be fully appreciated without consideration of the individual's identification with the group-as-a-whole. In hospitals and clinics in which staff and patient turnover is frequent, the group's collective response to the introduction of new members or therapists and the loss of members or therapists evokes characteristic group reactions which, unless identified as a group emotion, may be confused with the personal and idiosyncratic meaning to the individual patients (12).

In addition, as I have indicated above, it has been my experience that there are identifiable collective group concerns with which all therapy group members must contend and that these occur in a more or less characteristic sequence of phases as a group develops. I refer to issues of trust when dependency concerns are preeminent, to issues of security when concerns about power and control emerge and to issues of self-interest when group members become preoccupied with intimacy. The awareness of these phase specific group concerns are necessary in order to distinguish or at least to explore the differences between group-evolved conflicts and personal idiosyncratic reactions. I agree with Anthony's observations that for many patients the analysis of their reaction to group-evolved concerns may serve as the primary group therapeutic work (1).

The application of the concept of phases of development in organizations to the planning and administration of mental health organizations involves, of course, different skills and parameters than that which applies to a therapeutic group. In the therapy group the knowledge of the influence of phases of group development alerts us to the psychosocial determinants of behavior in order to increase our understanding of the individual idiosyncratic determinants in a patient's adaptation. In an organization the knowledge of the influence of phases of development, if they do exist, would serve to distinguish individual idiosyncratic reactions from organizational developments, which may or may not accrue to the benefit of the specific individuals in the organization. Besides this sharp difference in goals compared to therapy groups, the ability to apply knowledge of the phases of organizational development has many constraints, including those of conflicting mandates imposed by the usual multiple authority structure. What might be considered a therapeutic intervention in a therapy group would be manipulation of personnel in an organization that infringes upon labor-management contracts or the individual's civil liberties. The power of the leader of an organization has many prerogatives but it also imposes many responsibilities upon the exercise of that power.

With all these limitations and constraints not withstanding, I would like to conclude by considering future directions to which the study and understanding of phases of organizational development may lead.

a) It has been recognized in the past that organizations require different leadership styles at different periods of time. If the hypotheses of predictable phases of development proves to have validity, planning for changes in leadership as well as the membership could be done without reflecting adversely upon the individuals. The use of "project management" concepts, as Bennis has recommended (3, 4, 23) or the transitional task organizations to which Rice refers (22), would gain additional support and allow us to begin to consider a more appropriate deployment of manpower.

b) Besides changes in management planning, another influence of the concept of characteristic phases of development in organizations would be in the change in organizational focus. Directors of organizations would not emphasize loyalty to the organization as much as commitment to projects or goals and the membership in turn would have less recourse to externalize blame upon "administration."

Above all, there would be the recognition that organizations can be expected, if successful, to change over time just as one would hope to see a maturing process among the individuals who compose the organizations. This entails a fundamental reorientation of our attitudes about the nature of institutional and social change which should enable us to develop a more sophisticated and realistic approach to organizations, which are a major source of human endeavor and occupation.

REFERENCES

1. Anthony, E. J.: Generic elements in dyadic and group psychotherapy. *Int J Grp Psycho, 17:*57, 1967.
2. Arlow, J. S.: Ego psychology and the study of mythology. *J Am Psana, 9:*371, 1961.
3. Bennis, W.: Beyond bureaucracy. *Trans-Action, 2:*31, 1965.
4. Bennis, W. G., Benne, K. D., and Chin, R.: *The Planning of Change.* New York, Holt, Rinehard & Winston, 1961.
5. Bennis, W., and Shepard, H.: A theory of group development. *Human Relations, 9:*415, 1956.
6. Bion, W. R.: *Experiences in Groups.* New York, Basic Books, 1961.
7. Blake, R. R., and Mouton, J. S.: *The Managerial Grid.* Houston, Gulf Publishing Company, 1964.
8. Bradford, L. P., Gibb, J. R., and Benne, K. D.: *T-Group Theory and Laboratory Method.* New York, John Wiley and Sons, 1964.
9. Freud, S.: *Group Psychology and the Analysis of the Ego.* Standard Edition, Vol. 18. London, Hogarth Press, 1955.
10. Jaques, E., and Brown, W.: *Glacier Project Papers.* London, William Heinemann Ltd., 1965.
11. Kaplan, S. R.: Therapy groups and training groups: similarities and differences. *Int J Grp Psycho, 17:*473, 1967.
12. Kaplan, S. R., and Roman, M.: Characteristic responses in adult therapy groups to the introduction of new members: a reflection on group process. *Int J Grp Psycho, 11:*372, 1961.
13. Kaplan, S. R., and Roman, M.: Phases of development in an adult therapy group. *Int J Grp Psycho, 13:*10, 1963.
14. Lewin, K.: *Field Theory in Social Science.* New York, Harper & Row, 1951.
15. Lewin, K., Lippitt, R., and White, R. K.: Patterns of aggressive behavior in experimentally created "social climates." *J Soc Psychol, 10:*271, 1939.
16. Miller, E. J., and Rice, A. K.: *Systems of Organization.* London, Tavistock, 1967.
17. Parsons, T.: *The Social System.* Glencoe, Ill., Free Press, 1951.
18. Parsons, T.: *Structure and Process in Modern Societies.* Glencoe, Ill., Free Press, 1963.
19. Rice, A. K.: *Productivity and Social Organization.* London, Tavistock, 1958.

20. Rice, A. K.: *Enterprise and Its Environment.* London, Tavistock, 1963.
21. Rice, A. K.: *Learning for Leadership.* London, Tavistock, 1965.
22. Rice, A. K.: Individual, group and intergroup process. *Human Relations, 22:*565, 1969.
23. Schein, E. H., and Bennis, W. G.: *Personal and Organizational Change Through Group Methods. The Laboratory Approach.* New York, J. Wiley & Sons, 1965.
24. Stock, D., and Thelen, H. A.: *Emotional Dynamics and Group Culture.* New York, University Press, 1958.
25. Winn, A.: Social change in industry: from insight to implementation. *J Appl Behav Sci, 2:*170, 1966.

CHAPTER XVI

SOME USES OF GROUP PROCESSES IN SCHOOL SETTINGS

Rachel M. Lauer

In this paper that reviews the emerging trends towards the more extensive employment of group process methods in one of the largest school systems in the nation, Dr. Rachel Lauer does more than review this development. Among the several issues she deals with is the entire question of the role of the psychologist in the schools. Primary among the roles that has been conceptualized is that of diagnostician and the utility of this role is challenged by her. Although this is one of the more traditional parameters of the school psychologists' and other mental health professions' functioning as well, its proximity to the whole issue of the medical diagnostic model and its relevance in the entire field of mental health is at issue. Rachel Lauer juxtaposes a newer approach and makes an excellent case for not only its pragmatic utility but for its theoretical soundness as well. As a viable alternative to the more traditional approaches, her description of its application is certainly attractive and exciting.

One can also see in her emerging vista a certain consanguinity to the newer conceptions of community mental health. In this model one attempt is to change the community in a positive fashion to make it more constructive for the individuals involved. It is a striving to make social structure work for change within the individual and then the individuals' change contributes to positive growth within that social system. In the myriad group projects that have been initiated under her auspices, she describes this inexorable cycle toward corrective change rather than destructive rigidity. The structures that she works with seem to be the relevant ones necessary to implement an extensive revision in the school community. The projects encompass the use of groups for staff development, administrative reorganization, child-teacher interaction, child-peer improvement, child-parent relations, and even the extension to the outside community. The potential for human growth within these more mobile and improving social situations is indeed impressive. The fact that this milieu therapy is at its beginning and the beginnings are so promising is also exhilarating.

D.S.M.
G.D.G.

GROUP METHODS USED BY PSYCHOLOGISTS
IN THE NEW YORK CITY SCHOOLS

IN THE YEAR 1969-70, Bureau of Child Guidance psychologists reported holding over 2,000 group sessions with 2,600 children and parents. Although this year's statistics are not yet in, I predict a large increase for 1971. Staff motivation for working with groups has paralleled their increased opportunity for training. The Human Potential Movement with its concentration of training facilities in New York City has inspired many of us to participate in intensive group experiences for the first time, and some of us have gone on to get training as group leaders. The Bureau of Child Guidance, itself, provides on-going, regularly scheduled programs for training staff to work with groups in both traditional as well as the newer modalities.

Despite training in new methods, our most common type of group at this stage of history is still the traditional activity group, consisting of a small group of children, each child referred for help with a behavioral or learning difficulty, led by a psychologist or social worker whose orientation is eclectic with Freudian or Rogerian emphasis. Typical groups gather weekly or semi-weekly in any bit of private space that school administrators can squeeze out. The children play, snack, and talk about the incidents that occur among them. The therapists try to help the children articulate their feelings and focus their energies.

Many other types of groups are beginning to appear more frequently in our repetroire. Behavior modification and reality therapy are gaining adherents. Some psychologists now conduct encounter groups and here-and-now sensitivity training sessions with high school students, faculty-parent groups and with their own colleagues. Others are becoming more expert in helping whole classes of children focus upon human relations issues. To generalize, I would say that the use of group methods by psychologists in the New York City schools is expanding rapidly, but by no means has it reached its peak. Our basic unit of work is still the individual child. In group work, we are in the stage of self-training and experimentation, although perhaps 10 percent of our staff could very well lay claim to expertise.

Some Examples of Group Work

P.A.G.E.S., or Programs to Accelerate Growth in Education and Self; Queens Center of the Bureau of Child Guidance

Under the skilled and wise leadership of Mr. Wallace Rose, the Queens psychologists, plus several social workers, have organized themselves into five separate but coordinated units each of which is an evolving center-based program providing services both within the center and within the schools:

*P*sychological Intervention Unit
*A*pplied Behavior Modification Unit
*G*roup Dynamics and Sensitivity Training Unit
*E*ducational Remediation Unit
*S*upplemental Diagnostic Services Unit

These units, which meet weekly to plan and evaluate their programs, are involved in a variety of innovative activities. In one district, for example, a program for disruptive children was started in which the district team shared with teachers and administrators ways in which behavior modification methods could be employed in the regular classrooms.

A "Guidance-discipline" program for a junior high school consists of a series of workshops for teachers in the application of Behavior Modification to classroom management. These workshops coordinate the efforts of the teachers, behavior counselor, guidance counselors and administration in providing a specific sequence of steps for approaching behavior problems. An aspect of the program includes the use of a "Time-out" room in which the student who must be temporarily excluded from class can continue in his work and study.

Another project helps children who are highly anxious about taking tests. It offers a series of relaxation exercises combined with desensitization techniques.

The very active group dynamics unit sponsors programs for children, school staff, and people in the community. One of the most popular has been an experiential in-service course offered each semester. Groups meet weekly for six weeks (3½ hours) plus a full day on Saturday at a local motel. Another is a human relations training course with Board of Education credit, designed around ethnic and cultural themes. This is held over a weekend at an out-of-town retreat plus follow-up sessions at the center.

The group dynamics unit trys to insure that its medium is the message; i.e. those persons selected for attendance at the weekend course represent an utterly heterogeneous mixture of professionals, youngsters and community people of different racial and ethnic background. Brought together for a weekend on a "cultural island," they are enabled to do much more than talk about human relations. They interact with each other around various structured themes or tasks and then share their very personal feelings about each other. Feedback from these programs has been highly positive to say the least.

At Van Buren High School, an actively concerned student body requested the unit to provide training for students and staff together to enable them to relate more effectively to each other as well as to others and to provide the abilities needed to man a crisis room where students with problems, drug or otherwise, could seek help. Over ninety students and teachers are involved in this training activity.

In one elementary school a group of sixth grade students with behavior problems were selected to work with kindergarten children. Sensitivity training sessions were held with students and teachers together to gain commitment to responsibilities and to explore problems as they arose. Improvement in the behavior of the sixth graders was noted.

Many other such programs have sparked the work-year at Queens; orientation of Head Start staff, parent and teacher workshops, a two day group interaction program to help two junior high school classes of gifted children to break down existing interpersonal communication barriers and to facilitate more creative interaction within the classroom, etc. Most recently the group dynamics unit staff is planning an in-service course for teachers who are employing humanistic approaches in the classroom emphasizing affective education. Further information about the many activities of P.A.G.E.S. can be obtained from Mr. Rose at the Queens Bureau of Child Guidance.

C.L.I.C., or Center for Learning Improvement in Children; Bronx Center of the Bureau of Child Guidance

A small group of dedicated psychologists with the remarkable leadership and determination of Dr. Libero Arcieri has created a program of activities and services for young children with learning difficulties. These activities are carried out in one large room of our Bronx center and also in various classes in the schools. With the help of a social worker and a psychiatric consultant these psychologists have conducted small group activities with such titles as developmental learning program, perceptual training, motor-percept-concept program, Piaget's concepts applied, skill training for retardates, etc.

What is unusual about this psycho-educational program is the extent to which group dynamics have been used first to plow through the administrative maze to get things going; second, to become a cohesive working unit themselves despite multiple pulls upon each worker; and third, to involve other relevant persons such as parents, teachers, and local university students. Teachers now come to the center after school hours with their children and work together with the parents right in the classroom. Dr. Lilyan Ruderman from Lehman College has been collaborating and providing students from her special education program. Sometimes the atmosphere has the morale elements of a good community block party; parents speak with emotion about how much they have learned and how their feelings about themselves and their children have changed.

The psychologists have greatly enjoyed both direct work with the children as well as teaching and counseling. Some have enhanced their motivation for and skills in conducting research. Others are mastering the newer technical tools and equipment for educational remediation and diagnosis. Unlike the average psychologist who often quails under the lonely burden of endless individual casework, these psychologists feel gratified as well as effective. To me, C.L.I.C., like P.A.G.E.S., is an example of group process which includes and affects the therapists as well as the clients. As such, it is doubly valuable.

Training for Group Work

Because of the insistent demands upon our overextended staff for service to an infinite supply of individual cases, our administration has had to work especially hard to create and protect the time for training programs. By no means is enough being done yet in my opinion, but with the impetus of staff motivation we are learning how to be flexible in finding and using training resources. Staff has also done a great deal with its own time and money.

Supervision for Group Leaders

For years now, Dr. Leslie Rosenthal has conducted a weekly seminar throughout the year for staff leaders of groups and another for supervisors. His seminars are partly experiential and partly didactic. A worker may attend this seminar for as long as two years before he relegates his place to someone else starting a group. All three disciplines are eligible.

In the last two years, the Bureau has launched a more extensive and formal training program in group therapy. A multidisciplinary committee representing staff from each of our eight local offices, presently led by Dr. David Hays, psychiatrist, and Mr. Harvey Goodman, social worker, and responsible to the Chiefs of each discipline, meets regularly to plan and evaluate what is now a three-year training program. All candidates for the training program are first screened and then required to progress through several stages: attendance at a weekly lecture series, participation as a member of a group, direct supervision as a leader of one or more groups, and finally, experience in training others in group process. Thus far, about forty persons are involved. Predictably, the number of group sessions held and children served has jumped dramatically.

Even those psychologists who are not in any special training program are all assigned to supervisors who routinely oversee all aspects of their clinical work. Supervisors are encouraged to share their special skills; they often form small groups of mixed staff to study particular topics or methods.

Psychologist-in-Training Program

Each year, the psychology department hires about twenty M.A. level students and provides a closely supervised, full-time internship. One day per week all year long, these trainees meet with me to study various aspects of group process. Our major source of knowledge comes from the interactions among ourselves as we organize for tasks ranging in complexity from ordering coffee to evaluating the total program. Trainees are taught how to be participant-observers, and they regularly give each other feedback on cooperative decision-making skills, communication patterns, leadership styles, conflict resolution techniques, patterns of influence, methods of attaining cohesion, creation and maintenance of discipline through group norms, etc. Whenever possible, through discussion or role-play, we apply whatever we learn about our own group functioning to the dynamics of classroom group management. Despite our concentration on this subject, I believe our seminars are only introductory; trainees feel they need much more experience in order to become adequate consultants to teachers whose classes are in difficulty.

The trainees say that they get the most out of the afternoons we spend "T-grouping." I divide them into two groups and alternately provide leadership for each group. For the past two years, the trainees split themselves evenly into one sub-group which wants to be involved in an intensive experience and one sub-group which wants to experiment with a variety of specialized techniques; e.g. music therapy, poetry therapy, psycho-drama, family therapy, etc. We manage to build ourselves a program to meet most of the needs.

Over and above the valuable insights and skills accruing from participating in the T-groups, I believe is the even more valuable sense of cohesion and camaraderie that develops among them. Some remain friends many years afterwards. Others try to recreate the good feelings of the training year by contributing to cooperative efforts of new colleagues at their assigned centers. Some become very deeply convinced of the importance of "belongingness" and cohesion as an antidote to alienation and lethargy; these psychologists tend to concentrate later upon helping teachers make their classrooms more communicative and warm.

One of my goals in working with the trainees each Thursday is to evoke and reinforce in them the desire for continued learning and planning. When they finish the year, they are aware of a great many resources, and they know how to go after them. Experienced in taking risks and secure in their relationship with me as an authority in a hierarchical structure, they often become the kind of staff psychologists who enjoy innovation. Often, they are the ones who demand more staff development programs, who try out new projects in the schools and who stir things up in general.

During the rest of the week, the trainees work in the schools under close supervision. Dr. Gertrude Bondel Ashur's trainees each adopt a class. With teacher cooperation, they conduct human relations discussions with the children. This last year, her group of five also undertook (and survived) a project to help a teacher with a highly chaotic class. The school principal just wrote a letter of appreciation. Dr. Claire Thompson's trainees are all located in one 600 school, a school in which every child has been assigned because of inability to adjust socially in a regular school. By living in that school four days per week, the trainees become thoroughly acquainted with every class and teacher; they learn about the importance to disturbed children of order, structure, and reliability in the whole system. And above all, they learn how to contribute towards creating a more accepting mental health atmosphere.

Application of Group Process to the Handling of Individual Referrals

As was said earlier, the psychologist's major entrée to the school system is still the individual "problem child" as referred by the teacher or guidance counselor. Rarely does anyone hand him a request to do a teacher workshop, a classroom diagnosis, or a parent education series. Yet, I believe that no individual case can be helped unless the psychologist understands and capitalizes upon the fact that each child is a product of group process, has an impact upon group process, and can be helped by group process (2).

During this last year, I started a small campaign against a stereotyped routine that unfortunately still exists in the practice of some psychologists. A few still do go through the following operations after accepting a referral: remove the child from the classroom to an "office," put him through a battery of tests, write a report recommending what the "school" could do to help the child, and talk with the mother and teacher to explain the findings. I have found that this routine usually consumes about eight hours of school time. All too often, however, neither the school nor the child does much changing. Unless the child is completely removed from his class and placed elsewhere (an enormous change indeed) a psychologist's recommendations have more chance of remaining on paper than of being implemented.

Based upon the assumption that the psychologist himself, being peripheral to the child's class, family and peer group, can do very little *directly,* I have arrived at the following proposition: Psychologists should spend most of their eight-hours-per-child working directly with the natural groups who are central to his well-being. The people who are most affected by a child's problems are usually the ones who, because they care the most, are the most willing and able to bring about changes. Therefore, I recommend that the psychologist spend an hour or two with the child's entire family, his whole class, his special group of friends, and with any other group which cares about him—the child himself being present, of course. During these hours, the psychologist conceives of his role not of doctor, expert, or professor, but of catalytic agent. He intervenes into each small system in such a way as to help participants become more aware of what is going on among them and to give thought to what each might do to improve things. Thus, the people who care the most do the "diagnosing" and come up with the "treatment" plan. Diagnosis becomes the plan of action itself, not a separate operation (1). Frequently, the acts of diagnosing and planning action become the treatment itself; i.e. the process of looking more carefully at each other, of considering how to make things better for each other, results in greater feelings of warmth, acceptance, and competence. Furthermore, every time a small group is successful in making itself and its membership happier or more competent, positive forces are set into action; group norms may be established which could provide support for those persons who ordinarily would not be referred for help.

Sometimes a child may have no group which is willing or able to help him. I remember such a child. Isolated in a rigidly quiet classroom, isolated as an only child in a home with an alcoholic mother and an absent father, too lonely and frightened to reach out to other children, she sat in the back seat of her class quietly masturbating. Because this child had no group, I brought together in one room every adult in the school who could contact her; her teacher, principal, school nurse, art, gym and music teachers, and librarian. Functioning as a group leader, I helped them first experience their empathy for the child and then to formulate a plan of action. They had no difficulty imagining the pain of loneliness nor the comfort of self-love. Their plan of action was simple. Each person committed himself to make a special effort every day, in the course of ordinary path-crossing, to say something, anything, directly to this child; "Good morning, my, what a pretty dress, would you rather have soup or an apple today, would you like to choose the game, I see you have a new school bag," etc. At first, the child's response was only silence, then surprise, then a word or two of reply, then a smile. All of these responses were experienced as gratifying to the cooperating adults. They began to respond with some genuine, unplanned warmth which in turn really lightened this child's spirits. Of course some of the other children took note of this child who was evoking pleasant attention; they, too reached out a little, if only experimentally. Predictably, the child was able to respond in kind, and she found herself a friend. Within a week, the symptom of masturbating had disappeared and within a month the child was again functioning within the normal range. As a psychologist, I had spent exactly forty-five minutes on this case. Sometime later, I made an opportunity to see the mother on other business. Two hours with her provided just enough leverage to evoke a commitment that she would find herself a supportive group, the local chapter of Alcoholic Anonymous.

There is nothing about having a group dynamics orientation that completely rules out the necessity for gathering data. At times, it is highly useful to know an I.Q., a perceptual deficiency, the meaning of some symbolic behavior, etc. Some of this necessary data, the psychologist has to collect for himself with his specialized tools, but it is surprising how often a skillful psychologist can involve others in collecting the data as it becomes relevant to their desire for insight and planning.

In order to do "diagnosis and treatment" of the case referral by the group dynamics method, the psychologist needs to orient his role to that of helping others to help themselves. I think that the operations involved in getting small groups of people to solve problems together, constructively and humanistically, can tax to the utmost the psychologist's every capacity as a human being and as a specialist with exceptional awareness of modes of human relatedness. But I am convinced that the rewards are greater in terms of professional effectiveness and personal satisfaction.

Incidentally, one of the effects of working effectively with natural groupings of children, teachers, parents, etc. can be that as they enjoy the process and feel their own cohesion and competence, they begin to look around for the resources open to them. Finding too few resources outside of themselves, they can become inspired to collaborate with other groups to get more resources. Thus, ripples have been started affecting the larger community, and the school psychologist has found himself new allies in his struggles to bring about better mental health in the schools.

The above proposal for working group style with individual cases is already being used to some degree by a few psychologists. But I would like for more of them to have the training that would enable them to function in this way more often and more effectively.

In conclusion, then, I would say that the use of group processes by New York City school psychologists is growing rapidly. Eventually, I visualize that nearly all of our work will consist of working with groups in one way or another in order to bring about a better learning and living atmosphere.

REFERENCES

1. Cameron, D. E.: A theory of diagnosis. In Hoch, P. and Zubin, J. (Eds.): *Current Problems in Psychiatric Diagnosis*. New York, Grune & Stratton, 1953.
2. Lauer, R. M.: Roles of school psychologists: an epistemological approach. In Gottsegen, M. and Gottsegen, G. (Eds.): *Professional School Psychology*, Vol. III, New York, Grune & Stratton, 1969.

CHAPTER XVII

GROUP PROCESS IN INDUSTRY
AND PROFESSIONAL
EDUCATION

Samuel B. Kutash

This paper by Dr. Samuel Kutash is an extremely extended one in that he has set for himself the enormous task of group work in both industry and professional eduction—although he focuses for the most part on industrial settings. Doctor Kutash indicates that the complexities of industrial settings requires a considerable range of skills on the part of the industrial consultant. Each situation, as he envisions it, has numerous outcomes possible dependent on the type and method of intervention. He advocates a thorough dynamic and practical assessment of the situation and an application of appropriate techniques to that structure. In a very thorough but concise manner he provides examples of the differing dynamic constellations that one might meet in industrial settings. He also offers a precise evaluation of different group approaches and their particular utility in a given situation. Again, the concrete explication of method and environment and their mutual interaction with the possible consequent results is fully and consistently drawn.

One of the most interesting comparisons Doctor Kutash makes is with the emerging area of community psychology. As with Doctor Lauer in her paper on on school psychology, the industrial or educational setting is viewed as a social structure. The possible effects of this industrial environment for the continuation or reinforcement of already established neurotic patterns or the precipitation of new neurotic conflicts is readily apparent. The importance of a constructive work experience for the individual's mental health is also so patently obvious that it hardly needs repeating. Additionally, of course, the indictment of modern industry for its possible contribution to and exacerbation of our national alienation and detachment is also fairly well documented in the literature. The use of group process methods to improve the social atmosphere and, thus, directly to set in motion more constructive forces within the industrial setting provides a possible lever for change in a major area of life. Of course, at this time the task before us is still a mammoth one that would require the active participation of the responsible persons within each industrial community. Even if the industrial settings become more generally available for group process intervention, the

233

intricacies of these social structures will still require consumate sensitivity and skills on the part of the consultant to put in motion the wheels of change.

D.S.M.
G.D.G.

TWO OF THE NEWEST FRONTIERS for the fruitful application of group process techniques and experiences are in the fields of industry and professional education. Both fields are in the midst of rapid change and ferment and are part of a drastically changing social, cultural, economic, and psychological environment. Industry experiences at first hand the effects and challenge of such current phenomena and social problems as environmental pollution, increased interracial tensions, all pervading apathy and lack of involvement among masses of people, the impact of automation and advanced technology on the personal growth and creativity of the individual, the growing number of labor-management confrontations and strikes, the tendency towards industrial mergers, the increasing growth of new inventions, new consumer demands, heightened competition, and a host of other changes, which result in taxing most severely the human resources and resourcefulness upon which it must rely for productive achievement. At the same time, professional education for psychologists is undergoing a revolution with an increasing movement toward the establishment of autonomous schools of professional psychology, preferably in university settings, with innovations and new designs in training applied psychologists to cope with the heightened demand for their services and the renovation of existing programs to include more emphasis on newer tools such as group process and group techniques. Group process and group psychological services have experienced a boom and a challenge from industry that has pointed up the need for revitalized and more intensive training in these techniques for the professional psychologist.

In spite of the wide open doors which industry has welcomed group psychological services they have not yet fulfilled their promise. As Maliver (13) has recently pointed out, "businessmen are often disappointed customers of group psychology services." "They complain about the lack of tangible results." More serious from the point of view of professional psychology is whether group psychology services really introduce humanism into the computerized, automated, dehumanized technological and corporate climate or whether group process in industry will go the way of its predecessors–industrial and personnel psychology which fitted in to the technologically advancing, increasingly efficient but dehumanized industrial settings which they served by such methods and aims as increasing efficiency, time and motion studies, quality control, incentive awards, promotional guidelines, paternalistic bureaucracies and the like, some of which were contributions in their time.

The major overall problem for industry and professional education which needs to be confronted in order to insure the productive utilization and growth of their human resources, is that of integrating personal growth and self-development with organizational objectives and goals. This is also the chief task in any kind of effective and healthy individual and group functioning. All of the existing systems of individual and group psychotherapy, counseling and guidance, conceptualize this in one way or another in terms of the appropriate actualization of individual needs, creative talents, abilities, and inner drives, so that they are at the same time integrated or in mutual harmony with external reality requirements, social objectives, and the needs of others as represented by organizational, societal and industrial goals. For the individual I have delineated in my chapter on the *Psychoneurosis* in the *Handbook of Clinical Psychology* (7), in terms of ego psychology and ego boundaries the ways in which imbalance in the homeostasis between inner drives and pushes, on the one hand, and external pressures and the influences of the outside world of reality on the other, can result in various kinds of neurosis and mild to severe personality disturbances.

Where group process experiences and techniques have failed in industry it has been often because of the failure to achieve this goal in one of two ways. Either personal growth and self-development has lagged behind and been squelched by overriding organizational goals or the reverse has been true and the good and welfare of the group organization has suffered as a result of individuals placing sole or primary emphasis on "doing their own thing." Group process experiences ranging from unstructured basic encounter groups through sensitivity or T-groups to intensive group psychotherapy seem to be the methods of choice for use in solving or working through this central goal of individual and group inter-actions.

One of the great advantages of group techniques for effecting personality and behavioral change is precisely the fact that in the group you have each individual striving to actualize himself in a milieu or group entity and you have a group of individuals repre-senting organizational, social, familial, and reality requirements or a microcosm of the outside world. Industry is one of the great testing grounds for individual effectiveness in carrying out self-satisfying goals which simultaneously advance the organizational purpose. The development of professional competence in those professions that work with people is another process which de-pends for its fulfillment on individual creative achievement, and sometimes teamwork, as measured by the effects on other people as in the professions of psychology, psychiatry, social work, edu-cation, medicine and law, in fact all those callings that involve the rendering of services to other people.

In industry the professionally trained psychologist or psychi-atrist who has acquired a thorough background and training in group process experiences including group psychotherapy has the opportunity of applying his expertise in the "natural habitat" in which people in our society actually do their daily work. It is here that each person's effectiveness as a productive human being is measured daily in the crucible of reality, where he interacts with other people, peers, supervisors, and employees for whom he may carry responsibility.

Group process specialists have learned from the ethologists who have demonstrated that more valid conclusions can be drawn con-cerning animal psychology and behavior by studying animals in their natural habitats than by observing them in the laboratory. It is a most professionally enhancing experience to emerge from the clinic, hospital, or consultation room, and use psychological methods for effecting individual and organizational changes in the context of people's everyday work lives in industry or in profes-sional training. The consumer of what you have to offer is not a patient but may be a remarkably practical, effective, hard-nosed realist who will not hesitate to question what you do, take issue with you, show you whether the results justify the expenditures, and get rid of your services if you do not deliver the results that your contract promises.

Because of the test of reality which is applied to group psychological services they must of necessity be problem-oriented rather than technique-oriented. Experience in industry has convinced me that the group process consultant or consulting group must have available skills, background, and training in a variety, a full armamentarium of group modalities. These should include encounter groups, sensitivity or T-groups, analytic group process experiences, marathons, interpersonal skill groups, Bion or Tavistock type conference groups, group dynamics, discussion and educational groups, Gestalt groups, task-oriented groups, psychodrama and role-playing techniques, group counseling skills, group psychotherapy, and group evaluative methods. Each group process consultant must, in my opinion, be fully trained and have had some experience with a fairly adequate sampling of the available group techniques and systems. He should not be a dogmatic adherent of one method or technique if he is to serve most effectively. He may, of course, with great benefit specialize in a particular modality or in a few provided that he has acquired first an adequate broadbased training.

In industry, sensitivity training, in particular, as well as encounters have had a field day. These methods undoubtedly have helped many people and perhaps not helped or even harmed others. I have elsewhere discussed the values and dangers of group process techniques (8). In addition to the safeguards recommended in my article in the journal, *Group Process,* I would add now in relation to work in industry that the group process consultant must be aware of and have studied the research, literature and practices in the fields of small and large group behavior, applied social psychology and action research, industrial psychology, organization and systems development, group and individual psychotherapy, psychodiagnostics, community mental health, the psychology of prejudice and minority groups, and the full range of clinical psychological training besides. A relatively new body of knowledge is the new field of environmental psychology and there is now an excellent text by Proschansky, Ittelson, and Rivlin (16).

With a host of professional options open to him the group process consultant can set up group process experiences and programs that will meet the situations and problems presented to him. Preferably he should be part of a consulting group in which there are others with different skills and specialties. For example, in the consulting group, HDP Associates, Inc., we have an expert in multi-level communication and video-tape methods, a specialist in family therapy and role models particularly leader role models as they carry over from prior or present family influences, a specialist in analytic intensive group process experiences both short-term and long-term, a community based psychiatrist who is expert in community mental health, a director of a postdoctoral psychotherapy and training center, etc. while all the senior consultants are also trained psychoanalysts and group process experts.

One of the important decisions that the group consultant must make in choosing between sensitivity training experiences, encounter groups, marathons, Gestalt groups, or analytic groups for industry and professional training is whether these should be in the work context or in outside facilities, *in-house* or *stranger* groups. Generally this depends on a thorough diagnosis of the organizational climate and the goals for which the services are being recommended. When there is doubt as to whether the individual's benefitting from the experience will be well integrated with organizational goals it is better to refer the clients to stranger groups. When the goal is more directly related to organizational aims an in-house group is more suitable. Maliver (13), for example, quotes a study by Reddy (17) who compared the results of two T-groups led by NTL trained persons, with one psychotherapy and one control group. "The results pointed to a significant increase in pathologically deviant signs in the T-group members, and a marked decrease in those signs in the psychotherapy group."

Before going on to a consideration of the kinds of problems for which industry seeks help from group process practitioners, permit me to share with you an observation during an experience with a group of corporation presidents who were convened by HDP Associates for the purpose of learning from them the kinds of help they wanted in their industries. While the psychologists and psychiatrists present talked to some extent in terms of improving profits and productivity, the industrialists spoke in terms of wanting help in humanizing their industrial environment and in increasing personal creativity and fulfillment for their people, as well as improving the quality of life in their establishments. The professionals present realized quickly that they didn't have to assume that these leaders in industry were interested only in profits and productivity. They wanted satisfied, fulfilled people, a mentally healthy environment, and many other enhanced human values without sacrificing productivity or reasonable profits. Of course, these were relatively young leaders in industry with their eye on the future, not only of their industry but of healthy life on this planet.

Now I would like to give you a sampling of the kinds of problems for which industry seeks help. A research and development subsidiary corporation of a large international oil company sought help in improving and releasing the creativity of its large group of research scientists which included chemists, physicists, air pollution experts, geologists, engineers, etc. It was felt that group process could help these people actualize their creative potential while increasing their personal growth. Such a goal can usually be achieved either in basic encounter groups as conducted by Carl Rogers (18) or by intensive analytic group experiences, with provision for preliminary screening of those who need more individual private psychotherapy and for follow up in the event that a participant needs or wants a referral for more long-term therapeutic help.

Another frequent problem for which help is sought is in the area of motivation. A frequent complaint on the part of supervisors and employers is the lack of motivation and involvement on the part of personnel. Many industries are confronted with problems of minority groups, interracial tensions, black-white confrontations, protests with reference to discrimination against female employees, for example, in filling executive jobs. Problems of drug abuse, alcoholism, absenteeism, accident proneness, labor turnover, decreases in productivity, and many others, can usually be helped through group process experiences for supervisors and employees. Other areas of application involve on-the-job training and development of employees for supervisory, executive, and higher level management positions. The whole field of psycho-ecology and environmental improvement is receiving much more attention and not only for public relations reasons. Many industrial settings need assistance in improving communications, interpersonal relationships, morale, general productivity, job satisfaction, and in changing the organizational structure itself.

Industry is seeking new innovative methods for reducing costly executive emotional breakdowns, mental disturbances and disorders in employees. Short term group process experiences can be adapted by flexible creative practitioners into a useful method of improving executive selection and selection for all kinds of positions and roles which involve human relations and working with and developing people. Group process is already in use in the more advanced clinical psychology training programs both as an added method for selecting candidates for the program and as an important aspect of professional education as well illustrated by the program here at Adelphi University. Along these lines the recently published fact sheet announcing the new College of Professional Psychology which we are establishing in New Jersey states in part, "Students will learn to recognize their own motivations, and to understand the motivations of others. This is to be taught in classes using traditional lecture and discussion methods, as well as in seminars, in group process experiences, in tutorial sessions throughout the program, in personal therapy, and in formal observational experiences in all the areas of human life from birth to death" (4). Group process has similar application in helping to train and develop the managers of people and supervisors in industry.

Industry is receptive to the use of group psychological services either in a consultative capacity or in direct participation in negotiations involving mergers, acquisitions, labor-management problems, contracts, business agreements, and in the more fruitful, humanistic handling of the increasing variety of group confrontations. As a recent issue of *Newsweek* magazine makes clear, the American corporation is under attack from all sides. Many of the corporate leaders need more intensive and deeper understanding of the human factors and group phenomena involved. They themselves recognize the importance of mobilizing their own humanism and social responsibility. There is increasing demand for better integration of family relations and family life with career development and industrial life.

In setting up a group psychological program the consultant must early decide whether the problem presented is basically one in which the stress should be on those group process techniques that aim primarily at restructuring and/or changing the organization or system or whether the emphasis should be on techniques aiming primarily toward personal growth and/or the release of individual creative potential. Some group modalities such as the Bion-Tavistock approach, Psychodrama and Role-Playing, Interpersonal Skills Groups, Discussion and Brainstorming Sessions, and Group Dynamics Methods, lend themselves better to changing organizations. On the other hand, Encounter groups, Gestalt groups, Marathons, Esalen and Human Potentials Type Groups, and Multi-Level Communication Groups, have a better chance of releasing individual creative potentials, improving personal awareness and growth, and promoting self-actualization. Sensitivity Groups, Analytic Group Process Experiences, and Group Psychotherapy may handle both by aiming more directly at integrating the individual's personal fulfillment with optimal organizational development. Deciding which modality or varieties of group should be applied in the solution of a presenting or long-term problem depends on thorough study and diagnosis.

In a large corporation or industry the best strategy often is to start with the top echelon of management and to apply at this level the group process experiences that are best oriented toward increasing self and interpersonal awareness and actualizing creative capacity in the context of integrating them with the needs and feelings of others. These influential people in the organization could have a salutory effect in revitalizing the total organizational structure and in humanizing the entire organization. In middle management, at the first line supervisors level, and in the lower echelons, a variety of short-term techniques may be applicable including specialized workshops, marathons around particular tasks, communication groups, and the like.

An important issue both in group process work with industry and in the training of professionals is whether to aim at changing perception or the meanings that people attribute to stimuli, persons, environments, feelings, and events or to attempt direct behavioral change. This is a carry over of the contrast in clinical work between the perceptual therapies which include analytically oriented, experiential, and humanistic psychological approaches and the behavior therapies which include conditioning, desensitization, cognitive dissonance, and the like. In a volume edited by W. H. Ittelson and S. B. Kutash (6), I proposed in Chapter II that mental health be defined in terms of optimal perceptual flexibility. At this time when the problems in the industrial and corporate environment as well as in the new breed of clinical, counseling, and industrial psychologists which we are spawning, seem to be centered around the loss of individuality in people, the standardization of men and behavior, the computerized mechanized environment, and the like, it would seem that the behavior therapies and the group techniques derived from their basic philosophy can only lead to more mechanized, hollow men who fit into the organization by expected behavior but at the expense of individuality, creativity, and personal happiness. Group process methods must, therefore, in my opinion, aim at making people more flexible by increasing the range of their perceptions in relation to behavior, events, problems, and feelings. As Rosenbaum (19) has indicated many of the encounter and sensitivity groups are conducted in a way that implies a behavioral approach as when individuals are encouraged to express feelings openly and to act them out without regard to their perception of the situation or the perceptions and behavior of others. In industry, this has been one of the major causes of dissatisfaction with sensitivity groups. These groups do not have to be conducted in that manner. The leader must have a sound theoretical rationale, have sufficient perceptual flexibility and aim at helping the participants re-perceive and thus become more creative and contributory. I thus advocate what I would call a "Perceptual Change Group" to be added to the armamentarium. This could have various applications and could be applied both on a general basis as in encounter, sensitivity, analytic, and Gestalt groups but could also have more specialized aims such as re-perceiving a task in industry so that new creative solutions can be evolved on a group basis.

I should like to address myself next to some practical examples of applications of group process. The industrial community as well as the college and university community are two of the most important and influential milieus for the application of the community mental health approach. The community mental health centers that have proliferated all over the country have more and more had to develop group process methods and to depart from the one-to-one relationship in treating emotional disorders, delinquency, drug abuse, etc. The first signs of these problems often turn up in the work setting and environment. In some of my early articles published in the *Management Review* (9), *Supervisory Management* (10), the *AMA Management Report* (11), and in a chapter in the book *Leadership in the Office* (12), I have stressed the fact that many emotional disorders and kinds of neurotic reactions can be handled effectively in the industrial setting without necessarily removing the employees from the job, provided that a preventive mental health approach is present or developed in the industry. Some would, of course, still need referral to outside practitioners for more intensive help. To these suggestions, I now add the group process experience designed to prevent emotional disability. The institution of such groups requires an enlightened administration and a clear understanding of their value to the industry.

With reference to group process applied to labor-management negotiations the Association for Group Psychoanalysis and Process recently had as a guest speaker at one of its workshops, Dr. Enzo Spaltro of Italy, who has developed some innovative techniques that are most valuable not only in labor-management confrontations but in many other types of controversial negotiations. While the role of the labor mediator has most often been one of attempting to bring about harmony and agreement by striving to get the parties to agree and compromise, Spaltro and his group process colleagues in Italy aim at bringing into the open all the disagreements, controversies, and hard feelings. His only requirement is that the parties become authentic, honest, open, and truthful. After the hectic confrontations when the parties become real and authentic to each other the entire situation is perceived differently and real meaningful agreement based on mutual understanding is reached. In the past methods the compromise agreement is only the beginning of a new struggle between the parties and may be based on victory of one over the other with the need for the loser to recoup his strength and organize for the next encounter.

Another relatively new group process technique is the adaptation of what we have learned from family therapy to the industrial family. I have found that not only in family businesses but in corporate and industrial settings where the leadership structures itself like a family, the techniques of sculpting, group interaction, and helping the participants become aware of how they are unconsciously perpetuating earlier family patterns and structures is quite helpful.

During my years as a Field Selection Officer and Expert Consultant with the U.S. Peace Corps in which I shared some group process experiences with Gordon Derner we had as one of our major responsibilities the function of presiding over so-called Selection Board meetings in which the Psychiatrists, Field Assessment Officers who were psychologists, Physicians, Project Director, Faculty of the training installation, Training Officers, Language Instructors, Overseas Directors, etc. all participated in order to select the Peace Corps trainees who would go overseas as Peace Corps Volunteers. I began to conduct this as a group process experience and this was most valuable in preventing the capricious, prejudicial elimination of individual creative mavericks who later made excellent contributions overseas. In addition we stimulated the inclusion of group process experiences for the trainees which became a factor both in helping them decide whether to stay in the program and how to integrate their individual needs with the organizational objective. The techniques which worked best with the Peace Corps, when applied by fully trained experienced clinical or counseling psychologists as Field Selection Officers, are now in use in some industrial and university settings.

At present I am engaged as group process consultant at the Jersey City State College where under the initiative of Dr. Ann Marie Walsh, the Director of the Graduate Program in School Psychology, we have established as a required course one which is called Techniques of Group Dynamics but which is given by me as a course in group process techniques and another in Human Relations which I conduct as a group process experience. Through the cooperation of the school the group process experience is limited to twelve students per semester and all students who attend all sessions and become active participants are given an "A" for the course and they are told this in advance. In a group meeting with the faculty and in conferences with the students, the feedback was that two different groups of students last year and this year had found this personally helpful in learning at first hand human interactions, emotional processes, psychodynamics, group dynamics and self-awareness as well as understanding of others, through experiencing meaningfully and emotionally what they may have "learned" intellectually from books or lectures. They also felt that they picked up first hand knowledge of the techniques and felt better able to apply them in working with teachers and school personnel as well as school pupils, instead of relying most heavily on the one-to-one relationship. As mentioned previously group process is rapidly becoming a recommended experience for doctoral candidates in clinical psychology.

In spite of our interest as clinicians in the individual development of each person, we must not neglect the value of the application of group process and applied social psychological techniques in changing organizations and systems. In the May 1971 issue of the *American Psychologist* the latest article by Robert Cooper of the University of Liverpool and Michael Foster of the Human Resources Center of the Tavistock Institute of Human Relations, describes sociotechnical systems (3). They state that "current perspectives view organizations as dynamic complex structures in symbiotic relationship with their environments. The organization-environment matrix constitutes one total system in which understanding of the behavior of any part depends on the extent to which it is seen as being integral with other system parts." They elaborate an intricate rationale and structure for changing sociotechnical systems and organizations. What started essentially with Bion, the psychoanalyst, has evolved into a group process model geared toward changing the system or organization with the goal that individual and group behavior within the system may become more effective or productive. This approach fits in with the philosophy of organism espoused by Alfred North Whitehead (20) who described the modern factory as "an organism exhibiting a variety of vivid values" and said, "what we want to train is the habit of apprehending such an organism in its completeness." The existing research, techniques, and strategies of changing organizations is well described in the excellent text by Warren Bennis (1).

The Bion type of group training which is often referred to as a Tavistock type conference concentrates upon the functioning of groups as wholes rather than upon individual personality. The consultant, in this type of group, interprets to the participants the intra-group process and dynamics and encourages the exploration and study of how the group experience modifies or enhances the individual as a member of a social unit. In industry it often takes the form of a task oriented study group. Goldberg (5) in his volume on *Encounter: Group Sensitivity Training Experience* indicates that there is a sharp contrast between the study group and the T-group approaches–"The T-group trainer acts like the best group member should behave while the study group consultant acts as if he is speaking only to the participant as a social unit and not directly as an individual."

One approach which has been adapted for use in industry in rather unique ways is the *Psychodramatic Approach* (15) which has been described earlier in this conference by James M. Sacks. Most useful adaptation aims at effecting organizational change through a format requiring members of the organization to switch roles and interact. Thus, in one group process experience conducted by the Director of Training of a large corporation for whom I acted as consultant, we set up a series of critical incidents drawn from actual occurrences in the corporation in past years and assigned different roles to the key executives involved. Thus, the Controller became the Director of Advertising, the Director of Advertising became the Production Manager, the Production Manager became the Personnel Director, etc. The ten key people than handled the incidents in their new roles. After each "solved" session there was active interaction around the issues involved. Various attitude measures and ratings of positive and negative valance as well as sociometric measures indicated distinct improvement in inter-group relationships and mutual regard among the participants. Role-playing has been to some extent incorporated in many of the other group process approaches. The Bion-Tavistock approach has been relatively popular in industry with administrators and corporate officers while role playing models have appealed more to the industrial consultants, psychologists, training directors and other professionals.

In the ordinary course of problem solving and working together in the industrial or corporate setting many group activities, meetings, and conclaves break down in their effectiveness and in the accomplishment of their aims. The literature of social psychology is replete with social psychological diagnosis of such events and about 300 papers in the field of industrial psychology are published annually according to Meltzer's recent survey of papers listed in *Psychological Abstracts* (14). One group modality that we might call variously the *group dynamics* approach or the applied *social psychological* approach has the psychological consultant sit in on the working groups and diagnose the group problems in accomplishing their aim. For example, Bradford, Stock and Horwitz (2) discuss "How to Diagnose Group Problems" and report the information back to the group to get the group going again. The many variations of this approach have been an old standby in industry for the purposes of organizational development but have been revitalized by our new knowledge of psychodynamic group processes.

If we accept the major thesis of this paper that group process experiences in industry must orient themselves toward the integration of personal individual aims with group organizational objectives then we should conclude with a consideration of the possibility of adapting the analytic group psychotherapy modality or the psychoanalytic group process experience for use in industry and professional education. The assumptions that psychoanalytically oriented group therapy must be long term and must aim at helping the individual to the detriment of the organization or the employer are based on experiences with clinic, hospital, and private practice patients. But not only patients have the problem of integrating their personal needs or instinctual drives with reality requirements or social and group interests. This is precisely what industry wants and needs and what can re-introduce humanism in our technologically tainted corporate and industrial settings thus promoting individual and self-realization and organizational goals. With proper screening out of people suffering from disabling emotional disorders and the use of analytically oriented group experiences either on a marathon, short-term, or longer-term as part of human resources maintenance, with relatively mentally healthy people, a great deal can be accomplished. The words "psychoanalytic" and "psychotherapy" do not appeal to industry because of their pathological inference so that these modalities may be referred to as "intensive group experiences" or "integrative groups." The "industrial intergrative group" aims primarily to use psychoanalytic insights and what is available in role playing, encounter, sensitivity training, Gestalt principles, group dynamics, social psychology, etc. as technical tools designed to actualize each individual in a context of awareness of his impact on others, the organization he works for, the society he lives in and the interests of humanity.

REFERENCES

1. Bennis, W.: *Changing Organizations.* New York, McGraw-Hill, 1966.
2. Bradford, L. P., Stock, D., and Horwitz, M.: How to diagnose group problems. In Golombiewski, R. L., and Blumberg, A. (Eds.): *Sensitivity Training and the Laboratory Approach.* Itasca, Illinois, F. E. Peacock Publishers, 1970.
3. Cooper, R., and Foster, M.: Sociotechnical systems. *American Psychologist, 26:*467, 1971.
4. Fact Sheet, Organizing Council for a College of Professional Psychology, 1971.
5. Goldberg, C.: *Encounter: Group Sensitivity Training Experience.* New York, Science House, 1970.
6. Ittelson, W. H., and Kutash, S. B.: *Perceptual Changes in Psychopathology.* New Brunswick, Rutgers University Press, 1961.
7. Kutash, S. B.: Psychoneuroses. In Wolman, B. (Ed.): *Handbook of Clinical Psychology.* New York, McGraw-Hill, 1965.
8. Kutash, S. B.: Values and dangers of group process experiences. *Group Process, 3:*7, 1971.
9. Kutash, S. B., and Strong, L.: The problems people bring to the job. *Management Review, 50:*4, 1961.
10. Kutash, S. B.: Problem workers—or workers with problems. *Supervisory Management, 6:*2, 1961.

11. Kutash, S. B.: Dealing with emotional disturbances in industry. *AMA Management Report, 24:*125, 1958.

12. Kutash, S. B.: Problem workers or workers with problems? In Haskell, P. C. (Ed.): *Leadership in the Office.* New York, American Management Association, 1963.

13. Maliver, B. L.: The organization as a test crucible for group psychology. *Group Process, 3:*13, 1971.

14. Meltzer, H.: Industrial psychology in Psychological Abstracts, 1927-1969. *The Journal of Psychology, 78:*125, 1971.

15. Moreno, J. L.: *Who Shall Survive?* New York, Beacon House, 1953.

16. Proschansky, H. M., Ittelson, W. H., and Rivlin, L. G.: *Environmental Psychology.* New York, Holt, Rinehart, and Winston, 1970.

17. Reddy, W. B.: Sensitivity training or group psychotherapy. *Int J Grp Psychother, 20:*366, 1970.

18. Rogers, C.: The process of the basic encounter group. In Bugental, J. T. (Ed.): *Challenges of Humanistic Psychology.* New York, McGraw-Hill, 1967.

19. Rosenbaum, M.: The responsibility of the psychotherapist for a theoretic rationale. *Group Process, 3:*41, 1971.

20. Whitehead, A. N.: *Science and the Modern World.* New York, Macmillan, 1925.

CHAPTER XVIII

SOME ASPECTS OF MY THEORY AND PRACTICE OF THERAPY

PETER HOGAN

Dr. Peter Hogan is a psychoanalytically trained psychiatrist, a former director of the Adelphi University Mental Hygiene Clinic, and a pioneer in innovative practices in group psychotherapy. In this paper he presents a thoughtful and conceptually meaningful personal integration of both the etiology of man's psychopathology and the manner in which treatment methods uniquely, directly, and effectively contribute to the curative process. To do this he amply and effectively uses personal and clinical illustrations that elucidate and vivify his point of view.

In this chapter Peter Hogan comes through as a thoughtful student of man in his culture. He incisively outlines the multitude of familial and societal forces that help evolve and perpetuate a malignant social process. This process is one that undermines the individual's self worth by fostering a life long dependency state. It does this in his opinion by helping to create and maintain the infantile polarity of powerlessness and omnipotence. Thus, society interferes with the development of an adequate sense of self based on effective behavior, appropriate expression of emotion, and accurate assessment of one's self in the world.

Following Doctor Hogan's theoretical section on the origins of neurosis in man today, he describes in detail using clinical examples that elucidate the helping process of group psychotherapy. The process of change is accomplished by assisting people in getting in touch with their internal feelings and inner-selves and by undoing the self perpetuating isolation established by the introjection of the attitudes of the parent. His techniques in group treatment are variations and modifications based on Reichian, Gestalt, and Transactional theories. Three basic group treatment approaches are illustrated by clinical material that epitomizes his unique approach. His technical innovations: 1) The use of "helper-helped" pairs to administer a muscle pressure massage to the shoulders and neck muscles of each other in order to relieve muscular tension and get at buried feelings; 2) The use of video playback and closed circuit TV to overcome isolation. This enables a person to compare his internal experience with the external manifestations of them, and allows the patient to role play his own image as viewed on the video screen; 3) Last, his group treatment room does not have conventional furniture and lighting (which he feels conveys the cultural message to "cool it"). In their place, he has especially designed recessed fluorescents with colored sleeves for mood lightning and mats and pillows on the floor.

Thus, this paper provides the reader with a fascinating glimpse of a man and his method of helping people. In this very easy to read and clear paper, we see Peter Hogan's theoretical stance on the nature of man's present day dilemma—his dependency which has undermined his self worth and self assertion—and his particular methods of treatment which are geared to combat these difficulties. It is an innovative approach with a well integrated theoretical base.

D.S.M.
G.D.G.

I N HIS RECENT BOOK on group therapy (19), Irvin Yalom discusses the themes revealed in the "top secret" T-group encounter game. This exercise, given to non-patients at Stanford University who were "primarily medical students, psychiatric residents, nurses, psychiatric technicians and Peace Corp volunteers," resulted in just a few common themes, the most frequent being "a deep conviction of basic inadequacy–a feeling that if others could really see him, they would know of his incompetence, his intellectual bluff." The other two themes he mentions, were that "they do not or cannot really care for or love another person," or "that they are concealing some variety of sexual secret." But these are variations of the theme of inadequacy, in my opinion. In a footnote, Yalom goes on: "One cannot but reflect on . . . how disquieting it is, that representatives of our intellectual elite, students in one of our leading universities, should be so imbued with a sense of incompetence. Surely there is a malignant process at work in a culture which generates these feelings in its youth."

Well, if this malignant process exists, what is it and how is it related to group therapy? A thorough attempt to answer that question is beyond the limits of this paper, however, a direction can be developed within those limits. In my opinion, there *is* a malignant process, culturally induced. I define it as dependency, by which I mean the internal and external pressures to maintain, in the adult, the infantile polarity of powerlessness and omnipotence. This continuing polarity is easy to see directly in psychotics. In my experience, everyone in our culture has some form of dependency in some area of living.

I would like to show how, in my view, the processes that lead to this polarity also lead to the results of the "top secret" game. The necessary precondition for the maintenance of the infantile polarity is the biological requirement for physical and emotional contact during infancy, if normal human development is to occur. This was first reported in psychoanalytic literature by René Spitz (17, 18), who investigated an orphanage and found that children were dying even though they were very adequately taken care of in terms of sanitation and diet. Those that survived were physically and mentally retarded. This finding has been confirmed in non-institutional settings, such as in deprivational dwarfism (13). Jane Goodall has demonstrated strikingly similar needs and results in chimpanzees (5, 6).

The important consequence of this need, in my opinion, is that the infant and child will distort themselves in any way that will enable them to maintain contact with an emotionally nurturing person. In the absence of a response from a nurturing person, the infant will first give evidence of distress (12), then lapse into apathy, retardation and even death (5, 6, 13, 17, 18).

This finding had, of course, been known empirically long before scientific investigation began. Solitary confinement has been notorious as the most dreaded punishment in prison short of the death sentence itself. One form of brainwashing is based on the need for contact alone as the coercive force. If the prisoner gives the "wrong" answer, he is returned to solitary.

The middle-class equivalent of solitary confinement is being sent to one's room until one is "fit to associate with"; or, among peers, being "sent to Coventry." Even more powerful, because self-perpetuating, is isolating the child from his peers by a variety of techniques every therapist is familiar with. One striking example was related by a woman who recalled wanting to go out to play with friends as a child. Her mother suggested that she stay at home, sit on the mother's lap, suck her thumb, and tickle her mother's ear. The child chose to play with her friends. When she returned home, she found her pet chickens dead and dressed for the evening meal. The girl was threatened with injury to her dog if she revealed anything to her father about the incident, and so had dinner with the rest of the family. One wonders what emotions this child was swallowing along with the food.

While this incident is extreme, subtle episodes occur in any family in which the child must make a choice between disowning his feelings, behavior, or perceptions or losing the approval or love of the parent. Almost always, the former is the easier loss to bear. For example, I observed this scene in the lobby of an apartment building: On a mild spring day, with the lobby door open and most adults wearing street clothes only, a young, warmly dressed boy of about two began walking toward the door. His mother then said to him sweetly, "Darling, it's so cold outside." The boy protested that it was warm, but his mother repeated her words. I left before the episode went any further; however, it was clear to me that the mother obviously wanted her child to stay with her, but did not say, "Stay with me" or "Don't go out the door." Instead of a direct order or request she gave a double-bind message. One level was a command to the boy to deny or distrust his visual and temperature perceptions; the other level suggested that she was speaking out of loving feelings alone. The alternative of holding on to his perceptions and seeing that his mother was using her "love" to manipulate him, would be an extremely difficult one for the boy to stay with.

A similar incident in adult life was reported by a patient. His brother and parents were visiting him, the first family reunion in several years. His mother wanted to take a photograph of her two sons together. As she aimed the camera, John, my patient, said, "Mother, is that a flash cube on that camera? You know I hate a flash going off in my eyes." "No, darling," she replied, "It isn't a flash cube." Then, as she took the picture, the flash cube fired. The resulting print showed John looking to one side, since he preferred to believe his eyes rather than his mother's words. His brother, on the other hand, was looking full into the camera. "I was surprised by the flash. I believed her," he remarked later.

The above three examples have to do with family pressures (usually unconscious and unwitting) for the child to remain relatively powerless by giving up his ability to perceive and act independently and effectively. In the first example, the pressure used was the child's love for her pets, the "hostage" technique (a form of blackmail). In the next two examples, the threat was the loss of "love" or emotional closeness. Similar examples can be found in all areas of a child's developing mastery of his body, actions, emotions, perceptions, and the like. When the pressures are extensive enough, a child will disown even his own biological needs, in that they are no longer experienced as a part of his sense of self but rather as a part of the external, coercive world. For example, a man living alone once forgot to shop for food on his way home from work on Friday night. When he awoke in the morning, there was nothing to eat. He remained hungry in his apartment for the entire weekend "because nothing is going to make me do what I don't want to."

It is not only the ability to perceive and act independently that the child disowns, but also his right to feel and express emotions. If the expression of an emotion brings the threat of punishment or isolation, the emotion will first be suppressed and ultimately repressed. This repression can become so thorough that even under the most favorable circumstances it may be broken through only with great difficulty. In a special group I conducted, in which all the "patients" were psychiatrists or members of "people-helping" professions (social workers, etc.), one man, a psychiatrist, was undertaking a role play with another. This man had a prying, snooping, "loving" mother, and he had been having great difficulty in expressing his anger with her and his desire for her to stop. In the role play, the mother was played by another man. The exercise went on for fifteen minutes, and even though the patient was badgered, prodded, and subjected to blatant guilt-evoking tactics, and even though he reported feelings of anger arising in him, he was unable to do more than laugh helplessly and manage a mild "stop it" or two.

All of these examples illustrate that, to please the parent or escape punishment, the child will disown various aspects of the self that contribute to his potential mastery of his world. This disowning leads to powerlessness and inadequacy, and interferes with the development of a sense of self based on effective behavior, appropriate expression of emotion, and accurate assessment of one's self and the world. The sense of self or value then remains connected with evoking a "taking care" of response from others, which is the necessary case in infancy. That is, one develops a sense of being "special" or unique not through one's realistic activity, but from evoking approval and being "taken care of" by others–in effect, by remaining an infant. (Being "taken care of" is confused by most adults with "being cared for" or "being loved.")

The consequence of this process is that the center of one's feelings and behavior is placed in others rather than in the self. Others are responsible for what one feels and does. That this is a widespread cultural phenomenon is suggested by the language of most popular songs (and the language of most marital pairs and families in therapy). "You made me love you, I didn't want to do it!" "You made me leave my happy home." "You made me so happy." etc.–as well as Flip Wilson's "The Devil made me do it."

The centering of power in the other is of course normal for the infant, who must be taken care of by others until he develops to the point of being able to effectively take care of himself or to ask for help openly and directly. The idea of being "special" or "unique" not out of one's activity but simply out of existing is also natural to infancy, where the child's needs, expressed non-verbally and perhaps without conscious awareness, are "magically" translated and responded to. The transition from being translated to expressing one's needs clearly is at best made imperfectly in our society. In fact, in many families, open requests are punished, and "true love" is expressed by understanding and responding perfectly to the needs of family members, with no clear verbal communication. "After all," family members say, "we would have to give to anyone who asked"; whereas a "special" relationship is implied by getting without asking.

The sense of being "unique" or "special" can also be maintained directly by telling the child how "wonderful" he is or by behavior that implies the same, giving to the child without his effort or expression of need. One father told me unhappily of his daughter's humiliation at losing badly when she played chess with a classmate for the first time. Previously, she had played chess only with her father, who always arranged for her to win. As a consequence, she believed herself to be a master chess player, when she had learned little beyond the basic moves.

But perhaps the most powerful technique of maintaining the dual feelings of grandiosity/inferiority while simultaneously eroding the sense of effective action is guilt-evoking blame.

For example, a child scribbles on a wall with crayon. A typical response of the guilt-evoking mother would be something like: "My God, what have you done? You've ruined the wallpaper, you've given me a sick headache, and I've got to go to my room and lie down." For the rest of the week she is likely to bring up reminders of how sick he has made her. For his part, the child might reasonably say: "I didn't mean it; I'll clean it up." But the mother will not allow this. Her words and attitude will be that he has done enough: he has destroyed the wallpaper; all he can do is make it worse.

By her reactions, this mother has delivered a two-pronged message to her child. The first is that the child, who is physically weaker than the parent, through an inadvertent action (assuming that it is inadvertent) has nonetheless brought about this pronounced effect on the parent. He has, that is, this magical, grandiose, evil power—he can "make" his mother have a sick headache, shut herself in the room, and be sick for a week. The second message is that he cannot repair the damage he has done, and this reinforces his sense of helplessness or inferiority or ineffectiveness. The ultimate message is that the child is responsible not for himself but for the feelings of others; that their feelings take precedence over his; and that it is necessary for him to suppress and deny his own feelings for the sake of theirs.

Concurrently, as one accepts "power" over the feelings of others, one gives others this same power over one's feelings. Again, one comes to depend upon other people for a sense of value, through approval of praise or acceptance of one's behavior. Thus, the focus of one's activities is not on the doing of the activity but on obtaining the approval of others.

Some years ago I was at a skiing resort for families. On one morning, I observed as though for the first time the small children skiing and playing near the lodge. Those who were left to play by themselves, more or less unattended, were enjoying their play in the snow. Those who had a relative with them, or a babysitter, were not absorbed in having fun on the skis; they were tuned in instead to the relative. "How am I doing? Am I doing it right?" "You're doing wonderful, you're marvelous, you're terrific!" A skiing lesson that afternoon offered an enlightening contrast. The author was attempting to follow the directions of the instructor as earnestly as he could; and finally, when the procedures fell into place she (the instructor) said—*not* "That's right" ("That's wonderful; that's terrific")–but rather, "See how that feels inside? Doesn't that feel good?" The author had been totally unaware of his internal sensation; all attention had been directed toward obtaining the instructor's approval. But her reaction led to the understanding that the purpose of following her directions was not to please her, but to learn how it feels internally to ski well.

But–it has been the argument of this paper thus far–most children in the American culture are brought up to disavow their internal feelings and in fact to please the nurturing adult, or at least, to avoid displeasing that adult. The consequence of the disavowal of the self is dependency on others.

I can now return to the original question: What is the "malignant process" that generates a "sense of incompetence" in the "elite" of today's youth, that creates a "deep conviction of basic inadequacy"? I believe it is as follows: As a result of the cultural pressure to remain dependent upon others for a sense of self-esteem and value, most children in our culture have an almost "universal" experience. At some time in his development the child realizes that he is not loved unequivocally and in every aspect, that something about him is unacceptable to his family (wetting his pants, crying, being effective in a way that threatens a parent). In the black-and-white terms of childhood, this realization is translated into the experience "I am unlovable," or "there is some defect in me that is irreparable." At this point the child begins to dissociate not only from specific behavior patterns or feelings, but also from a whole aspect of himself. That is, that behavior, those feelings and attitudes that appear to be unacceptable, begin to go underground as a constellation and to form the "Child" ego-state of the personality.*

With many people this process begins before words are learned. In that case, there are no words to express this aspect of the personality, only dreams, images, sounds, behavior patterns, somatizations, symbolic symptoms, etc. Even when the process begins or develops when language is present, the verbal aspect may be dissociated from awareness. In some cases, especially when connected with magical destructive power over others, one feels not

---

* While accepting Berne's formulation of Parent-Adult-Child, I differ in my understanding of when and how these ego states develop, and how they interact.

only unloved, but that one is a monster. For instance, a man reported a fantasy of putting his hand on the knee of a friend's mother. In his fantasy, she immediately developed a terminal cancer under his hand.

The awareness of not being totally and unconditionally loved is also experienced or translated as, "If my parents, who really know me, can't love me, how can I expect anyone else to love me once they find out what I'm really like inside?" The same man who had the cancer fantasy had another fantasy of his mother saying to him as an infant, "You are so ugly that only a mother could love you, and even she has difficulty."

When the aspects of the child that are unacceptable to the family have gone underground, there may be a number of further developments. The acceptable aspects of the self are kept up front and are in conscious awareness (the "front stage" of Goffman (4) or the "public area" of the "Johari Window" (19). Other aspects of the self are screened from public disclosure but remain in conscious awareness and can be revealed to trusted persons (the "back stage" of Goffman and the "secret area" of the Johari Window). Still other aspects of the self are not in conscious awareness but are vislble to others (the "blind area" of the Johari Window). And finally, there are aspects of the self, including memories, emotions, and impulses, which are screened from both the self and others (the unconscious self).

Once the child aspect of the self has gone underground, the dependency process becomes self-perpetuating. Perhaps first in importance is the identification-with-the-aggressor facet of the introjected parent. This protective device serves to perpetuate both the powerlessness and the grandiosity of the child: by continuing the criticism of the child's activity as inadequate or inferior, by maintaining grandiose expectations, and by continuing the guilt-evoking of the original parents or parental surrogates. Of course, no credit is deserved for activities of the public self; after all, it isn't the "real" self, it is phony, etc. At the extreme of this process is the schizoid split and the "divided self" of R. D. Laing (11). Staying within cultural norms, we arrive at the results of the "Top Secret" exercise reported by Yalom, with which this paper began.

In summary, I have suggested the existence of a universal dependency constellation in our culture, and I would now like to outline, very briefly, some of the processes and manifestations of this constellation as they appear in patients entering therapy.

To repeat, the dependency constellation consists of two poles: grandiose ideas, and inferiority feelings. The grandiose ideas result from parental activities that tend to perpetuate beyond infancy the infant's need and ability to evoke a "taking care of" or approving response from his parents. In the ideal situation, the infant's developing sense of effectiveness shifts from the ability to evoke such responses to the evolving ability to care for himself. In the cultural actuality, his primary sense of self and his sense of effectiveness tend to remain connected to the ability to evoke a response from others. Grandiosity also has a negative aspect, manifested in feelings of exaggerated power to do (unwitting) harm. The man whose touch, in fantasy produced cancer exhibited this aspect. Grandiosity appears in addition, as exaggerated expectations of oneself.

At the other pole, the inferiority feelings develop out of the parental handling of the original physical powerlessness of the infant. In our society, the child's sense of self, based on the development of his physical and mental skills, is interfered with. The child's accomplishments are minimized or negated. He is not allowed to truly possess his constructive activities. As a result, even when a child has learned to act in an effective manner, he frequently cannot give himself credit for it, as when he "modestly" attributes his success to luck, or minimizes his achievement ("It was nothing, really"). Further, while he denies real accomplishments, he is also suggesting that he obtains results without effort. He is therefore unable to increase his self respect with increasing constructive ability. (There are also ways in which the child's ability to act effectively is undercut while his sense of grandiose power is simultaneously enhanced. Guilt-evoking blame is one example.)

On reaching physical adulthood, then, most people are not self-directing individuals but are impaired in many areas of activity, because of their dissociation from themselves. As a result of this dissociation, many varieties of dependency result. For example, dependent persons may require the recognition of their needs by another and the permission of that person to act for themselves. Or again, they may be able to act without the permission of another, but require a response to and approval of their acts in order for the acts to have any meaning.

On the one hand, this dissociation from areas of oneself makes one vulnerable to feelings of low self worth (inferiority). On the other hand, the ability to evoke approval and the gratification of one's needs by another person leads to feelings of being "special" in the grandiose sense. Note, however, that an important requirement for the feeling of being "special" is the seeming lack of connection between one's behavior and the responses of other people. The person must gain approval or love out of the "spontaneous and voluntary" reaction of others to one's existence, not from an open request for recognition. This reenacts the infant's relationship to his parents.

In the end, the dissociation from "owning" one's behavior, and the dissociation from the effects of one's behavior on others,* together with the necessity to maintain the idea of being "special" in the grandiose sense, form a constellation which is accompanied by difficulties of seeing and evaluating both oneself and other people in an accurate manner.

We arrived then, at the patient entering therapy: isolated from himself and others, divided against himself, dissociated from his emotions and his body, feeling ineffective, unlovable, and powerless, and not seeing the value of his activity to others or the value of other's activity to him in the group process. There he is, grandiose, inferior, and expecting to be taken care of by the therapist.

From one standpoint, group therapy can be seen as a way of helping people get back in touch with their internal feelings and inner selves, and undoing the self-perpetuating isolation–the isolation that is in fact perpetuated by all the internalized attitudes of the introjected parent. Toward this end, while I continue to use

---

* Except where grandiose responsibility enters. On the one hand, the dissociated person feels that the other's good opinion of him arises spontaneously, out of no actions on his part. On the other hand, he feels that the other person will feel good or bad (or get cancer or not) on the basis of how he behaves toward that other person.

conventional interactional techniques, I also use techniques that lead to more concrete experiences. That is, the goal is not simply insight of an intellectual nature, it is a concrete experiential activity which then leads to insight. That experiential insight, as has been often described, is of a different nature from the intellectual (16). To put it in other terms, the Parent-Adult-Child terms of Berne (3), it is necessary to bring the Child/Parent aspect of the personality out into the open, to give it a voice, and to develop a dialogue with the Adult before the insight can be used most effectively. The Adult and the Child need to come into contact with each other without the intervention of the Parent.* The various ego states can operate synergistically with each other rather than being compartmentalized and divided.

What is usually found in American society, with middle-class neurotics at any rate, is that they have identified the Adult with the parental introject; they say "I" when they are being self-critical. One of the functions of many kinds of group therapy, including Transactional and Gestalt therapy, is to externalize that introjected parent, to place it back outside the person so that it can be seen as separete from the original self. When the sense of identity is shifted from the introjected parent, that part of the personality can be recognized for what it originally was, a protective device to shield the child from emotional injury. Then, with the expulsion (if only temporarily) of the introjected parent, the Child aspect of the personality can be experienced, and expressed, directly.

As mentioned above, once the Child has gone underground it is largely dissociated from the verbal processes, and may not be readily uncovered by verbal techniques. On the other hand, non-intellectual techniques (such as free association, fantasy, role play, sounds, body awareness and movement and the enactment of dreams) bypass the intellectualized defenses and permit the beginning expression of suppressed emotions, attitudes, and memories.

As long as the Child aspect of the personality is buried or dissociated from, various symptoms are likely to be present; then, to

---

* The technical aspect of dealing with the Child/Parent as two aspects of the same basic personality function, I have dealt with in more detail elsewhere.(8)

undo the dissociation is to undo the symptoms. This is, when a person has the right to have his effectiveness, his feelings, and his attitudes, to experience them directly and to express them directly, he no longer has the need for indirect, symptomatic expression through behavior, somatization, or symbolic distortion.

To illustrate (though not to prove) this point: A young post-hospital schizophrenic woman had been doing quite well in her life until, in a single month, her individual therapist went on vacation and her boy friend broke off with her. She came into her regular group therapy session after these two events actively delusional but not hallucinating. Her delusional system involved the discovery that the world's ills were due to lack of love. In addition, she was responsible for making sure that the sun rose each day. The members of her group had experience with getting into intense feelings rapidly to relieve symptoms, and, although wary of her particular symptoms, encouraged her to express her feelings of loss and anger. She refused, since to do so would have gone against her "mission." She had sufficient trust in me, however, to risk getting into emotions through the use of muscle pressure (which I will describe later). Soon she was expressing her rage at being "abandoned" and, shortly thereafter, her grief about being alone. By the end of the session, her delusional system was not operating. As might be expected, this was not the end of the delusional system, although it did not return for several days.

The symptoms related to the suppression of intense emotions associated with present or past events are relieved when the emotions are expressed. But, as Freud discovered in his early work with abreaction, emotional release does not change the life attitudes that are also related to these incidents. The attitudes and values have to be "worked through." This necessity was rediscovered in World War II, when sodium amytal was used to help soldiers "relive" a traumatic event. If the event was less than six months old, "reliving" with abreaction was usually sufficient to relieve symptoms. After six months the experience was so integrated into the self structure that several abreactive experiences were not sufficient to relieve symptoms. Conventional psychotherapeutic techniques were also required for relief.

Most patients quickly empathize and act helpfully toward the

Child aspect of others in the group. When the Child aspect of themselves is expressed, however, only the Parent seems to be around to participate in a dialogue. The Adult is in a separate compartment, available only to others. Closed-circuit TV and videotape are especially helpful in dealing with this "blind" area and promoting Adult/Child dialogues.*

As an example, a man started therapy in an ongoing group and related to others in a warm, encouraging, and supportive way. While discussing his own problems, however, he displayed harsh self-criticism and often self-contempt. He could not see that he was acting Parentally towards himself, even though he could clearly see others acting Parentally towards themselves. When asked to do a role play where another group member played himself, he remained harshly critical. He could not accept warmth and concern from others either directly or in a role play. One day we used TV in the group when he was presenting his problem. On playback, he could see the suffering in his face and hear it in his voice, and could finally use the Adult information, warmth, and concern available to others for the Child in himself.

In general, the techniques of group therapy that I use can be classified into two broad categories: those that work from the outside in and those that work from the inside out. That latter is characteristic of the Gestalt approach (14), which tends to work toward the increasing awareness of repressed emotions through such techniques as "here and now" exercises, fantasy, and internal role playing. These activities, of course, in no way prevent the person from relating back to the group, so that the "external" aspects need not be neglected. Most often, my groups begin working from the outside in, most commonly through verbal interaction but occasionally through non-verbal encounter interaction. In the latter, the internal resistances are bypassed; the focus is primarily on the external environment as exemplified by group contact, and the internalized aspects of the self may be left unverbalized. Generally, to start from the inside is to deal largely with the Child/Parent polarity: to work from the outside in is to deal primarily with the Adult aspect of the personality. Non-verbal touching

---

* Barbara Hogan has been active in developing this area of therapy.

techniques tend to make contact in a supportive way with the Child aspect of the personality while bypassing the Parent aspect.

One way in which my use of the above techniques differs from usual practice is that I emphasize the recovery and full expression of intense, basic, dissociated emotions. I have found in my group work that the most rapid and effective method of reconnecting with and reowning effective activity is to first reconnect with and express these dissociated emotions and the underlying attitudes linked with them. A more unusual technique I have explored in this connection apparently works from the outside in, but is in reality more closely related to the internal Gestalt techniques. It involves an application of the "body armor" concept of Wilhelm Reich (15). According to Reich, the body armor results from the suppression of primarily sexual energy; the author's experience has been that it results from the suppression and repression of emotions generally, including anger, fear, pain, pleasure, and a sense of strength. When these emotions cannot be fully experienced and expressed, sexuality usually cannot be fully experienced and expressed. The use of this technique has developed gradually over the past three years.

Very briefly, I have found that the presence of muscle tension is the first level of somatization of emotions. Muscle tension can then serve as a short cut to reaching suppressed emotions initially and then repressed emotions. It can be used in a number of ways.

One way is as a part of a feedback system between the helped and the helping person. On the assumption that muscle tension reflects suppressed feeling, the helper suggests that the group member experiment with expressing and feeling a basic emotion by making a sound associated with it. (Many people have an initial resistance to working with sound, and working with fantasy can be substituted.) When the muscle tension begins to diminish, the emotion somatized in that particular way is identified and then can be intensified by words, sounds, actions, role plays, etc. The full expression of the emotion is signified by complete relaxation of the tense muscle.

The easiest area to locate and work with in this regard is the trapezius, the large muscle running between the top and back of the neck and shoulder area on each side. The masseter (jaw muscle) and temporalis muscles (the temples) are next easiest to locate and work with. The neck area is a frequent source of chronic tension, but is a rather complicated area to work with since closely adjacent muscles may reflect different emotions. (Further muscle areas will be detailed in a later article.) While working in this way–allowing himself to experience the emotion associated with the muscle tension–the person frequently has associations, images, memories, and even odors related to genetic events of the past. The main resistance to this method is Parental–"This is ridiculous," "What good will it do?," etc.

Next, when a person is blocked, when the usual methods of reaching inner awareness (including muscle tension feedback) do not work, additional pressure on the tense muscle leads not only to pain, but again to a rapid experiencing of emotion, images, etc. However, this method has a price–a number of resistances are encountered that do not develop with the gentler feedback method. The chief resistances are related to the idea of being "worked on" or "forced," or being physically hurt "for one's own good." People who resort to endurance or dissociation from pain as a major defense experience the pressure as a power move unless well prepared for it. "You can't make me feel," "you can't make me admit to having a feeling" are common responses. At a further extreme, some people have a sense of self so separated from their bodies and emotions that to "give in" to feelings is a betrayal of the self and is experienced as a humiliating defeat.

An important aspect of this method, then, is to give responsibility to the group member for regulating the amount and length of pressure that will be helpful to him. If errors are made (through an unconscious anesthetic response, for example), valuable information is gained for correcting future work. For example, one group member was reluctant to allow another member to use muscle pressure with him. Investigation revealed that the previous time they worked together, the reluctant member had developed a skin abrasion. Further investigation revealed his misunderstanding that the goal of working with muscle tension was to produce pain, and that the pain might lead to emotion. Since the pain seemed to be necessary, he saw no way to deal with the situation other than refusing to work with the other group member. It was explained to him that the goal in "muscle work" is to connect with and express the emotion, with pain being an occasional byproduct. Also explained was the importance of his learning to differentiate between the pain produced by pressure on a tense muscle, and the pain produced by friction on the skin. If a genuine emotion is expressed but that emotion is not connected with the muscle being worked with, the muscle tension remains the same or even intensifies.

Both ways of using muscle tension as a shortcut to emotions may lead to further resistances if the person connects with basic emotions more quickly than he is prepared for. The fear of losing control or being overwhelmed is common; so are psychosomatic manifestations of choking, or the development of nausea. When these resistances are worked through, an extremely intense fear often develops–of suffocating or actually dying. (This is sometimes preceded or accompanied by excruciating pain in the tense muscle–even though, at that time, very little pressure may be applied.) This intense fear is connected with core defenses or dissociations protecting the underground or original self. These are usually the final defenses; when they are worked through, and the intense basic feeling is fully expressed (or the fantasy fully experienced), the group member experiences himself in a significantly different way. The sound he makes changes from the basic emotion to a strong assertive sound. He feels his body and strength fully, often with sexual overtones. Often, sex is fuller and more enjoyable for a period afterwards. I should like to report that these are permanent changes, but they seem to last for several weeks at the most. However, it becomes easier to reach this state again, so that the effect is somewhat cumulative.* In addition, the awareness (which often comes as a complete surprise) that such a state of "self-togetherness" is achievable by him can provide strong motivation for further work (in therapy and in redirecting his

---

* This state can be reached by any technique that results in the full expression of a repressed emotion, and many of my group members have achieved it starting from encounter techniques. But muscle pressure is usually a shortcut here also.

life), and strong support when he encounters the fears attendant on both situations.

In addition to the defenses mentioned, a variety of dissociations may occur. The group member may seem to be fully expressing emotion in the view of others but may feel no emotion within. He may hear his voice and recognize his emotion intellectually, but deny that it is a part of him. He may connect with the feeling and deny or forget a short time later that he experienced it at all. Or he may dramatize an emotion to meet group norms while being unable to experience it internally. These are indications that the person is going beyond his capacity to integrate the emotions expressed and to benefit from such expression.

When these basic emotions are fully connected with, however, psychosomatic changes frequently occur in areas that were not dealt with directly. Some psychosomatic manifestations that have been relieved are: constipation, diarrhea, chest pains, menstrual irregularities, chronic sinusitis, asthma, hypertension and thyroid insufficiency. An interesting case was that of a woman who had eight years of chronic pain in her left arm. While working with an area of muscle tension there, she remembered–almost as though reliving it–a decision to abort a third child. The decision had been made at her husband's insistence; she herself had wanted the child. She had never expressed any grief at its loss. After reliving this experience through the muscle pressure feedback technique, she was unable to sleep that night, and expressed grief for almost twenty-four hours. At that point the pain left and never returned. That pain was accompanied by a partial loss of function; and this raises the commonly accepted idea that hysterical paralysis is rare these days because people have become too sophisticated. Its place may be taken by many psychosomatic equivalents, instances where a person is not paralyzed but, for effective purposes, his not functioning well is an expression of the repressed emotion.

To return to muscle tension in therapy, it may be used diagnostically by the therapist as a part of the screening interview. I use it in the following way: before explaining some theoretical aspects of muscle tension, I ask the prospective patient's permission to check his shoulders for muscle tension. After so checking, I inform him that I am going to do something further without discussing it, but will discuss it afterwards. I then exert moderate pressure on an area of muscle tension in the trapezius. The nature of the person's reaction to this sudden physical pain is diagnostic of his characteristic ways of dealing with emotional pain, and of dealing with other people whom he experiences as inflicting pain–especially authority figures. Further elaboration of this use will be made in another paper.

I have stated that I emphasize the recovery and full expression of intense basic dissociated emotions, and that this, in my experience, leads to reowning effective activity. This process furthers the development of a sense of self based on effective activity, rather than a sense of self based on being "special" to others without effort. Since the expression of intense emotion goes against the universal dependency constellation that I have postulated as arising from the basic fear of emotional isolation, considerable emotional contact and support are necessary to tolerate the anxiety that develops. The first impulse when contacting intense basic feelings is to shut off the emotion to avoid being isolated, or to isolate oneself "voluntarily" in order to express the emotion fully.

To illustrate: A professional man had worked for several years on the prohibition, as he experienced it, against rising above his family's station in life (blue collar). After almost flunking his studies several times, he succeeded in overcoming all obstacles and was licensed in his profession. On the day of his licensing, he came into his group in a panic. His fantasy was that he was on a space walk with only the "umbilical cord" keeping him attached to the space capsule and the possibility of eventual return to earth. The alternative prospect was that he would be cut off from all contact with earth and float in space forever, with no contact again with another human being.

Since emotional contact and support seem so vital to reowning oneself, these techniques risk the possibility of reinforcing the dependency constellation. I have attempted to deal with this problem in a number of ways, three of which I will present here. First, I believe that the function of a group leader is to help the group members become leaders themselves; that is, to take responsibility for themselves and for others in an effective way (without however, becoming magically responsible for others). To that end, I teach group members the techniques that I use and encourage them to work in pairs with these techniques during a certain portion of the group time and during alternate sessions.

This practice has a number of consequences. All power for reaching buried emotions and attitudes does not reside in the leader. The responsibility for finding an effective way to work is shared by the helping person and the helped person in the working team. The helping person is often surprised, at first, to find his efforts useful and appreciated by another group member. The goal is to develop a feedback system between the pair that provides an opportunity for both people to experience themselves as effectively developing autonomy. Since unconscious contracts can easily develop within a pair that always works together, it is suggested that group members work in different pairs from week to week. Also, reluctance to work with a particular other person can reflect strong repressed incidents or emotions and alternating partners will often bring about fruitful confrontation. On occasion, I leave the group room during "pair work." This helps to elicit dependency reactions, both from the patients who "cannot work" if I am not around, or who feel that as official therapist I owe them my presence, and those patients who "work much better" if I am not there.

Another way that I deal with the dependency problem is to stress that the person being helped is in charge of the pace and intensity of the work he is doing. This helps to avoid the disowning implied by the "you pushed me too far" type of reaction, gives the member responsibility for monitoring himself and others working with him (including the author), and helps to develop trust in oneself and others. It also helps to develop trust in the therapy process by giving the person the means to protect himself from a repetition of the childhood experience of helplessness, of feeling overwhelmed by emotions and experiences beyond the ability to integrate. The person being helped has the right to say "no" to any suggestion at any point. Testing this point enables the group member to take greater risks with manageable increases in fear.

Finally, I make it clear that it is the responsibility of the working pair (including the pair of group leader and group member) to find a step that is effective for the person being helped. The problem here is that so many people (helper and helped) are caught by a Parental bind which says, in effect: "Any step that you can accomplish is too easy and therefore meaningless when done. Any step that has any value is too much for you right now." The result is that no feeling of effectiveness results regardless of what step is taken. (This bind is related to the competitive value that anything less than 100 percent is equivalent to zero.)

One further problem is mitigated by these methods, and that is the problem of the group leader "owning" the patient's therapy activity or progress, as parents may "own" a child's marks at school. However, a thoroughly dependent patient will do anything to "please" the group leader, even taking apparent "responsibility" for himself. ("See what a big boy I am.") To some degree this response is inevitable. Hopefully, the growing person will eventually connect with himself for his own internal gains rather than as a method of "pleasing" the leader.

Another highly useful tool in undoing isolation involves videotape and closed-circuit television techniques, a field in which the author has been active since 1965 (1, 2, 7-10). The unique value of these techniques is that they help people work from both directions, outside-in or inside-out, either at the same time or sequentially. Videotape, for example, is for all practical purposes the only therapeutic tool that allows a person to compare his internal experiences with his external manifestation of them, and allows a group of people to compare the internal intent of their communications with its external effect on others. Videotape, that is, allows a person—including the therapist—to see both sides and then talk about them.

A few years ago, I was leading a demonstration group in videotape techniques, and at one point, in response to the expression of pain on the part of a group member, extended sympathy toward that person. Afterward, I was distressed to find several group members attacking me for being unfeeling, for not really caring, for not being sympathetic at all. When the tape was played back, a careful observer could detect a slight tremor in my voice, a sure sign—to me—that I was deeply involved and genuinely sympathetic. It was clear, however, why nobody else had had this response since my appearance was "stony." After viewing the tape, I was able to re-express my feelings in a way that was clear and believable to others, including those who had previously attacked me.

The ability to see and understand and make use of information is a property of the Adult part of the personality. But videotape is also useful in helping to reach the Child, particularly with people who are not accustomed to exploring intense feelings, or are anxious at the prospect, or are not ready to "face" themselves. Videotape allows them to describe what is occurring internally, how they were reacting to another person or a particular event. At the actual occurrence of the event they may have expressed no reaction; but seeing themselves on television, they feel free to discuss their earlier emotions.

In contrast to videotape, closed-circuit television can provide a different kind of approach. One way of using the television monitor is to treat it as another person in the group. That is, a group member can encounter himself directly, talk to himself, do role-playing; the dialogue with the "person" on the screen can help the person in the room differentiate between Parent, Adult, and Child. Or a person can have a dialogue between his right and left halves, looking first at one side of his face on the screen and then at the other side, and talking back and forth between the two. One woman working in this way saw on the left side a tough young boy who was left over from childhood, and saw on the right side a mature, adult woman. At the start of the dialogue she wanted to rid herself of that tough, young boy, who had once done her a service but was no longer necessary to her; but he spoke up for himself, and finally they came to a compromise. In effect, she was able to accept his earlier help and his present existence, and also accept the fact that occasionally she disliked that tough aspect of herself. This kind of acceptance of oneself, especially of the wounded Child, is a major step in reestablishing contact with oneself and connection with others.

One final note, concerning my group room. I believe that chairs and furniture convey an implicit cultural message to "cool it," to stay fixed in place. In the past several years, I have used cushions as the only furniture, to promote mobility and spontaneous activity. I use gym mats on the floor both to encourage the full physical expression of basic emotions, and to protect participants from accidental physical injury. Occasionally, I have used an alternative lighting system to help intensify basic emotional expression.* My group room has "concealed" lighting, provided by fluorescent tubes mounted vertically behind open-sided panels along the front and back walls. The alternative system involves the use of a smaller number of fluorescent bulbs surrounded by colored plastic sleeves. The original sleeves were blue, but the effect was often peaceful or tranquilizing, in contrast to what I had hoped for. At the suggestion of Millard Hoyt, M.D., I changed to red sleeving with satisfying results.

In summary, I have suggested that a dependency constellation is universal in our culture[†] and that in Transactional terms it results in a diminution of the Adult portion of the personality and a magnification of the Child/Parent duality; and I have discussed some of the methods I use to help group members take Adult responsibility for their lives.

---

* At the suggestion of lighting consultant Lesley Wheel of Wheel-Garon, Inc.
† I have developed these ideas more fully in an unpublished manuscript, *Dependency, a Universal Constellation in American Culture.*

CHAPTER XIX

VIDEO IN GROUP PSYCHOTHERAPY

Milton M. Berger

Milton M. Berger, a psychiatrist and group psychotherapist, has become one of the major figures in the utilization of video techniques professionally today. He edited one of the first books in the field on video in training and treatment as well as chaired the American Psychiatric Association committee in this area. Closed circuit video and video playback techniques have enormous potential in clarifying the multi-level in and out of awareness communications that occur within groups. They can be utilized by therapists of any theoretical persuasion with patients of all ages and degrees of illness. Their impact on group psychotherapy is just beginning to be felt and a paper such as this provides us with new insights into this recent innovation in the armamentarium of the group therapist.

In a comprehensive paper Doctor Berger first introduces his reader to broad theory and applications of video techniques before going into greater detail on specific uses. He illustrates the particulars of diagnoses and working through regressive behaviors in patients utilizing an interesting clinical case. A slight digression from his format into an interesting history of the utilization of video techniques in psychotherapy is followed by further examples of their application. He discusses the subtle sensitivity and art required of the therapist in using the confrontation by video. With ample use of case material Doctor Berger provides some startling effects occurring during replay indicating how video clarifies roles and attitudes, makes for an immediacy, intimacy, and confrontational impact. Following his analysis of use of confrontation at all stages of therapy there is a major section on specific technical concerns. In this part he addresses himself to whether the cameras should be exposed or hidden, the meaning of the first playback experience for the patient and detail of the multitude of uses of playback. He concludes the paper by a summary of what effects playback has on group members.

Milton Berger has given us a thorough verbal picture of the potential and actual uses of video in group psychotherapy today. His expertise has made this presentation clear, vivid and, in perspective, video playback techniques a most useful tool.

D.S.M.
G.D.G.

INTRODUCTION

Today's understanding of group process not only relies on an awareness of psychodynamic formulations of the individual, dyads and groups, but even more importantly upon the clarification and understanding of the multilevel multi-patterned systems of communication which occur at any one given moment within the group's life. The use of closed-circuit video and videotape replay allow the attention of the therapist as well as other group members to be tuned in to those multilevel and multi-channel systems which carry unconscious and conscious data. Such data serves to express, control, program and regulate individual and group behaviors and process. Video permits more accurate diagnosis of process and makes data not only accurately retrievable but also available for repeated review and study which enables the group members a second chance to work through crippling psychopathology or nonpotentiating impediments to growth.

Videotape playbacks can be used in psychiatric treatment by a therapist with any theoretical view of personality dynamics which acknowledges: subconscious or hidden motivation for one's behavior or attitudes; the significance of signs and symbols which regulate and arrange relationships; resistance; transference and the impact of the concomitant communication of emotion, behavior and thoughts through multiple levels and multiple channels in human relationships. Therapists interested primarily in modifying behavioral states by suggestion, direction, education or desensitization methods can also utilize video constructively to some degree.

A new theoretical framework for encompassing the multiple contemporary concepts of body images and self-concepts is presented by Bahnson (3) within which each self-experience may be described in terms of position on three independent dimensions: genetic developmental level, degree of consciousness, and experiential quality (conation–emotion–cognition). Developmentally, successive layers of self-experience form around each other as layers of an onion, with some of these layers referring to body, others to self-images. The concept of regression under the stress of self-confrontation to earlier self-perceptions is introduced as a working hypothesis in his study of a population of hemophiliac children, adolescents, and adults who participated in a longitudinal study investigating personality and psychodynamic correlates to hemorrhaging in hemophiliacs.

Bahnson found that younger children most often were excited and pleased about seeing themselves and exhibed frank narcissism as they perceived the film image as an extension of a barrierless self. Older children were concerned with the way they appeared to others, but the self still was experienced in terms of physical body aspects. Older children and young adolescents often made use of denial to cope with these self-perceptions. Adolescents frequently used conscious self-concepts as a defense against threatening covert images, and their self-reactions had interpersonal reference.

Adults perceived self-confrontation as a social situation calling for self-criticism, and their self-experiences were more abstract, cognitive and partly conscious. They struggled to improve control over perceived "give aways" of underlying dangerous self-images.

DIAGNOSING AND WORKING THROUGH
REGRESSIVE BEHAVIORS

Regressive moments occur often in group interaction. They become available for diagnostic interpretation and therapeutic intervention through mostly unconscious nonverbal behaviors such as the look of a terrorized child, lip biting, fingers brought into or over the mouth, fingers crossed, a nose-wipe, or an attempt to bury or hide one's face.

Such moments of regression can clue the therapist and other group members into levels of psychosocial fixations and hang-ups triggered by transference reactions to the therapist or others. Once out in the open, such moments are available for repeated review and working through if on videotape.

The following example of working through in group therapy indicates the significance of zooming in on nonverbal data to successfully expedite the psychotherapeutic process. Initially one group member, Cathy, commented on how she had observed Ralph noticing his image in one of the monitors and then "taking an adjustment" and becoming more relaxed as if he had moved himself towards his more familiar social masked portraiture of himself.

The process of group therapy is one with many rapid shifts and changes in the group's focus. I, in noticing Cathy's body movement as she spoke of Ralph's adjustment, commented on her adjustment, and then suggested a replay in response to the sexual message she was sending about herself which I decided was worth exploring. This shift in the group's attention to Cathy and her conscious and unconscious psychosexual conflicts led to a profound cathartic experience in which the dramatic dimension of her unresolved fixation at a child's level concerning her sexuality was manifested to all involved. Many group members identified with her. As a group we attempted to give her permission to grow up and to accept that she is, indeed, "a sexy babe." Her internally incorporated strict parental injunctions against being sexual were manifested in the guilt and anguish expressed in her almost-panicky-frightened eyes, her grimacing, biting lips, her twisted, anxious, tense finger actions, and the attempts she made to move towards an almost fetal-like infantile sitting position as she tousled her hair and buried her head between her knees because she is sexual and her sexuality is being publicly noticed, acknowledged and reacted to by others, male and female alike.

HISTORY

Reports on videotape in group psychotherapy have increased in the past few years. They cover aspects of training, treatment, its use in various settings, the psychotherapeutic process multi-levels of communication, the impact of self-confrontation with in-patients, outpatients, and alcoholics, and increasingly refine and detail the artistic and technical aspects involved in the use of the video equipment itself.

Amongst the earliest reports on the use of television in the teaching of group psychotherapy was that of the weekend teach-in at Tulane University School of Medicine in 1964. Berger and Gallant (7) found "that the closed-circuit television system can be of immeasurable value in studying the details of group process as well as in expanding the size of the student audience. The tele-vised group therapy session adds emotional interest to two impor-tant aspects of learning: the method of presentation of material and the motivation of the viewer. The workshop leader, by bring-ing himself and his reactions into the training situation, both in the meeting with patients and the following meeting with students, af-fords the students someone to identify with, to incorporate, to emulate, to resist, to compete with, or to react to in other ways as each student establishes and defines his own identity as a psycho-therapist.

"The enthusiastic response of the workshop audience can be ex-plained by the following factors which are essential to a true learn-ing experience and which are inherent in this type of televised demonstration: the student must be an active participant in the learning process; he must be in actual contact with the problem that is presented; the practical application of theoretical concepts must be revealed early to the student to stimulate his motivation further; and he must be allowed to form his own judgments about the realistic material that is offered to him.

"Students can perceive and appreciate that process is of greater significance than content in psychotherapy, although both process and content are integral parts of the therapeutic mainstream. They can also learn that nonverbal communication, alone and in con-junction with lexical languages, is of major importance not only as a medium for expression, communication, and imparting in-formation, but also to establish, maintain, or regulate relation-ships. Their attention can be drawn to overt psychosomatic symp-toms such as blushing, sweating, scratching, facial and bodily tics, dermotographia, belching, and borborygmi."

In 1967 Alger and Hogan (1, 2), two major contributors to the use of video in group psychotherapy, published articles on the use of videotape recordings in conjoint marital therapy in private prac-tice and on the impact of videotape recording on involvement by patients in group therapy. The use of videotape in group psycho-therapy with juvenile delinquents was also reviewed in that year. Videotape has been used quite innovatively. For example, group psychotherapy with chronic hospitalized schizophrenics was televised from a special hospital television studio to the patients on other wards and had very positive effects on the participants. Videotape playbacks have also been used in marathon groups.

By 1968 the number of articles on videotape in group psychotherapy increased by leaps and bounds. It has been reported that when playbacks were used with in- and outpatient psychotherapy groups that the rate of rehospitalization in those patients who had experienced the video playbacks was less than that of other patients treated on the same service during the same period. The use of videotape self-confrontation in psychotherapy as a clinical and research tool was reviewed as well as the use of television videotapes to enhance the therapeutic value of psychodrama. In addition, group therapy has been shown on commercial television and the rationale for such exposure of group psychotherapy patients to public television has been noted. A series of articles also appeared on the uses of focused feedback for accelerated interaction in marathon, encounter, counseling and therapy groups.

CLINICAL DATA

Confrontation in treatment is a form of psychotherapeutic intervention (9). However, whether video self-confrontation serves as more of an interference or intrusion than a constructive intervention will depend upon the scientific and artistic skill of the therapist, his intuitive sense of timing, and the goals envisioned by the therapist for each confrontation (5).

Startling Insights During Replay

Reivich and Geertsma (14) mention the strong reaction in some patients to recognition of an unconscious identification with a significant relative during playback. For example, they refer to a woman suddenly recognizing her similarity to her despised and hated grandmother whom she had discussed with great feeling in several previous interviews. In my experience with videotape in private practice, I have seen such a recognition trigger startling "shock" reactions which were important milestones for therapeutic insight and progress.

Clara, an overweight, quiet, passive-aggressive thirty-five-year-old married mother of two school children, was taken aback by experiencing a selected videotape playback of herself in interaction during a group session. She had been reared in an unloving home with a double-binding, inconsistent mother and a cruel, intermittently absent, ne'er-do-well, alcoholic father. Immediately after her self-confrontation she said, "I looked at myself and saw my mother, I nearly dropped dead." It's like a look of distaste or suspicion and as if she smelled something bad. "God, I never realized that I had this look–that I looked like this in repose and when I was just looking at somebody. And I also noticed this real ploppy-blobby expression and with a real double chin. I never knew that. And I realized that I looked a lot like Mary–like organic–like a sleepwalker–like one-half asleep and dopey." (Mary is a former alcoholic group member who dropped out of the group and was in a sanitarium at this time.) "My husband has been telling me that for years. I look sleepy and all doped up and I thought of my father too–ugh! It was quite a surprise–I never knew I looked that way! And oh! my voice. (pause) It's this high little girl voice with a definite pattern of rrr-rrr-rrr-rrr–and up and down singy-songy effect." Though the video playback brought forth many painful expressions of her self-hate and awareness of ways she had unconsciously incorporated her mother and father into her character structure, she definitely became more clearly motivated following this disturbing confrontation to work more actively toward giving up her alienation, her resignation and her passivity.

Selections used for focused confrontational feedback may range from a few moments of audiovisual playback to the playback of a single visual behavior without sound in order to trigger insight, awareness or free associations in a patient or family or group. *It is often necessary to play back segments of the preceding complex social interaction taking place over a period of minutes in order to confront and then review with people the arrangement they unconsciously make with others through their nonverbalized communications* (4). There is no longer a reliance upon the patient's or therapist's ability to recall, as we now have a system much more reliable and better than his memory or the therapist's memory, notes or even audiotapes, because it provides para and meta communications as well as context.

The continued effects of videotape confrontation in groups are somewhat different from the primarily self-image preoccupation which occurs initially. Subsequent playbacks lead to a more profound awareness of pathological interaction and characteristic styles of being and relating. Repeated confrontations enable patients to identify their own self-defeating patterns, to become more quickly identified with and to join the therapist in a pro-therapeutic position as they see and hear their over-reactions and under-reactions and inappropriate ways of reacting. It is as if the process of nonverbalized experiential awareness through the playback itself demands the giving up of blind spots and denial systems. *Further, where change is achieved, patients are often best able to see it in the playback session, when they can be more objective and less interactionally or defensively involved than in the on-going experience of a regular group session.*

Video Clarifies Roles and Attitudes

Sarbin (15) in clarifying role theory, stated, "Implicit in social interchanges is the portrayal of roles. . . . Roles are portrayed through acts such as verbal communication, accent, intonation, facial expressions, posture, movements, gait, dress, adornments, grooming and visible emblems such as tattoos, uniforms or silver badges. These behaviors may be perceived and organized by observers into role concepts. . . . Enactment of roles may be used to indicate what is to be expected of an individual, his position in a hierarchy and to affect others in a particular way. It is also a way to conceal or deny feelings to oneself or to others. The degrees of awareness and intensity of the role played varies widely from one person to another and in differing social contexts."

Paredes and Cornelison (13) aimed to bring into awareness for the alcoholic the nature and context of his role conflicts. Their playback of sound motion pictures served to confront the alcoholic with certain aspects of his behavior in order to help him examine the characteristic roles he enacts as he talks about his life problems, and hopefully to understand the self-destructing desires he has used to escape from uncomfortable conflictual personal issues. They emphasize that the anatomy of an attitude serves not only as a response to social expectations, but also to affect others in particular ways. "Attitudes are composed of a variety of individual actions including facial expressions, posture, gestures, mannerisms, etc. They possess qualities such as mood, fluidity (ease of flow of the sequence of movements or actions) and social appeal. They indicate ascendancy and gender and have functions such as: affective (indicating feelings); attributive (e.g. pointing with a finger); mimicking (imitation of a person, animal, or mechanism); preening (smoothing the hair with one's hand); courting (e.g. rubbing the sides of the thighs, hips and waist with the palms of both hands); autistic (seemingly idiosyncratic movements, probably unconsciously determined); coping or instrumental (such as grabbing a glass) and postural" (12).

Television Magnifies

Television magnifies. There is an immediacy, intimacy and powerful confrontational impact from seeing the closeup of a portion of a face, or of hands anxiously twisting a kleenex or matches, or of someone unconsciously taking off and putting on alternately their marriage band while talking about the difficulties in their marriage. The impact of magnification is equally at home in treatment as it is in training. However, it must be kept in mind that as accurately as video can reflect a person as he is, there is no modality which can reproduce a person exactly as he is.

Confrontation as Process

Confrontation involves an almost endless variety of processes and subsystems which range on many levels simultaneously through the whole gamut of human actions, reactions and interactions. Feelings, thoughts and behaviors are intricately and intimately expressed during confrontation and the prescience and experience of the therapist help to determine which processes to engage in with each individual patient at specific times in therapy. Some confrontation processes which may be utilized in the later stages of psychotherapy may be ruled inappropriate and nontherapeutic in the early stages.

All the subtle and blunt processes which make up the totality of confrontation are witnessed more clearly by both therapist and patient in videotape playback and their impact is reinforced during such additional self-confrontations.

The author is cognizant of the fact that many of these processes occur in all stages of therapy. In the early phase of therapy we are more likely to experience the following processes as examples of confrontation: acting, acting-out, accepting non-judgmentally, activating, advising, anticipating, assuring, cajoling, clarifying, conditioning, controlling, demonstrating, desensitizing, directing, encouraging, exhorting, frustrating, intervening, persuading, praising, predicting, and questioning.

In the middle phase of therapy we are more likely to experience: altering, analyzing, being authentic, catalyzing, challenging, coercing, commanding, contradicting, depriving, forbidding, implanting, influencing, inhibiting, instigating, interpreting, limit setting, provoking, role playing, silencing, and teaching.

And in the final or terminating phase of therapy we are more likely to experience: criticizing, demanding, discounting, emphasizing, evaluating, insisting, mimicking, opposing, pressuring, prodding, reminding, repeating, reviewing, and synthesizing.

The Cameras

Factors of importance concerning the use of television cameras while conducting group therapy include: 1) whether the cameras are exposed openly to patients or are hidden; 2) the number of cameras being used; 3) whether the cameras are fixed or mobile; 4) whether the cameras are used by the therapist(s), the patients or technical personnel not directly engaged in the psychotherapeutic transaction; 5) whether the camera itself is used as an observer-recorder or catalytic provocateur; 6) whether monitors are exposed during the recording; 7) the impact on the group of the major goal for videotaping, that is, if the goal is treatment, training, research, or the making of a film devoted to a specific aspect of group process or communication.

Wilmer (16), Alger and Hogan (1) and I have concluded it is less likely to stir up patients' resistance or paranoid potential if the cameras are open to patients than if they are hidden. When the cameras are hidden one can see patients intermittently scanning the walls and ceilings of the room they are meeting in to see if they can locate the cameras and can determine who the cameras are being pointed at. This curiosity and concern may reflect more health than pathology.

The First Playback

The first playback experience has profound impact on each member of the group, although the impact may not be fully known to each participant, let alone acknowledged at the actual moment of the playback. In the first playback patients are fixed primarily on an examination of their own ongoing self-image and particularly on their physical appearance. Though narcissism and neurotic egocentricity are a common basis for this initial hyperfocus on self-image, there may also be aspects of healthy curiosity and real self-interest in operation. The process of social self-evaluation and self-criticism occurs almost universally in those exposed to their self-image played back for the first time. A differential diagnosis as to the depth of pathology in a person can be made upon the basis of this initial self-critical response. The healthier a person is the sooner he stops making negative comments about his self-image and begins to notice and comment on something positive about his appearance, his manner, his bearing or his tone. If he only makes negative comments and persists self-hatefully in ruminating upon these, his prognosis is less favorable. If he denies any reaction to the initial self-image confrontation with himself then he may be a poor candidate for psychotherapy.

In general, the majority of initial playback reactions in both neurotic and psychotic patients includes remarks indicating preoccupation with appearance and sex appeal in women and masculinity or its absence in men.

The continued effects of videotape confrontation in groups are different from the initial over-preoccupation with self. Through the therapist's guidance on what he considers to be significant aspects of their manner of interacting, patients develop a broader and more discerning sensitivity for what they and other group members do which disrupts, disturbs or confuses their communications and interpersonal relationships. The basis for such disruptions representing transferential hangups is rapidly made available for psychotherapeutic working-through when a segment of video-tape is played over and over again until group members perceive the trigger-mechanisms which they are allergic to interpersonally.

As the framework of perception and understanding increases for each group member, the degree of motivation and commitment to the mutual work of the group is increased and the group now functions with more aliveness, zest, cohesiveness and expertise in moving towards greater awareness and insight which can lead to working-through and change.

Video Playback

Video playback of a patient's participation in his group meeting one year previously often has salutary effects similar to those noted by Berger and Mendell (8) in their report on patients' concurrent participation in more than one group. Participating in a here-and-now group meeting which can experience itself in a there-and-then meeting which occurred one year previously allows for an objective overview with less defensive mechanism likely to be mobilized. Each person can see himself through a more expanded observing ego than was operative a year previously. Some examples of the values in such a replay are:

a) A thirty-four-year-old single woman, Nancy K., who was an only child and is very shaky in her evaluation of how she is being accepted by others, notes the degree of sincere interest and caring demonstrated repeatedly by various group members towards her. She sits somewhat aghast and says, "Wow! It really is true. You people really do care for me. What a fool I've been to deny it for so long and not to really enjoy your warmth and offers of friendship this past year."

b) Mary S., a married school teacher of forty-two, who had not received adequate satisfaction for her dependency needs in childhood was able to observe the frequency and destructive consequences of her oppositional behavior. She became more motivated to examine how simple repartee with her could lead to irritability and argumentation in which she wound up feeling misunderstood, confused, abused and victimized as well as alone and somehow different from the other people in the group.

Playbacks Affect Cohesiveness and Intimacy

A separate playback session or a playback during a regular group meeting rapidly becomes an important experience for its own sake, heightening group cohesiveness and intimacy. Perhaps it is the fact that each member of the group, including the therapist, is equally vulnerable to the possibility of exposure of private areas of self, that heightens this sense of intimacy and breaks down separating barriers in isolated patients previously so fearful of closeness and intimacy.

The additional intimacy engendered in the playback meeting results not only in the development of greater cohesiveness and trust but also of sharing and caring among group members. For example, during playbacks group members engage in more nonverbal activity than during regular meetings. Group members who had never cried in regular sessions cried during replay sessions. In the non-demanding silence of the playback patients tend to feel deeply and let go of their usual defenses. There is also more compassion for self and others shown during the playback sessions. The use of the tape for self and others diminished the pressure (real or fancied) for involvement to exist primarily through words. The lessening of this kind of pressure results in an increased availability to quietly be with and feel with others. This speeds up the process of intimacy and enhances the possibility of change being risked in an atmosphere of mutual trust with close, significant others.

It has been the history of many patients that intimacy is primarily experienced in time of trouble and consequently they unconsciously attempt to provoke crises in order to experience closeness. In the playback sessions patients learn to know and experience intimacy outside of a framework of emergency, trouble or crisis.

Listening to and viewing the tape allows another dimension of intimacy not usually available: experiencing silence as non-threatening. Prolonged periods of non-threatening shared silence allow for increased reflection and integrative processes to occur without self-consciousness, embarrassment, guilt or demands to perform, impress or talk. This in turn leads to more shared experiences, caring and group cohesiveness. It should be noted, however, that usually it is only after a group is well established and has gone beyond the need to verbalize that it is able to experience silence in this way. This process is akin to what occurs in a solid marriage or friendship.

Clarifying the Therapist

Another value of the playback session is to clarify the nature of transference attitudes towards the therapist. In the use of video playback, the patient who is seeing himself differently also has an opportunity to more objectively experience the subjective person known as the "therapist." He is able to assess through his own reflection the nature and degree of the therapist's capacity for caring and what the therapist is as a person more realistically. If he can believe in the warmheartedness of the therapist and in the therapist's sincerity, wholeheartedness, integrity and human capacity for caring which is being made available to him at deeper levels of his own being, he may be able to move more rapidly in the group.

CONCLUSION

Videotape replay of parts of a group session have various general effects such as clarifying or bringing into awareness how and to what degree a member does or does not: 1) Initiate or contribute to the problems or goals of the other group members or the whole group by spotlighting, questioning, defining, summarizing or seeking an explanation of a change in group process or atmosphere. 2) Ask others for clarification, information, suggestions, opinions, feelings and attitudes about a problem or task. 3) Spontaneously offer information, opinions, facts, generalizations or his own experiences in relation to the problem of an individual or the group. 4) Elaborate, clarify, illustrate or examine openly the relationship or ramifications of various ideas, suggestions or behaviors. 5) Express group standards, mores, values or expectations concerning the group as a whole or an individual member or a kind of behavior among group members. 6) Cooperate in performing technical group procedures which expedite the group's movement towards its goals, e.g., making photocopies of an article or poem for all other members, writing a report of a specific group meeting or happening to be shared with other members. 7) Encourage or support risk-taking "participation" by others and suggest new ideas or options for conflict-resolution. Expressing appropriate concern, caring, warmth, acceptance, praise, appreciation, annoyance or anger are valuable contributions towards reality-testing and learning the art of living with others.

Video, by providing repeated opportunities for feedback and validation of nonverbal as well as verbal impact (6), aids in the more rapid fulfillment of most of the following goals of individual and group psychotherapy: 1) the development of an expanded observing ego; 2) the clarification and giving up of projective and externalizing mechanisms which confuse realistic assessment of "Who does what to whom?" Such mechanisms foster the festering injustice and rejection-collecting which underlie the chronic abused reactions, bitterness, and vindictive needs which in turn are the basis for each neurotic's idealized image and self-hate; 3) the clarification and more or less resolution of transferential reactions as group members give up their allergic hypersensitivities to each other and to the group's leader; 4) the reduction of non-involvement, detachment, passive-aggressivity, inertia and resignation as the capacity for spontaneity, risk-taking and healthier self-assertion are expanded when group members develop a more realistic self-image and self-concept and assume responsibility for themselves while learning the living-meaning of "If I am not for myself, who am I? But if I am only for myself, what am I? and not later, but now!" (11).

REFERENCES

1. Alger, I., and Hogan, P.: The impact of videotape recording on involvement in group therapy. *J Psychoanal Groups, 2:*50-56, 1967.
2. Alger, I., and Hogan, P.: Use of videotape recording in conjoint marital therapy. *Am J of Psychiatry, 123*(11):1425-1430, 1967.
3. Bahnson, C. B.: Body and self-images associated with audio-visual self confrontation. *J Nerv Ment Dis, 148:*262-280, 1969.
4. Berger, M. M.: Nonverbal communications in group psychotherapy. *Int J of Grp Psychotherapy, 8:*161-178, 1958.

5. Berger, M. M.: Self-confrontation through video. *Amer J of Psycho-analysis, 31:*48-58, 1970.

6. Berger, M. M. (Ed.): *Videotape Teachniques in Psychiatric Training and Treatment.* New York, Brunner/Mazel, 1970.

7. Berger, M. M., and Gallant, D. M.: The use of closed circuit television in teaching a group psychotherapy. *Psychosomatics, 6:*16-18, 1965.

8. Berger, M. M., and Mendell, D.: A preliminary report on participation of patients in more than one psychotherapy group concurrently. *Int J of Soc Psychiatry, 13:*192-198, 1967.

9. Garner, H. H.: A review of confrontation in psychotherapy from hypnosis to the problem-solving technique. In Berger, M. M. (Ed.): *Videotape Techniques in Psychiatric Training and Treatment.* New York, Brunner/Mazel, 1970.

10. Geertsma, R. H., and Reivich, R. S.: Repetitive self observation by videotape playback. *J Ment Nerv Dis, 141:*29-41, 1965.

11. Hillel, Rabbi: In *The Talmud, Ethics of the Fathers.* Chapter 1, Par. 14.

12. La Barre, W.: Paralinguistics, kinesics, and cultural anthropology. In Sebeok, T., Hayes, A., and Bateson, M. C. (Eds.): *Approaches to Semiotics.* London, Mouton, 1964.

13. Paredes, A., and Cornelison, F. S.: Development of an audiovisual technique in the rehabilitation of alcoholics. Unpublished manuscript based in part on paper presented at the 19th clinical meeting of the A.M.A. in Philadelphia, November 1965.

14. Reivich, R. S., and Geerstma, R. H.: Experiences with videotape self-observation by psychiatric in-patients. *J of Kans Med Soc, 69:*39-44, 1968.

15. Sarbin, T. R.: Role theory. In Lindsey, G. (Ed.): *Handbook of Social Psychology.* Cambridge, Addison-Wesley, 1954.

16. Wilmer, H. A.: Technical and artistic aspects of videotape in psychiatric teaching. *J Nerv Ment Dis, 144:*207-223, 1967.

AUTHOR INDEX

289

SUBJECT INDEX

293